PRISONS AND THE

AMERICAN CONSCIENCE

A HISTORY OF U.S. FEDERAL CORRECTIONS

Paul W. Keve
With a Foreword by Myrl E. Alexander

SOUTHERN ILLINOIS UNIVERSITY PRESS
Carbondale and Edwardsville

94   93   92   91   1   2   3   4

Frontispiece: The pride of Leavenworth.

Library of Congress Cataloging-in-Publication Data

Keve, Paul W.
   Prisons and the American conscience : a history of U.S. federal
corrections / Paul W. Keve, with a foreword by Myrl E. Alexander.
      p.   cm.
   Includes bibliographical references and index.
   ISBN 0-8093-1710-9
   1. Corrections—United States—History. 2. Prisons—United
States—History.
HV9466.K48   1991
365′.32′0973—dc20   91-2833
                                                              CIP

You were speaking of the Last Judgment . . .
I shall wait for it resolutely, for I know
what is worse, the judgment of men.

God is not needed to create guilt or to
punish. Our fellow men suffice, aided
by ourselves.

—Albert Camus, *The Fall*

CONTENTS

ILLUSTRATIONS

FOREWORD

Only in the last two centuries has confinement in penal institutions become the basic penalty for criminal behavior. In earlier times, offenders were sentenced to a wide range of punishments: executions, tortures, banishment, slavery, transportation to penal colonies, public flogging, or exposure to public ridicule in the stocks.

In the past two hundred years, penal systems have undergone substantial evolution, impacted by emerging social and economic developments, legislative reform, drastic effects of war, new insights evolving from management experience, and research in the social and behavioral sciences.

The United States government had virtually no penal institutions until the early twentieth century. Persons convicted of federal law violations were housed in state institutions by contract. William Sidney Porter, sentenced for a federal crime, was committed to the Ohio State Penitentiary, where he began writing and became known eventually as O. Henry, his pen name.

This book, by Professor Paul Keve, experienced correctional administrator and writer, is a history of the United States government's prison administration, with expanded emphasis since 1930 when the Federal Bureau of Prisons was created by Congress. In its sixty years of existence, the Bureau has introduced many correctional innovations. This record of those events becomes a valuable source of information for staff, academicians, and the general public.

In the mid-1980s, Bureau director Norman Carlson, recognizing the need for gathering and preserving a vast range of valuable historical documents and memorabilia, appointed a task force to propose a solution. The report of the committee led to an important decision—

to create an office of a Bureau of Prisons Archivist. Professor Keve's historical research was already underway when John W. Roberts was appointed as the Bureau's archivist, a fortunate and effective move. The result was the collection and organization of the ever-growing wealth of historical material, from wide-ranging sources.

The history of the Bureau provides invaluable insight into the bases on which the present rests, and it becomes a significant resource for current and future administrations. As Sanford Bates, the Bureau's first director, wrote years ago, "The Bureau's philosophy was not predicated on fear of a man's past so much as it is expressive of hope for his future." And as the sequential relationship between the past and future is studied, one is reminded of a truism written long ago by Santayana: "Those who cannot remember the past are condemned to repeat it."

That truth was also expressed by the essayist Bacon, two hundred years ago, in the quotation carved in stone on the proscenium arch over the stage at the United States penitentiary at Lewisburg, Pennsylvania: "That which is past and gone is irrevocable; wise men have enough to do with things present and to come."

Myrl E. Alexander

PREFACE

Having finished a book that recounts the story of one federal prison (McNeil Island), and having caught glimpses thereby of the richly interesting experience of the entire federal system, I inevitably began to think that a history of the Federal Bureau of Prisons as a whole should be written. Norman Carlson, director of the Bureau of Prisons, was warmly encouraging and assured me of the Bureau's cooperation. I started work in 1986, with the hope that the book would be no more than a two-year project— a hope that was much too optimistic, for the task required interviews and the perusal of voluminous materials in many parts of the country. Much was done in Washington, D.C., where the Bureau of Prisons headquarters, the Library of Congress, and the National Archives were primary sources. It was necessary also to visit state historical associations and other specialized archives in Massachusetts, Connecticut, New York, Pennsylvania, Texas, Kansas, Georgia, and California.

Such wide-ranging research was needed when it became evident that to write just a history of the Bureau of Prisons would not be enough; the Bureau had been created only sixty years before, but its roots are found in the gradual evolution of federal justice over the many previous decades. It seemed essential to start the story at an earlier time, and that meant starting at the birth of the republic itself. The consequence is that this has become a history of federal imprisonment since 1776.

The history can be divided into three phases. The first phase lasted from 1776 until about the end of the nineteenth century. During this period the government maintained no federal jails or prisons, but boarded federal prisoners in state or local facilities.

xiii

The second phase began at about the turn of the century, following Congress' passage of the "Three Prison Act," in 1891. By the beginning of the twentieth century, the federal government had made a start on the enormous task of providing its own prison cells. Construction was underway at Leavenworth and Atlanta, and the old territorial prison at McNeil Island in Washington had been given regular federal penitentiary status. Eventually a reformatory at Chillicothe, Ohio, and a prison for women at Alderson, West Virginia, were built. But still, there was no bureaucracy, no effective supervisory force to make a prison *system*.

In 1930, the third phase began with creation of the Bureau of Prisons, and since that time the Bureau has evolved into an effective, centrally controlled system with progressive standards.

The development of federal imprisonment practice is intimately tied to other facets of the nation's social, economic, and political history, and so it is important here to show the most significant of these relationships. Also, those individuals who were effectively influential in promoting a federal prison system often were not governmental officials, but were perceptive, respected men and women from outside the system; prominent in business, in the church, or in organizations for social change. Between them, these articulate individuals spanned several decades during which they successively pricked the federal conscience about its insensitive neglect of federal offenders. They did not live to see the positive effects of their efforts, but their influence did lead eventually to development of a new, highly principled governmental conscience, with humane concern for custody and treatment of prisoners. Their places in the emergence of the federal prison service, though important, are today seldom remembered, and so they are entitled to appropriate recognition here.

Some will think that the book is too brief and superficial. Depending on what the reader is seeking, the complaint may be valid. However, the amount of information available on this topic is massive and if fully used would result in an encyclopedic tome of intimidating size. Thus, the principle I followed here was to delineate the major social, political, or cultural factors that shaped federal imprisonment practices prior to this century, and to describe the federal prison system since then, in terms of what gives it its own character and distinguishes it from state or local correctional organizations.

An inevitable question in writing the history of an existing agency concerns the proper cutoff date. While it is tempting to carry the story through to the time of the writing, this involves the dangerous task of writing current events as history. I decided that the end of the Carlson administration, July 1, 1987, was a convenient and logical place to conclude the account. Much of significant interest has taken place since that time, but it will be told more reliably by a future historian.

Although the early history of the federal prisons included some courageous and dedicated leaders, it was also seasoned with a few examples of defective policies, inept and sometimes corrupt management, and problem-plagued institutions suffering distressingly meager support. With creation of the Bureau of Prisons and with its subsequent growth under the leadership of a succession of astute, highly principled directors, the system matured into an effective, disciplined bureaucracy, currently of outstanding quality. And therein lies a potential problem for an author who attempts to depict such an organization responsibly. To praise the agency that has given unstinted cooperation to a study of its history and present condition raises understandable questions about the writer's objectivity, or even his integrity. I have been keenly conscious of the challenge this presents and my appraisal of the Bureau's operation is as honest as I can make it. If it falters in its objectivity and balance to any appreciable degree, undoubtedly articulate critics will not hesitate to challenge my observations.

This research and writing would not have been possible without wholehearted support from three Bureau directors: Norman A. Carlson, his predecessor Myrl E. Alexander, and his successor J. Michael Quinlan. To all three I extend my most grateful thanks for their cordial interest and solid contributions. I am especially indebted to Bureau archivist, John W. Roberts, for his enthusiastic and knowledgeable guidance in locating the more elusive source materials. David Ward, University of Minnesota professor and authority on Alcatraz history, is due my earnest thanks for his immense help in reviewing and suggesting improvements in the chapter on Alcatraz and the Marion penitentiary. Beyond these, I face the futility of naming names; additional contributors are far too numerous to list without the likelihood of regrettable omissions.

Among those to whom I pay appreciative respect are researchers and librarians at the National Archives who helped with the daunting task of locating needed data from within the enormous volume of records related to the prison system. There were similarly useful and appreciated librarians at the many state and historical association archives.

Warm thanks are due to an incredible number of employees within the Bureau of Prisons. These people include managerial and support staff in the national and regional headquarters offices, and wardens and staffs in the more than forty federal institutions that I visited across the country. And as usual with any historical research, a particularly appreciated source has been retired Bureau personnel; I held rewarding interviews with former wardens and other retirees who added richly to the perspective on the Bureau's last several decades.

The interviewing was not all one sided. In addition to Bureau of Prisons loyalists, I was aided by some of the articulate critics of the Bureau, including those prominent in the Moratorium movement and those involved in opposing the Marion penitentiary.

And finally, closer to my home base at Virginia Commonwealth University, others earned my genuine appreciation. I could hardly have done the work without the general support of the University and the friendly encouragement of the department chair, David Farmer. Faculty colleague R. Michael McDonald, virtuoso of the word processor, provided real and practical help. Had he not always been at hand to guide me through the mysteries of that wonderful but intimidating invention, the job would have taken longer and would have been far more difficult.

PWK

PRISONS AND THE AMERICAN CONSCIENCE: A HISTORY OF U.S. FEDERAL CORRECTIONS

THE FIRST CENTURY:
AT THE MERCY
OF THE STATES

In the spring of 1777 a small party of armed
horsemen escorted a rider along the quiet country roads leading
northwestward from Middletown, Connecticut, to the village of Litchfield. There, they stopped at an undistinguished, two-story log building fronting on the village green—the Litchfield jail. The letter of
commitment handed to the sheriff along with his new prisoner informed him that he was receiving William Franklin, late governor of
the colony of New Jersey and son of the well-known patriot, Benjamin
Franklin. The prisoner was to be held in solitary confinement for an
indefinite time and was to be allowed no writing materials and no
conversation with anyone except the sheriff, unless exceptions were
authorized by Connecticut governor Jonathan Trumbull.

Federal crimes and federal prisoners were not yet so well differen-
tiated from state or local offences and offenders as they are now, but
clearly Franklin's crime of treason was federal, and his imprisonment
by order of the Continental Congress made him one of the earliest
of federal prisoners. For the first century, and more, the federal
government had no prisons of its own, but was dependent upon state
or local jail space it could rent as necessary. After federal courts were
created in 1789 they counted on their marshals to scout for prison
cells to be utilized at the most moderate fees possible. And far too
often the space available was not tolerable at all, except for the lack
of anything better.

William Franklin found the space chosen for him to be onerous
indeed, but Congress had little choice. In a war that was then going
poorly for the Continental armies, quiet Litchfield was usefully remote
from the fighting. Although New York City was in British control,
General William Howe was preparing to strike out from there toward

1

the south and Philadelphia. That city would, in fact, be in his hands by late September. For the time being, the New England area, except for Rhode Island, seemed to be free from likely incursions of enemy troops, and so it was judged a safe enough locale for holding prisoners whom the British would be likely to rescue if they had the opportunity.

Franklin's imprisonment was the culmination of a painful break in what had been a warm, close relationship between father and son. Though William was illegitimate, Ben Franklin had always accepted him and had given him every advantage possible. But when the country declared its independence, the father joined solidly with the patriots of the revolution while the son remained staunchly royalist. When the several royal governors were asked to relinquish their posts, Governor Franklin refused and continued his active support for the Crown. The Continental Congress took no pleasure in arresting Franklin, but found it necessary to remove him from office and to separate him from his New Jersey contacts. He was committed to a form of house arrest in Connecticut, where Governor Trumbull agreed to accept him. Franklin was allowed to rent a room in a private home in Middletown, but he was required to remain within a six-mile radius and to engage in no activity with or for the enemy. Because he believed it was his duty as a loyal Tory to aid the royalist cause and hinder the revolution to the best of his ability, Franklin violated his parole flagrantly. [1] When he persisted in actively aiding the enemy, Congress ordered the former governor into actual imprisonment.

Trumbull responded as Congress directed, writing to John Hancock, president of the Congress, on May 5, 1777, to report:

> I received your letter of the 23 ultimo inclosing the report of congress regarding Wm Franklin Esq. late governor of New Jersey and paid all the attention to it that you can wish or expect. I gave immediate orders to have him conveyed under proper guard to Litchfield in this State and confined in the jail there. . . . Wm Franklin is without question highly inimical to the rights and liberties of the United States and disposed to do everything in his power to injure them. [2]

Franklin's previous high status brought him no special consideration as a prisoner. In fact, his accommodations were painfully uncomfortable. His room was tiny, with one small barred window, filthy straw on the floor, and no furniture or bathing or toilet facilities. In July he wrote to George Washington to plead for some relief, describing the dismal jail conditions and also the suffering of his wife who was acutely dependent upon him and was reported to be in an ominous decline.

Washington expressed sympathy, but Congress refused to grant Franklin's release; Mrs. Franklin died while her husband was still in prison.[3] After eight months of solitary confinement, and with his health seriously impaired, Franklin was allowed to move to a private home in East Windsor, still a prisoner. In November 1778, Congress exchanged him for John McKinley, a British prisoner who was the patriot ex-governor of Delaware.

When the new U.S. Congress enacted the country's first federal criminal statute in 1790, it defined explicitly those crimes that were to be subject to federal prosecution. Treason, such as in Franklin's case, was of course one of these offenses and in fact was one of several that were punishable by death. Franklin was among the first of many prominent political figures who have spent time in federal custody, and he was not different from thousands of others in being held in local facilities at the expense of the federal government.

Franklin was not the only federal prisoner during the struggle for independence. He serves here only as a useful example. Indeed, the Revolution, by its very nature, tested the loyalties of a great many people, making arrests for treason common. At the same time Franklin languished in the Litchfield jail, other federal prisoners were held under equally bad, if not worse, conditions a few miles away in Simsbury. This notorious prison was a former copper mine adapted by the state of Connecticut in 1773 as its colonial prison. Officials believed that the underground cavern, with one vertical shaft as the only access, would be virtually escape-proof. At the surface, a walled enclosure and several shop buildings were built in which convicts made such products as nails, barrels, and shoes. At night prisoners were confined to the caverns below. Darkness, slanting floors, low ceilings, and continually dripping water made this prison grossly uncomfortable and injurious to health. Nor was it as escape-proof as the state had hoped.

Whether or not Washington was aware of Simsbury's dismal conditions, he had little choice of custodial facilities. In December 1775, the Simsbury mine, then named New Gate Prison, held the usual collection of felons sent by the colony, plus five men accepted from the Continental Congress after their courts-martial. Washington's order of commitment was a letter to the Simsbury committee of managers:

> Gentlemen:
> The prisoners which will be delivered you with this, having been tried by a Court Martial, and deemed to be such flagrant and atrocious villians that they cannot by any means be set at large or confined in any place near this Camp, were sentenced to be sent to Symsbury in Connecticut; you will therefore be pleased to have them secured in your jail, or in such other manner as to you shall seem necessary, so that they cannot possibly make their escape. The charges of their imprisonment will be at the Continental expense.[4]

As a typical example of the group, John Short, convicted of desertion and theft, was sentenced to serve two years or the duration of the war. But Washington's appraisal was correct; Short did attempt an escape, which ended fatally for himself and a fellow prisoner.[5]

From the time the first Continental Congress convened in 1774, there was a gradual increase in the number of criminal cases that were peculiarly federal in nature and not within the obvious jurisdiction of any one state. Other than treason or crimes within the military, the first obvious type of case that can be categorized as federal was that which arose in maritime situations. Borrowing from British law, the colonies had developed admiralty courts to deal with the many matters involving such problems as captured vessels, crimes at sea, and disposition of wrecks. The first such court on this continent appeared in 1615, and more were founded gradually during the century.[6] In 1696, Parliament acted to give system and definition to these courts, which from then to the Revolution gave the colonists experience in adjudicating issues between or beyond single colonies.[7]

The outbreak of war with England quickly brought a substantial increase in the demands on the admiralty courts. Soon after taking command of the Continental Army in June 1775, Washington asked the Congress for guidance in disposing of the many cases related to ships and cargoes taken as prizes of war. In the following November,

Congress resolved that the colonies try such cases in their own courts, but that the Continental Congress retain the function of an appellate prize court.[8]

The colonies did assume this responsibility, but the resultant courts were of little help as the Continental Congress had no way to participate authoritatively in their operation. For the time being, even such obviously federal matters as cases of treason had to be tried by the state courts. Congress could be represented by its attorneys in such actions but had no other means of affecting the prosecutions. It was one of the various problem areas that pointed to the crucial need for a new, stronger form of government.

During much of the time before the constitutional form of government became operational in 1789, the federal government followed procedures that were made expedient and necessary by events, even though proper authority was not clearly established. As crimes were committed, the Continental Congress and the states did what had to be done, case by case, and gradually the elements of a criminal justice system evolved. In 1776, Congress provided that state and county prisons could be used to confine prisoners charged with federal crimes, even though there were few such prisons. At that point, the only facility of any size, other than Simsbury, was the new Walnut Street Jail in Philadelphia. The older jail, the Old Stone Prison at Third and Market streets, was still usable, although it was in dismal condition and due to be replaced by the Walnut Street facility. However, plans for the latter were frustrated by the events of the war. Soon after the Walnut Street Jail opened, it was commandeered by the Continental Congress for federal use, an action that would seem to qualify this institution as the first federal prison in the United States.

Federal accession of the prison is noted in the minutes of the Congress for July 20, 1776. "The convention of Pennsylvania having directed the common prisoners to be removed from the new jail to the old, and the new jail to be given up to the Congress for the use of the state prisoners; Resolved that Robert Jewell be appointed keeper of the said new jail, and that he take custody of the prisoners committed to his charge."[9]

Though Jewell had no special credentials for the warden's job, he was a politically attractive candidate because he had lost an arm the previous year during the ceremonial firing of a cannon at a patriotic rally.[10] His appointment made him, in effect, the country's first federal prison warden. At that point, with his institution reserved for those imprisoned by order of the Continental Congress, Jewell sometimes signed his letters "Keeper, State's Prison," but just as often he signed, "Keeper, United States Prison." If indeed it truly qualified as a federal prison, was the Walnut Street Jail a military prison or a civil prison? The answer is unimportant. Being the only federally operated prison, it accepted either type of prisoner that the Continental Congress sent. The Walnut Street Jail was not the only such resource, however. The inconvenience of travel made it useful to board some prisoners closer to their homes or points of arrest. The Journal of the Congress for May 3, 1777, notes such an instance: "To the committee of York County in Pennsylvania for the board of 10 prisoners from the 3 July to the 23 November, nineteen weeks at one dollar per man per week, a ballance of 180 dollars."

In Philadelphia, Jewell's administration was interrupted in September 1777 when the British armies broke through the American defenses and occupied the city, forcing the Congress to move to York. While General Howe and his troops wintered in the comparative comfort of Philadelphia, the jail was redesignated the "British Provost Prison."[11] In June of the next year, however, the British evacuated Philadelphia, and again the jail was available for Continental prisoners.

During the occupation Jewell had left the city, and his post was filled by a British appointee. But with the British departure, Jewell returned and resumed his duties. In 1779 he was feeling badly used on the minimal salary afforded by the Congress and repeatedly petitioned for relief. His brother, Joseph Jewell, was the assistant keeper and was similarly troubled. In an appeal dated September 2, 1779, Joseph reminded the Congress that he had been better paid while in military service, but now "his pay which amounts to only thirty shillings per day as Assistant to his brother is by no means sufficient to maintain him and family."

Only a month later Robert Jewell sent his own request for better pay for himself and his assistants. Apparently there was no satisfactory response, for the keeper again wrote on April 24, saying, "The salary allowed your Petitioner is so small that he cannot therewith procure the common necessities of life." Jewell sent other petitions during the following months, with the last one dated January 17, 1781, pleading that he had spent his funds to procure necessary supplies for the jail; a lengthy list of those items was appended. But two weeks later Robert Jewell was dead of "spotted fever." Despite the low pay of the now vacant job, Congress began immediately to receive applications from those eager to be appointed. One letter, dated February 8, was from Joseph Jewell, and within a week, six other men had applied. A further clue to the federal character of the prison is given in the application submitted on February 9 by Elijah Weed. "Upon the death of Robert Jewell, late Keeper of the Goal which for the confinement of prisoners of war and state prisoners is assigned to the United States of America, your petitioner presumath to apply."[12]

For well over a decade the new United States governed itself in a weak, groping, indecisive manner because of its conditioned fears of submitting to a strong authority so soon after throwing off the authority of the Crown. The ineffectual Continental Congress attempted a stronger structure in 1781 when it adopted the Articles of Confederation and a new designation, "the United States in congress assembled." While this was an improvement, it still left the government short of the strength needed to meet the demands upon it. Just as there was no strong and well-defined criminal justice system, so were all other areas of governmental authority still inadequate. Inevitably the country had to move toward an authoritative constitutional government.

In September 1787, the Constitutional Convention in Philadelphia completed its work and presented its proposed new constitution to the states. A year later the necessary nine states had ratified the Constitution and Congress scheduled March 1789 for the new government to start operating.

A most important item in the agenda of the first Congress was the authorization of a federal court system, a matter the legislators promptly and effectively tackled. While the new court did not evolve directly from the admiralty courts or their appellate prize court in the Continental Congress, experience with that special judiciary largely shaped the design that emerged in the Judiciary Act of 1789.[13] As one historian notes, of the several laws enacted by the first Congress, "none was of greater prospective force than this act; none more astutely contrived."[14] In addition to establishing the Supreme Court the Congress divided the country into districts, each with a U.S. district court having jurisdiction over crimes "cognizable under the authority of the United States." Specifically these were the lesser crimes that carried penalties of fines up to one hundred dollars, prison up to six months, or whipping with up to thirty stripes. There also was a circuit court with jurisdiction over any federal matters not reserved to the district courts. The act provided that the justices of the Supreme Court (which in its first years was not very busy) were to try cases as needed in the circuit courts.[15] Also created by the Judiciary Act were the positions of U.S. district attorney and U.S. marshal for each district.

The Constitution did not define certain other principles important to a federal court operation, as some of the statesmen were keenly aware. A bill of rights was needed, but was not enacted then to avoid delay in establishing the new government. However, work started promptly on preparing twelve amendments that would comprise the Bill of Rights. In September, only seven months into the government's first year, ten of those amendments were agreed upon and submitted to the states. They included such crucial elements as the right to trial by jury, a speedy trial, and due process in criminal cases.

Meanwhile, dependable custodial facilities were needed for federal prisoners. At the same time the Judiciary Act was passed Congress formally resolved the following: "It be recommended to the several states to pass laws making it expressly the duty of the keepers of their gaols to receive and safe keep therein all prisoners committed under the authority of the United States, until they shall be discharged by due course of the laws thereof, under the like penalties as in the case of prisoners committed under the authority of such states respectively; the United States to pay for the use and keeping of such gaols at the rate of fifty cents per month for each prisoner."[16]

As a matter of obvious necessity, the courts went into operation without waiting for the ten amendments to be ratified, but functioned with a respectful eye upon the prospective principles. The Bill of Rights became effective when ratified by Virginia on December 15, 1791, and as noted by one authority, "Meanwhile, the new federal courts had been functioning for two years, unbound by the pending constitutional restrictions; contrary to the expectations of some, the skies did not fall."[17]

Also established by the First Congress was the position of attorney general—but not a Department of Justice. The attorney general, a man with no department under him and with enough free time to maintain his own law practice, was simply to be a legal advisor to the president. Even sixty years after the office of attorney general was created, the staff consisted of only two clerks and a messenger.[18] It was not until 1870 that the Department of Justice was created; meanwhile, many of the responsibilities later given to that department were distributed among other secretariats, including State and Treasury.

Although the Judiciary Act had authorized the appointing of district attorneys, the attorney general was given no control over them or any other governmental functions. Here again, the Congress was avoiding any invitation to strong central rule that might infringe on states' rights. The frugality of the Congress also served to defeat the potential strength of the attorney general's position, for the office operated with a minimal salary, almost no supporting staff, and no funds for operating expenses.

Often the early criminal cases in federal courts resulted from shipboard offenses. A notable example occurred in the same year that the Judiciary Act was passed, when a sailor named Thomas Bird shot and killed the captain of his sloop, *The Mary*, while off the coast of Africa. Bird was tried in the federal court in Portland, Maine, in June 1790, convicted, and sentenced to death. Judge David Sewall noted in a report to the secretary of state, "This capital conviction is probably the first in the nation since the establishment of the Federal Courts under the new Constitution."[19] Bird sent a petition to President Washington requesting clemency, but his appeal was not granted and the execution took place as ordered.

A similar but more notorious case was tried in Philadelphia in 1800 when three men were convicted of murdering three crewmen of their schooner, *Eliza*. Joseph Burser, Peter Peterson, and Joseph Baker, on order of the court, were executed by hanging. The sentence was carried out on an island in the Delaware River, on May 9, 1800.[20]

A more sophisticated crime tried in the same court in 1793 was committed by Peter Barrici who was charged with violating the neutrality of the United States by furnishing France with "two great guns, one hundred cannon shot, two gun carriages, fifty pounds of powder and four gunner's handspikes."[21]

For a few years after the Revolutionary War, the Walnut Street Jail continued as a federal resource; at some point it returned to state operation, though conditions gradually deteriorated under the problems of overcrowding and inadequate financing. Meanwhile, the marshal regularly brought federal prisoners to be held at the jail. Typical cases included Joseph Ravara, admitted May 15, 1793, for extortion from the British ambassador; John Singletary, admitted May 31, 1793, for joining with a French schooner in attacking various British vessels; Francis W. Henry, admitted May 27, 1794, for stealing sixteen blank coins from the mint.

Often the jail's governing board was able to take an interest in individual prisoners; the minutes of July 27, 1798, recorded the following: "The board considering Robert Worrall, a prisoner under the laws of the United States an object worthy of the clemency of the President, it is mutually agreed that the chairman do sign a recommendation for a remission of his fine to the President of the United States."[22]

Imprisonment was not the only punishment available to the courts. In addition to execution in capital cases, the federal courts were free to use the various corporal penalties that were common at the time. For example, in 1790 two defendants in a piracy case were convicted in the U.S. district court, New York City, and were sentenced to stand in the pillory for one hour, to receive thirty-nine stripes each, and then to serve six months in jail.[23]

The Walnut Street Jail, when expanded after the Revolution, was the first of the penitentiary type of prisons—implementing the new effort to use fewer harsh corporal penalties and resort instead to solitary confinement with labor. Soon afterward, and ahead of most other states, New York invested in the new penitentiary idea by building massive prisons at Auburn (1819) and Dannemora (1845). Auburn became the great, internationally visible proponent of the silent system with congregate workshops. The rigid enforcement of silence was accomplished only by vigorous daily use of the whip, making Auburn a highly controversial prison. Nevertheless, the facility was an impressive resource that was regularly host to federal prisoners for a century or so. Prison receipts for the year ending September 30, 1845, showed a total of $1,115.58 for board of federal prisoners. Based on a guess of the daily fee being charged then, the year's receipts suggest a daily average population of about ten federal prisoners then at Auburn. Sing Sing accepted fewer federal prisoners, and the marshals seem not to have used Dannemora, probably because of its remote location.

The use of Auburn increased dramatically during the 1880s. A peak year was 1891, when Auburn admitted seventy-five federal inmates.[24] Prisoners often arrived in bunches, as a marshal would bring a group from some distant place. For instance, in 1891, nine men from Tennessee were admitted on one date. On several other dates, groups of prisoners were accepted from the District of Columbia.

Pennsylvania's answer to New York's Auburn prison was the Eastern State Penitentiary, opened in Philadelphia in 1829. Supplanting the Walnut Street Jail, which was later closed in 1835, the new structure was the country's most monumental commitment to the penitentiary concept. In fact, it was the largest building constructed in the United States to that time. The cells were extra-large, and each had its own walled garden. Every prisoner lived and worked entirely within his cell and was supposed never to encounter any other prisoner.

On October 25, 1829, the first state prisoner was admitted to the Eastern State Penitentiary, and four months later the first federal prisoners were received. U.S. Marshal John Conard wrote to Warden Samuel R. Wood about two men, George Wilson and James Porter, charged with robbing the mail, men who were "most likely to escape" if held in the inadequate local jails. The marshal commented, "I am well aware that the Penitentiary was built for certain convicted offenders of the state, and was not intended to be used as a bridewell for untried prisoners. We do not therefore ask this as a right, to be used as a precedent at any future time, but as a favor and for the furtherance of justice." The board accommodated the marshal without objection.[25] And, precedent or not, the prison long continued to be a resource regularly used for federal prisoners.

During the first few years of the nineteenth century other penitentiaries were built in the eastern states, and most, if not all, accepted federal prisoners from time to time. In Richmond, Virginia, one of the country's earliest penitentiaries was built by the state from a design by Benjamin Latrobe and opened in 1800. Latrobe later was retained by President Thomas Jefferson to carry forward the design and construction of the United States capitol. The Virginia penitentiary had three floors arranged in a horseshoe-shaped building; exposed balconies gave access to the cells. In one very special case, the state of Virginia advised the federal court of the availability of "apartments in the third story of the public jail and penitentiary house for the reception of such persons as shall be directed, under the authority of the United States, to be confined thererin."[26] This pronouncement followed an event in the spring of 1807, when a small contingent of mounted soldiers from Fort Stoddert, in Mississippi Territory, found and arrested a fugitive for whose capture a reward of two thousand dollars had been posted. The culprit, charged with treason, was the colorful Aaron Burr, former vice-president of the United States. Brought back to Richmond, Burr had to be held in custody for several months during his trial in the federal district court of Virginia. Burr was given privileged accommodations on the third floor of the penitentiary, with use of three adjoining rooms. Though large, the space was spartan and cheerless, but it had at least the advantage of privacy.[27]

The persons involved in Burr's trial included some of the major political figures of the day. An opening appearance for the prosecution was made by the U.S. attorney general, Caesar A. Rodney, while the bench was occupied by Chief Justice John Marshall who was taking a turn as a trial judge according to custom at that time.[28] Burr ultimately escaped the ordeal of serving a prison sentence; he was released upon the jury's odd finding that he was "not proved to be guilty."

The Virginia penitentiary served well enough for Burr's detention, but the federal government did not see fit to use it regularly. Over a period of time certain of the state prisons became favored and were more heavily used than others, depending on factors such as geographical location in relation to busy federal courts, reputations of the particular prisons and their wardens, nature of their accommodations, and management. The volume of federal offenders was not great, however, and there was no central coordinating office or statistical accounting.

The first systematic attempt to gain any comprehensive knowledge of the number and distribution of federal prisoners came in 1846 when the secretary of the treasury sent a circular inquiry to all U.S. marshals, asking what prisoners they then had in custody. The returns provide a useful picture of the volume and nature of federal crimes in a day when fewer offenses were designated as federal and when there were surprisingly few federal prisoners. Fourteen of the marshals reported they had no prisoners at all. Sixteen others listed one or more in custody. The northern district of New York reported the largest number, with twelve prisoners. The southern New York district was next with eight, while eastern Pennsylvania had six, Georgia had five, and Maryland four. The eleven other districts reported in with either one or two prisoners each. Some of the marshals reported the fees they paid for the board of prisoners; these amounts ranged from sixteen and one-half cents to twenty-eight cents per day. The reported categories of crimes and the number of prisoners in each category are shown below.[29]

Theft or embezzlement of U.S. mails	19
Counterfeiting	8
Assault on the high seas	3
Manslaughter	3
Mutiny at sea	3
Slave trade violations	3
Forgery	2
Perjury	2
Theft of government property	3
Assault	1
Attempting to create a revolt	1
Larceny	1
Total	48

The fact that this information was collected by the secretary of the treasury and not by the attorney general reflects some of the illogical expediencies of government organization at that time. For a long time Congress had refused to give the attorney general a staff or a bureaucratic function, and instead lodged various justice responsibilities with other bureaus. In 1820 the Treasury Department was authorized to employ an "agent" who would give direction as needed to U.S. district attorneys for civil suits on behalf of the United States.[30] This agent also served as a liaison with the marshals. The agent's work and the heavy demands for his services helped to demonstrate the need for a law department under the attorney general. The issue sputtered intermittently; in 1830 a compromise of a sort resulted in creation of the position of solicitor in the Treasury Department. The solicitor, asking advice from the attorney general when he should so choose, was to instruct district attorneys and clerks, oversee all civil litigation, enforce customs laws, and instruct the marshals as needed.[31]

In 1849 the Department of the Interior was created and was to supervise the accounts of district attorneys and marshals. Later, as territorial prisons were built, the secretary of the interior was made responsible for site selection and acquisition and for construction of such institutions.

Advocacy for a department of law persisted, but it was not until after the Civil War, and with the extra impetus given by its fallout of greatly increased cases of litigation, that the new department could be planned and achieved. Finally, the act to create a Department of Justice was signed by President Ulysses S Grant in June 1870, and the department came into being on July 1, headed by a new attorney general, Amos T. Akerman.[32] As its duties gradually were defined the Justice Department assumed responsibility for control and disposition of all federal prisoners, although there was still no move toward having federal prisons. Boarding of prisoners in state or local institutions was still to be the unquestioned practice.

Following the pattern started in 1820, on March 3, 1873, the position of "agent" was authorized for the new department, with duties that included oversight of prisoner placements. By a decade later, the title was "general agent," and there were three subordinate positions for "examiners" who traveled to make on-site inspections and report on all prisoner matters.[33]

Meanwhile a few of the state prisons were regularly, sometimes heavily, used for federal cases. One of these was the Albany County Penitentiary in New York, and it illustrates well the conditions that gradually led to pressure for federal institutions. Albany County Penitentiary was opened in the 1840s under Amos Pilsbury who became one of the country's best known wardens. When Pilsbury died in 1872, his place was taken by his son, Louis D. Pilsbury, who later left to become superintendent of all New York state prisons. Another who later achieved prominence was Zebulon R. Brockway; at age twenty-four Brockway became deputy warden at Albany and eventually was famous as an innovative warden at the Detroit House of Correction and, later, at the Elmira Reformatory.

In its early years, the Albany institution seemed well favored with a beautiful location by the Hudson River, good industries, and more than enough space in a suitable building. Pilsbury made a point of accepting prisoners at a fee from several other New York counties, as well as from federal courts, making his operation a profitable one apparently.[34] The marshals regularly brought prisoners from most of the eastern seaboard, using Albany particularly for District of Columbia prisoners.

Eventually, however, other prisons became more competitive, while there seemed to be new reasons to make less use of Albany. By the 1880s, the attorney general was receiving letters of complaint from Albany prisoners who protested about being whipped. Whipping was a form of punishment in use generally among prisons at the time, but the federal government was trying to restrict or forbid its use for federal prisoners. In the context of New York practice, the whipping at Albany was not as severe as at other prisons; at the Auburn institution, for instance, Warden Elam Lynds had made for himself and the prison a reputation based on the ferocity of the whipping. After Lynds was transferred to Ossining in 1825, to build and then operate the new Sing Sing prison, the whipping at Auburn continued, and the regime at Sing Sing became notably harsh.[35] Such conditions continued until the 1840s, when public criticism was strident enough to force prison inspectors to modify the disciplinary policies and legislators to order a retreat from uncontrolled whippings.[36] Notwithstanding the assertion of the Auburn warden that the "cat" could not be dispensed with safety, in 1847, the New York legislature prohibited whipping, except in self-defense or to suppress a riot. Two years later, the board of inspectors noted with satisfaction that the prisoners were better behaved and worked more productively.[37]

At the same time, Albany officials noted that fewer federal prisoners were being supplied to them, while the Auburn state prison and the Erie County (Buffalo) penitentiary were getting such prisoners. The nature of the competition is seen in the explanation furnished by the general agent. "It was understood that the U.S. prisoners were removed from Albany to Auburn because they had been whipped and because the Penitentiary at Buffalo offered terms more favorable to the United States."[38] One advantage offered by Erie County was their willingness to transport the prisoners to the penitentiary from the courts, and then to their homes after discharge, without charge to the government. The Auburn prison officials matched the Erie County offer and managed to hold on to some of the profitable business. On one occasion, the attorney general directed the marshal in Nashville to go to the Tennessee penitentiary and pick up several prisoners: "Having made written application to me to be transferred to a more healthful place of confinement, now therefore . . . you are directed to take the said prisoners . . . to the Warden of the Auburn prison."[39] By the following year, the Tennessee federal courts had designated the Erie County penitentiary as the place of confinement for any prisoners they might commit.[40]

As a general practice, the Department of Justice looked for humane treatment in the handling of its prisoners, but the department was hampered by backward conditions in most of the state prisons and also by the government's own penurious approach to boarding-out arrangements. The attorney general seemed always to be looking for bargains. Thus, for instance, when the marshal in Providence submitted his account of payments made to the state of Rhode Island for jailed prisoners in January 1881, headquarters responded that the bill would be paid, but thereafter the marshal should make every effort to get the jail rate reduced to thirty cents per day.[41]

At the same time, marshals in other states were urged to persuade state prisons to take federal cases without charge. The picayune level of this concern is seen in letters telling the marshals to protest any extra charges for such items as clothing, medicine, or laundry. It was the attorney general's opinion that prisoners could do their own laundry. As with any other kind of market, the rates usually depended upon demand in relation to supply. At one point, the state of Iowa, needing more prisoners to meet its contract labor obligations, inquired about getting federal men. The general agent, Brewster Cameron, replied to the warden that "the principal penitentiaries of the country are now supporting, furnishing guards, clothing and medical attendance and returning the prisoners to the place of conviction free of all expense to the government. If you desire to make a similar proposition the Department will give it due consideration."[42]

In his annual report of 1879, the attorney general noted that "where prisoners have been sentenced to long terms, and there was no suitable penitentiary in the district where they were convicted, they have principally been sent to the penitentiaries at Detroit, Michigan, or Albany, New York." When the Detroit House of Correction opened in 1861, Zebulon R. Brockway was brought from Albany to operate it and there began building his reputation as the country's most respected warden. In his decade of service in Detroit Brockway worked conscientiously to provide a rehabilitative setting. The federal courts obviously appreciated Brockway's work and sent ninety-nine prisoners there during his tenure.[43] Brockway makes a cryptic comment about them as a group. "Taken together, they were an interesting contingent possessed of positive characteristics in marked contrast with the characterlessness of the misdemeanor prisoners."[44]

By the 1880s the federal population at Detroit had climbed considerably, and more than one hundred such prisoners were on hand. At the same time, Pennsylvania's Western State Penitentiary and the New York institutions at Albany and Auburn had substantial federal contingents. The federal government by this time had housed its prisoners in borrowed space for something more than a century, without serious thought of creating its own institutions or facing the inevitable future demands for more space and quality control. But now, with its dependence on rented space, the Department of Justice was encountering problems severe enough that this arrangement was intolerable—and getting worse. Federal institutions would have to come, and, considering the time normally required to convince and energize Congress to take action, the campaign would have to be vigorously pursued. The attorneys general, one after another, made the point at every congressional session, and fortunately some notable citizens added effective voices to the effort.

2

THE DEMAND FOR FEDERAL PRISONS

In his annual report for 1875, Attorney General Edwards Pierrepont worried that federal prisoners, when confined in prisons of any state or territory, were to be subject to the same control, treatment, and discipline as the prisoners of the state. "Under this law," Pierrepont said, "great wrongs are done and cruelties are practiced, which call for immediate redress." He went on to give a stinging indictment of the widely prevalent contract labor practices.

> In some of the States the system prevails of letting the prisoners to work for cruel task-masters, and while the United States pay for the keeping of their prisoners from 70 cents to $1 each per day, these same prisoners earn a large amount of money, which goes to the keeper of the prison, and of which no account is ever rendered to the United States, while the prisoners are often driven a long distance to work for those who hire them, are improperly fed and clothed, over-worked, sometimes severely beaten for slight offenses, and are made a source of large profit to those who avail themselves of this kind of forced labor. While working under this system of letting, large numbers of United States prisoners have escaped. . . . The Attorney General is empowered, when at the time of conviction there may be no suitable prison in the District, to designate some prison in a convenient State or Territory; but he has no power after the criminal is consigned to a State prison to change his place of confinement or relieve him from inhuman treatment. Such authority might easily be given by Congress.[1]

Pierrepont was right that Congress could grant the attorney general power to exercise more control over conditions of confinement in federal cases, but Congress would not take such a big step hastily. It was not until 1887, during the first administration of Grover Cleveland, that Congress finally acted to forbid any contracting out of federal prisoners.[2] That step became a potent factor in eventually forcing the federal government to authorize its own prisons, for the states in many cases virtually closed their doors to federal prisoners when they no longer could sell their labor.

During the economically difficult years after the Civil War the states developed several stratagems for employment of their prisoners. Among these alternatives were the contract system, the piece-price system, the public account system, and the lease system. State authorities were not concerned with beneficent ideas of work therapy or trade training, but only with saving state money.

Under the contract system, prisoners worked in prison shops operated by outside contractors. The prisoners were directed by the contractors who paid an agreed upon daily price for the labor.

With the piece-price system, the prison operated the shops and directed the work, while outside contractors furnished the materials or parts and paid the prison for finished products at an agreed piece price.

Using the public account system, the prison operated its own manufacturing shops and sold its products to the best available market.

Under the lease system, the prison sent prisoners out to a contractor who leased them for his own purposes and worked them at his discretion, at a site he maintained.[3]

Of these four systems, the latter was much the worst. "Under the lease system, a private citizen, group, or business would negotiate a legal contract for either part or, more often, the whole of a state's convicted felons. While such leases might specify minimum standards of security and maintenance, the distinguishing characteristic of the lease operation was the total control it vested in the lessee. The lessee alone determined the type and amount of labor done by prisoners and the conditions of confinement."[4]

The self-supporting prison was a goal eagerly sought by all the states. Variations on the leasing or contracting out of prisoners were tried nationwide, although the more insidious examples were in southern states.[5] While the contracting out process brought substantial savings in state prison costs, the side effects were reprehensible in the views of many. Humanitarians were disturbed by the gross hardships and high mortality rates among contracted out prisoners, especially in leased labor camps, and both labor unions and manufacturers were critical of the competition from prison labor. Particularly through the last three decades of the nineteenth century, the various states groped for solutions to the prison labor problem and experimented with legislation to keep labor unions placated and prisons productive. For a time, the states profited by taking federal prisoners, but when the Department of Justice stopped allowing its prisoners to be contracted out, the states quickly lost interest in accommodating them, unless board rates were increased. In any event, available space was substantially reduced, even while the number of federal prisoners steadily increased. Because fewer facilities were usable, the marshals had to make longer and more costly trips to deliver prisoners.

After the Civil War, throughout the southern states there were almost no prisons available for use by the federal government. Prisoners often were brutally and callously exploited for their labor, and while economic conditions were not sufficient reason to excuse the abuses, they did make the practices understandable. The South was seriously short of prison space, and it faced an enormous task of industrial rebuilding everywhere. With no money available to build prison cells or to support prisoners in them, the leasing of prisons to private contractors, or the contracting out of prisoners to work on roads, railroads, canals, or mines was an inevitable expedient. A preponderance of southern prisoners were blacks and the penal system consigned them to a new and particularly callous form of slavery. In Louisiana, for instance, "Plantation work was adopted after the Civil War at a time when the vast majority of convicts were Negroes. There was much cotton picking and cane cutting to be done in the 1870s, and because most of the inmates (as slaves) had been experts in this line of work, sending many of them back to the fields seemed the natural (and most profitable) policy to pursue."[6]

Less than ten years after the Civil War, one man from the deep South wrote and lectured so effectively about abuses of the convict lease systems that he was heard nationwide. George Washington Cable was a New Orleans newspaper reporter and author of Creole stories when, in 1881, he was put on a grand jury investigating local prison conditions.

Impelled by his dismay over the treatment of prisoners, Cable persuaded his city to create a nonpolitical Board of Prisons and Asylums Commissioners. One thing led to another. Cable was next asked to write articles about prison reform for the New Orleans *Times-Democrat,* and he soon obliged with a series of seven articles in which he described brutal treatment of prisoners and blamed public apathy for the appalling conditions. "In writing of the parish prison he alluded to matters that would soil the page if he recorded them. . . . He marshaled horrifying details of facilities and management, but his main thesis was that the public was responsible and was itself ultimately the sufferer."[7]

Cable was invited to address the 1883 National Conference of Charities and Corrections in Louisville. As one conference member later observed, "The most notable event in the Louisville Conference was the presentation of a monumental paper upon 'the convict lease system' by George Washington Cable, the famous author from Louisiana. It occupies thirty-five pages of the conference report and still remains the most accurate and vivid exposition of the subject ever written."[8] Cable detailed the abuses of convicts in the leased labor camps in twelve states across the South, combining an effective emotional appeal with hard supportive evidence of facts and statistics. The speech was printed in *Century* magazine and circulated nation wide; Cable achieved national status when he was elected a vice-president of the National Prison Association.

Cable was an astute investigator who looked past the banal self-congratulatory prose of official prison reports and found the human tragedies they masked. He told how prisoners spent their lives and health to make money for the operators in building railroad tunnels, quarrying stone, and constructing roads, canals, or levees. His scathing observation was that a sentence to such imprisonment was, in effect, a life sentence, as most men could not survive the brutal conditions. His facts argued that "ten years, as the rolls show, is the utmost length of time that a convict can be expected to remain alive."[9] In forming his conclusions about the whole contract system Cable bluntly asserted "that it kills like a pestilence, teaches the people to be cruel, sets up a false system of clemency, and seduces the State into the committal of murder for money."[10] Even if the Department of Justice had wanted to use prisons operated by lessees, it could hardly have continued to do so after Cable's revelations. Understandably, the attorney general, in his annual report for 1879, stated that U.S. prisoners sentenced to long terms usually were sent north, either to Albany or Detroit.

Cable's accounts were so convincingly researched and so soundly reasoned that they generally incited little or no rebuttal, even in the South. Nevertheless, southerners did not like their prisons to be compared with those in the north. A Cable biographer astutely observes:

> [The leased prisoners] Cable was talking about were for the most part Negroes. Jailed often on very slight pretext, given lengthy prison terms for what frequently were no more than simple misdemeanors, they were in effect being sold into bondage again, under working conditions that equalled or surpassed the very worst that antebellum slavery had to offer. Without actually saying so, therefore, Cable was by implication attacking the South's treatment of Negroes. Though the states of the former Confederacy had ostensibly acquiesced in the abolition of human slavery, Cable implied, widespread involuntary servitude was nevertheless still being carried on under the guise of penal correction.[11]

While the worst examples of the lease system were in the South, in both North and South state officials failed to set and enforce any standards of care and custody for their prisoners. This lack gradually narrowed the range of choices for places to assign federal prisoners; at the same time, it caused the cost of prisoner boarding to rise, inexorably increasing pressure for the federal government to provide its own prisons.

Cable's writings and speeches came at an opportune time to reinforce the growing interest of many people in this possibility. In fact, much of the history of the movement for federal prisons is revealed by the personal histories of outstanding individuals such as Cable; the movement can be fully defined only through an understanding of both the broad social conditions and the leaders who spoke effectively for needed change. Usually these leaders were from outside government, free of the political constraints that affected government officials. In addition to Cable, the best remembered is Enoch Cobb Wines.

The influence of Wines on the federal prison issue was indirect but important in creating a context that could nurture reform. His outstanding accomplishment was the part he played in the inception of the first national organization for corrections professionals. Central to Wines' life-long career was a strong, unquestioning religious zeal; though he achieved his distinguished reputation as an educator, he previously had served several years as a minister in two New England locations.[12]

In 1862, at age fifty-six, Wines was appointed secretary of the New York Prison Association and plunged vigorously into the task of making that organization an effective voice for reform. He soon teamed with another zealot, Theodore W. Dwight, to visit and survey the major adult and juvenile institutions of the time. Their investigative travels and correspondence, conducted shortly after the Civil War, led to their impressive 1867 *Report on the Prisons and Reformatories of the United States and Canada.*[13]

With his broad-gauged, creative intellect, Wines could not be confined to his own state agency, and it was he who suggested to his peers that a national meeting be called. That gathering of enthusiastic U.S. and foreign prison workers in Cincinnati, in 1870, was the well-known beginning of the National Prison Association—the modern American Correctional Association.

Whether anything was said at the Cincinnati meeting about the problems of federal prisoners is not important. What is significant is that, finally, a useful forum existed through which interested leaders could—and would—effectively attack the issue of federal prisons. Wines made his feelings on the subject clear enough in his writings, as he no doubt did at various podiums. In one book he expressed dismay that the federal government, without its own prisons, could not enforce decent standards for its prisoners. "It has no control, no voice, no influence over the discipline of the prisons to which they have been committed. That discipline may be cruelly severe or unwisely lenient. . . . But the Government . . . can only sit silent and let the work of corruption go on."[14]

Following the Civil War, and for the remainder of the nineteenth century, the general agitation for prison reform carried with it the side issue of federal institutions for federal prisoners. Among the prominent leaders who helped give the cause respectability was Rutherford B. Hayes, President of the United States from 1877 to 1881. As governor of Ohio, Hayes had welcomed Wines and the other corrections professionals to the meeting in Cincinnati and had stayed to take a genuine interest in the proceedings. On his return to Ohio, after his term as president, Hayes showed such a continuing interest in prison issues that in 1883 he was elected president of the Prison Association. During his decade with the Prison Association, he missed no opportunity to speak with well-informed sincerity about more effective and more humane ways of dealing with offenders. Hayes gave the association prestige and helped it become a gathering place for people of influence in penology. Inevitably, the programs at the association's annual meetings included presentations on the kinds of problems that argued for a strong federal role in corrections. [15]

Outstanding among the leaders who followed Hayes to the association and who took up the federal prison issue was another Ohioan, Roeliff Brinkerhoff. As a young lawyer and newspaper editor in Mansfield, Brinkerhoff had developed an active concern about political and social issues. During the war years, he left to serve in the Union Army; on his return, he started a new career as a banker. In 1879 he was appointed to the Board of State Charities, a position that exposed him to problems within Ohio's prisons and asylums. On his own initiative Brinkerhoff visited prisons in other states and became knowledgeable on the subject. He continued his regular career in the business community, but for many years he poured his considerable extra energy into the work of improving prisons and mental hospitals. Brinkerhoff joined the National Prison Association in 1883, at the same time Hayes became its president. When Hayes died, ten years later, Brinkerhoff was elected to replace him, and for most of the two decades after about 1880, Brinkerhoff was the single most vocal and effective advocate of a new federal role in corrections. [16]

One of the issues on which Brinkerhoff took an unpopular stand was the need for nonpartisan administration of prisons. Political patronage, including prison management appointments, was a taken-for-granted practice in Ohio, as in most states. Thus, Brinkerhoff was not appreciated by everyone when he gave the report of the State

Board of Charities for 1878 and in it called for an end to patronage in the prison system. The annoyed legislators voted not to publish the report, but an affluent member of the Board of Charities ordered 1,500 copies printed at his personal expense.[17] Despite such minor setbacks, Brinkerhoff's prestige grew at both the state and national levels. He became convinced of the value of the new idea of parole and spoke so effectively for it that Ohio set an example for the country and enacted a parole law in 1885. Brinkerhoff was less successful in his opposition to political patronage. Such appointments not only continued in the state systems but also became regular practice in the federal system when the new U.S. penitentiaries Brinkerhoff fought for were opened.

In 1880, while he was preparing a report to the National Conference of Charities and Corrections, Brinkerhoff wished to make reference to the problem of federal prisoners. He asked for statistical data from the attorney general, but the response he received gave him no real information. He next wrote to his congressman for help but the congressman only referred Brinkerhoff to the attorney general. Soon afterward Brinkerhoff was in Washington, so he used the opportunity to go directly to the Department of Justice:

> The head of the department was away, but his representative received me cordially, and turned me over to Mr. Haight, the young man in charge of the prison department, with instructions to afford me all assistance possible. After hearing my inquiries, he told me it would take a little time, but he would send answers to my hotel by the next morning. Not hearing from him the next day I called again, and then he told me he was not yet through but would send me a full report to my address in Boston. The outcome was I got no response whatever.[18]

At that time the Department of Justice was only ten years old and, with its minimal funding, had not yet developed a system to track the many prisoners it had in scattered placements. Brinkerhoff's difficulties in finding any basic data increased his determination to persevere in the search. By writing directly to state penitentiary wardens and by pursuing reports in the Library of Congress, he was able to assemble enough information to impress delegates to the National Prison Congress at Saratoga in 1884 with the seriousness of the issue. As organizations typically do, the Prison Congress appointed a committee, with Brinkerhoff as chairman, to study the problem and recommend ways for improvement of record keeping regarding federal prisoners in jails.

At the 1885 meeting in Detroit, Brinkerhoff did make his report; nor was that the end of it. He persisted in his data gathering and in his repeated admonitions to every appropriate audience that the time had come for separate federal prisons. During those years he was probably more precisely informed about the many aspects of the issue than the Department of Justice was. And despite his frustration with the department, Brinkerhoff could understand its problem. Regarding his critical speeches in 1884 and 1885, he later noted, "The department of justice very naturally was much disturbed at the revelations made, but did not dispute my statements. In reality, I think the department was doing the best it could under the existing conditions, and with the limited appropriations allowed."[19]

In 1895, Brinkerhoff was able to report that 2,516 federal felons were held in prisons in thirty states, compared to only 1,027 ten years earlier. During the same ten-year period, the number of federal pre-trial or misdemeanor prisoners in jails had increased from more than ten thousand to more than fifteen thousand.[20] Echoing Cable, whom he admired, Brinkerhoff noted that of the thirty penitentiaries used for federal prisoners, not one was in the South.

Probably Brinkerhoff's most poignant appeal on this subject was in his speech at the 1887 Congress of the National Prison Association. As vice- president of the association, giving the closing address, he put his considerable feelings into the issue of federal prisoners, noting that "there is now a substantial unanimity of conviction that they should be cared for in federal prisons, in charge of federal officials. For a great government like ours to convict its citizens of violations of its laws, and then turn them over to the tender mercies of officials over whom it has no control and in whose appointment it has no voice, is a shame and a disgrace which ought to be corrected, and that most speedily."[21]

The fact that the Department of Justice could not give any useful data about its roll of prisoners did not mean that it was unconcerned. Sensitive to the increasing criticism, it was evident that successive attorneys general saw the worsening problem and were more than willing to correct it if Congress would implement the means. The annual reports of the Justice Department repeatedly addressed the issue, often with cases illustrating the situation. Attorney General Akerman, in his first annual report (1871) after the new Department of Justice was organized, made a wry point about the weakness of the government's management of its prisoners.

> If Congress shall choose to leave the Government dependent upon the comity of the States for prisons, I suggest the propriety of a law which shall forbid unauthorized release of persons imprisoned under sentence of the courts of the United States. An instance has recently occurred of a release of such a prisoner by a jailer for the avowed reason that the law under which the prisoner was convicted was disapproved by that functionary, and the only known remedy is a prosecution in the State courts.[22]

The Congress eventually passed legislation that seemed to vindicate Cable's campaign against the leasing of prisoners. In 1887 it prohibited the contracting out of federal prisoners, an action that was probably more far-reaching in its effect than Congress realized at the time. It would be reassuring to think that the legislation was a high-minded move stemming from concern about the humane treatment of prisoners. More to the point, it was a political response to pressures from both unions and manufacturers that feared competition from the prison systems. In fact, during the previous year, manufacturers had organized the National Anti-Convict Contract Association.[23] But if the motivation was only political expediency, at least the effect was a solid step forward, and the act had one result that probably had not been anticipated. It closed many doors to federal prisoner placement and thereby increased the pressure for the government to establish its own prisons. When state prison wardens could not only charge board rates for federal prisoners, but could also sell prisoner labor for additional revenue, they were happy to house as many federal felons as space allowed. But as Attorney General

Augustus H. Garland noted, when sale of the labor was no longer allowed, the prisons in many cases either raised their board rates or declined to take the prisoners at all.

> There should be, in my opinion, provisions at once made looking to the erection of at least one United States penitentiary, and if possible, a reformatory. The objection in the minds of many, that the cost of conducting such an institution would be so much greater than the existing arrangement, is being about overcome by the fact that the favorable contracts which the Department has heretofore been able to enter into can no longer be made. This arises from the fact that laws passed recently by several of the States and by Congress . . . prevent the employment of prisoners on contract labor.[24]

During this same period, when the federal government was finding fewer state institutions open to its prisoners, it was also in the uncomfortable position of having to admit that some of its own institutions were substandard. The United States government did, in fact, own several prisons—the territorial prisons in the west—and they tended to be minimal in most respects. Not surprisingly, they reflected the raw, primitive quality of the frontier areas they served, sometimes giving the attorney general some twinges of conscience in having to use them. Not only the basic amenities, but also adequate security features were often lacking. Principally these were the prisons at Boise, Idaho; Deer Lodge, Montana; Salt Lake City, Utah; McNeil's Island, Washington; and Laramie, Wyoming.

Such facilities were under the general direction of the U.S. marshals in their respective territories, but responsibility for site selection and prison construction lay with the secretary of the interior. As each territory achieved statehood it was usual for the federal government to turn over to the state its territorial prison. The new states, always short of funds to carry out their added responsibilities, sometimes resorted to contracting out prisoners, a practice the federal government had proscribed.

In 1864 Congress authorized the Department of the Interior to designate which state prisons were to be used by the federal government and to pay the costs of transporting prisoners. An act of 1871 defined the attorney general's responsibility for supervising the marshals and their prisons. A year later, control of funds for the purpose was finally transferred from the Interior Department to the attorney general who was then shaping the function of his new department.[25]

Often prisoners had to be transported long distances to the Midwest or Northeast rather than being left in substandard territorial facilities. For example, in 1872, the attorney general designated the Michigan state prison at Jackson to be used for U.S. prisoners from Wyoming and Utah territories; while prisoners from New Mexico territory went to the Missouri penitentiary.

California became so populous following the gold rush that it achieved statehood in 1850, ahead of other territories in the West. Within another two years the new state opened a penitentiary at San Quentin, and the U.S. marshals made regular use of it. In 1889, when the warden prepared a list of all admissions covering the previous twenty-four years, it included 162 federal prisoner admissions. Most were from California, but a few were from Alaska, Arizona, Oregon, and Washington.[26]

Through the 1870s and 1880s, calls for a federal prison system were voiced with increasing urgency. The most insistent advocate continued to be Brinkerhoff, backed by the collective voice of the National Prison Association, and successive attorneys general made the needed prison system an issue in each annual report. Although the new Department of Justice gained authority over federal prisoners in the early 1870s, the attorney general possessed none of the management tools for the job. There was no central statistical service, and there was no machinery for central control of the prisoner placements until an act of 1873 authorized a position entitled agent. This agent was to serve the attorney general, performing various duties, including any matters that pertained to prisoners. By the end of the decade the "agent" had become a "general agent," and by 1882 the general agent had three subordinates entitled "examiners."[27] Apparently the Mr. Haight whom Brinkerhoff encountered in his futile search for prisoner statistics was this overworked general agent.

Having some staff to serve him in prison matters was a welcome advantage, but the attorney general still had little power to control imprisonments when the only prisons he had were the inadequate territorial facilities. He could not make any demands upon state prisons in respect to their care of federal prisoners, and he could not require them to supply routine reports.

The Fifty-first Congress, in the year 1891, took the first step toward providing the federal government with its own prisons. After a decade of trumpeting the need for this, Roeliff Brinkerhoff had the satisfaction of seeing the so-called three-prison act passed.

> The Attorney General and Secretary of the Interior be, and are hereby, authorized and directed to purchase three sites, two of which shall be located as follows: one north, the other south of the thirty-ninth degree of north latitude and east of the Rocky Mountains, the third site to be located west of the Rocky Mountains, and the same to be located geographically as to be most easy of access to the different portions of the country, and cause to be erected thereon suitable buildings for the confinement of all persons convicted of any crime whose term of imprisonment is one year or more at hard labor by any court of the United States.[28]

The credit for accomplishing this legislation goes to no one person; the law would not have come into being without the persistent pleadings of successive attorneys general, powerfully augmented by influential persons and organizations outside government. The bill was introduced in the House as H.R. 182 by a Georgian, John David Stewart, a second-term congressman, member of the Judiciary Committee, ordained Baptist minister, and former superior court judge. Stewart found the measure was not an easy one to push to enactment; the opening debate evoked a variety of opposition arguments and numerous attempts to amend the bill.

Arguing strongly for the measure was the attorney general of the time, William H. Miller, with backup help from his predecessor, Augustus H. Garland. Much of the opposition centered on the issues of probable cost and the organizational concept to be followed. The latter concern was voiced by William McAdoo of New Jersey, who viewed with alarm the proposed placement of the prison administration under the attorney general.

> I do not believe it to be a wise policy to intrust the administration of a prison to the prosecuting officer of the government. My own

idea has been that it is only in the comic opera where the lord high chancellor and the lord high executioner are one and the same and the duties of their respective offices are combined in the same individual. The Attorney General of the United States has a quasi-judicial function to exercise and it is his duty as such to protect the liberty of the citizen, on the one hand, as well as to enforce the laws of the Government on the other. But by the combination of the two functions as embodied in this bill you make the Attorney General the prosecutor in the first place and then the administrator of the jail. . . . I believe it will be a wise principle in this country, in the making of rules for the administration of these penal institutions, to separate these two functions, and that the conduct of the prisons should be given to the Department of the Interior, where it naturally belongs, and that it should rest there alone.[29]

On the other hand, Ezra B. Taylor of Ohio, chairman of the Judiciary Committee, was confident that the attorney general was the proper official for the responsibility.

In my opinion the officer of the United States best calculated to have charge of this matter of the care of prisoners is the Attorney General of the United States. From a humanitarian point of view I believe his services are more valuable in this capacity than those of any other officer of the Government, because he knows, it may be presumed, more about the subject than does any other officer. All the reports concerning the prisoners are made to him; he has the whole matter in his charge; he therefore has the opportunity to know more thoroughly than any other officer of the Government the needs of the various classes of criminals. . . . The Attorney General is not the active prosecuting attorney; he stands, as he ought to stand, defending the rights of the criminal as well as the rights of the public. . . . Aside from this, the Secretary of the Interior is already overburdened with business; and if this matter were placed in his charge it might result in a thoughtless administration of the law.

Other arguments, extensive and practical, were presented in favor of keeping the responsibility for prison administration in the Department of Justice, and eventually that view prevailed. The final act did give the secretary of the interior some responsibility for the acquisition of sites, a function that had been his anyway. But the act clearly stated "that the control and management of said prisons be vested in the Attorney General."

Congressman Stewart found that his most vocal opponent was a fellow Georgian, Judson C. Clements, who used the opportunity to champion the interests of some of his tobacco farmer constituents. Clements was hotly critical of the taxes that restricted the freedom of tobacco growers, and he found a thin thread to link this concern to the federal prison proposal. "The country needs legislation," he said, "that will avoid the cruel imprisonment of honest people under oppressive and un-American laws more than it needs prisons in which to incarcerate them." The object of his displeasure was "this oppressive tobacco tax which prohibits a man from cultivating, raising and selling freely in the open market, to the highest bidder, the product of his own land and his own toil." Though other congressmen sympathized with the need for tax reform, no one else saw it as relevant to the prison issue. Another opposing argument was the ancient and inevitable plea, what's wrong with the way we have always done it? William S. Holman of Indiana led the members who were oblivious to the gross abuses in the state prisons and the increasing difficulty of finding acceptable placements for federal prisoners.

> I think there is no existing evil which requires the remedy contemplated by the bill. There may be parts of the country where it is inconvenient to make contracts for the custody and safe-keeping of prisoners convicted by the Federal courts; but if such exists, it certainly cannot apply to any material extent of country or to any considerable number of states. Gentlemen should bear in mind therefore, in the consideration of this bill, that there are but few States of the Union which discourage or prohibit arrangements between the State authorities and the Attorney General for the keeping of the Federal prisoners.

Holman was badly misinformed. He also was alarmed about costs, and he offered the interesting argument that "while this measure will not diminish at all the number of State officials employed for such purpose, not by a single man—just see what an army of employees under the Federal Government you are providing for."

In rebuttal Congressman Taylor noted that "both the present Attorney General and the last one estimated this system as one of saving in the keeping of prisoners, instead of enlarging the costs." Undoubtedly both of the opposing arguments were defective on this issue.

Finally, some of the members made telling comments about the growing effect of the nationwide opposition to contract labor and the prospect that, in a few years, the Department of Justice would have serious difficulty in finding spaces for its prisoners.

The outcome was close. When the chairman brought debate to an end the measure was passed with a vote of 116 to 104, with 108 members not voting.

Months passed before the bill could get effective attention in the Senate, and there the debate was negligible. The measure depended upon the efforts of a prominent Senator from Massachusetts, George F. Hoar, whose real interests were in other fields and who was only superficially informed on the prison issue.

Senator Hoar, a member of the Senate Judiciary Committee, was a highly respected, widely known politician, a member of a Worcester family, noted in business, law, and politics. (The Senator's older brother, Ebenezer, had been President Grant's first attorney general and was the last to serve in that office before the Department of Justice was created.) Apparently Senator Hoar was approached about the prison issue just ten days before the debate in the House. A constituent, William S. Greene, general Superintendent of Massachusetts Prisons, wrote to Hoar:

> I have this day given a letter of introduction to Mr. F. H. Wines, Secretary of National Prison Association, which he will probably soon present to you.
>
> He desires to call attention to the necessity of action by Congress providing for for the establishment of a "Prison Bureau" under the Department of Justice, and also to the importance of a favorable response to the invitation of the Russian Government to this country to be represented in the International Penitentiary Congress at

St. Petersburg in Sept. 1890. I heartily endorse the subject and trust you may conclude after his presentation of the case, to take favorable action thereon.[30]

(When this letter was written Enoch C. Wines had been dead for just over a month, but his son had picked up effectively on many of his father's interests while developing a broad social service career of his own.)

Whatever Wines or Greene may have done to follow up on this start, they did succeed in obtaining Senator Hoar's support. However, the Senate Judiciary Committee members had a few ideas of their own. Though the House had debated and finally rejected the proposal to put the prisons under the Secretary of the Interior, the Senate came up with still another administrative design. It proposed an amendment to create an independent three-man commission, to be appointed by the president. This commission would plan the construction of three prisons, each with a capacity of six hundred, and "accommodations for juvenile convicts and first offenders." The bill went with Senator Hoar to a joint conference committee to reconcile House and Senate versions. The House was stubbornly unimpressed with the Senate version, and on February 29, 1891, Senator Hoar reported back to the Senate that the bill had no chance of passing as amended by the Senate. When Hoar then urged passage of the House version, the Senate made no further issue of the administrative arrangement. Hoar, in the only argument he offered in favor of federal prisons, stated lamely that "the Attorney General of the United States informs me that prisoners from the south under the present arrangement are committed to Northern prisons, and there is a great tendency among them to pneumonia and other diseases of the lungs; that the climate and air of those prisons is very injurious to many of them."[31]

It must be supposed that the Judiciary Committee, and undoubtedly other members of the Senate, had already heard far more urgent and persuasive arguments than that, for the Senate was ready to move on the matter. The Senate's amendment was withdrawn, and the bill was passed; in March it was signed and became law. The final form of the act specified that it should not apply to minors, but it provided that prisoners under the age of twenty should have cells and yard space separate from older prisoners, and that their management "shall be as far as possible reformatory." The contract labor issue, the most impelling factor behind the legislation, was reflected in the stricture "that convicts be employed exclusively in the manufacture of such supplies for the Government as can be manufactured without the use of machinery, and the prisoners shall not be worked outside the prison enclosure."

The three-prison act was a profoundly significant new development. For the first time, the federal government was committed to the idea of having its own prisons to house its own prisoners. Even so the new law was only a token start. Though the act authorized some funds for necessary planning, no money was appropriated for prison construction. The first ground-breaking was yet six years in the future.

3

THE FIRST
THREE PRISONS

The penitentiary at Leavenworth, Kansas, was the first of the three; and yet, to be strictly correct, there was one earlier federal penitentiary. Now virtually forgotten, it was built beside the Anacostia River in Washington, D.C. Although the facility was known as the United States Penitentiary for the District of Columbia, Congress authorized it as a national penitentiary. The prison opened in 1831, complete with a twenty-foot wall, guard towers, and shops for making brooms and shoes. It had 150 cells for men and 64 for women.

Because the Department of Justice did not yet exist, the penitentiary was placed under the direction of the Department of the Interior, and its warden was appointed by the president. Had it not been for the institution's location and the advent of the Civil War, it might still be in operation. But, adjoining the prison was an army base that needed extensive enlarging when the war started, so the penitentiary was closed in 1862, and the prisoners were transferred to state prisons, mostly to Albany.[1]

The institution was never replaced, and the concept of federally owned and operated prisons disappeared until 1891, when Congress authorized three prisons. Leavenworth, a small town a few miles north of Kansas City on the Missouri River, was picked as the site of the first prison, for the simple reason that a prison already existed there, and it could be taken over, at least temporarily.

Fort Leavenworth had its roots in early measures taken to tame the West. In the 1820s, increasing westward migrations made it necessary to establish a military base for protection of parties traveling the Santa Fe Trail or the Missouri River. The army assigned Colonel Henry Leavenworth to find a location for a new fort and to start its construction. The place he chose in 1827 was later given his name and became what is yet a major army base. In 1875, after a half century of growth and use, the fort was chosen as the site for a military prison; within a year Fort Leavenworth housed more than three hundred prisoners in a remodeled quartermaster supply depot building.[2]

The army used its new prison for only two decades and then had to give it up. With a federal civilian prison being badly needed and no congressional appropriation for one forthcoming, it was all too tempting to take over an existing one. In 1894, the secretary of war reluctantly conceded to the House Appropriations committee that his department could do without the military prison if it dispersed prisoners to small lockups on various other bases.[3] The following year Congress transferred the facility to the Department of Justice even though other army personnel did not agree with the secretary's agreeableness about the decision. "In spite of all arguments to the contrary, such a transfer was directed by Congress, and on July 1, 1895, the Department of Justice took over the plant and inaugurated the United States Penitentiary."[4] This move was the beginning of a symbiotic relationship between civilian prisons and military reservations, one that would persist and be important to both until the present time.

The commandant of the military prison, James W. Pope, whatever his own feelings about having the prison taken from him, was gracious and cooperative in easing the transfer. A civilian warden had to be selected, and numerous items of property had to be transferred or replaced. Hay for pillows and ticks, and cloth for prisoner uniforms were carried over. Pope recommended that a program for staff training be instituted, that a coal mine be opened, and new cell houses be built. Particularly he urged that the attorney general should select a highly qualified, professional warden to be hired on a nonpolitical merit basis, and that the salary should be at least five thousand dollars annually.[5]

Both of the latter suggestions were ignored, even though the first two wardens happened to be of professional stature. When the building was formally transferred to the Justice Department, Pope gave the keys to its new warden, James W. French. French, who came to Leavenworth after four years as warden at the Indiana State

Prison, had previously been a newspaper editor and a member of the Indiana Legislature. He quickly found a surfeit of problems that needed immediate correction. Shortly before French's appointment, General Agent Frank Strong had warned the attorney general of the problems ahead.

> The prison proper consists of two cell houses, with kitchens, shops, laundry, electric plant, boiler house, chapel and school room etc. surrounded by a stone wall, twenty feet high. The cell houses were not built for the purposes originally, but have been converted from three-story brick and stone dormitories by placing on each floor a row of steel cages about eight feet high, and some seven by nine feet in area. The tops of the cells are made of round iron bars (about ¾ inch) and about three inches apart. The partitions, ends and sides are of solid sheet iron or steel, each cell having a barred door. . . . The floors are of wood.[6]

Congressional leaders soon learned how unrealistic it was to expect a gift prison to be adequate. A substantial appropriation could not be avoided. The cell houses had wooden floors, ceilings, and stairs, and each dormitory of forty to ninety cells had only one door. The wardens worried greatly about the danger of fire during the several years this prison was used. Less than a year after the Justice Department took over Leavenworth, the House Judiciary Committee recommended that the facility be replaced.[7] On June 10, 1896, Congress authorized a new institution. The act decreed that the necessary acreage be taken from one edge of the military reservation property and specified that convict labor be used to build a prison with "a good capacity to accommodate at least 1,200 convicts."

Warden French did not delay; by the spring of 1897 he was marching prisoners every morning two and one-half miles from the Fort Leavenworth prison to their work at the new site. No federal prison was built so slowly as this one; the work went on for two and one-half decades. Labor-intensive methods were utilized by unskilled prisoners whose work days were shortened by the necessary count times and the long march daily between the fort and the construction site. For most of the time that was the only work to occupy the inmates.

The fort's prison, as French reported, had "shops fully equipped with the best machinery for making boots and shoes, tables, chairs, stools, and other furniture, harness, brooms, brushes, and all kinds of tinware, wagons, ambulances, carriages etc." But the shops stood idle; there was no market to serve. Because the work force now comprised civilian prisoners, the army would no longer buy the products.[8]

Under such conditions, the prison managers were fortunate to have the construction work, though it was miserably arduous labor for both prisoners and staff, French noted. "[The guard] must rise at 5 AM to be ready for duty when the gates open at 6. At 7 AM the convicts have had their breakfast and are in line to march to work. It is 6 PM before they are again locked in their cells and 7 PM by the time the guard has had his supper. This makes fourteen hours time, twelve of which were spent in continuous and active duty."[9]

Travel time from home and back again added to the daily strain. The prison, located about three miles from the town, was served by what was considered rather poor trolley service that cost a guard three dollars per month. With a regimen such as this, it would seem probable that most of the guards would have little energy left for frivolous activity, but the management took no chances. Rules recorded in 1898 specified that "guards shall refrain from whistling, scuffling, immodest laughter, profanity, boisterous conversation, exciting discussion on politics, or other subjects calculated to disturb the harmony and good order of the penitentiary." Nor were the guards given a much longer leash when off duty; they were forbidden to frequent saloons or gambling houses. To put some teeth in the rule the managers made this stipulation: "[the deputy warden] shall consider it his duty to make himself acquainted with the social habits and conduct of every subordinate officer and employee, and particularly whether, when off duty, he is a frequenter of saloons or other houses of similar resort, or associates with idle or loose characters, and report the facts to the warden."[10] For such a life the pay was sixty dollars per month, out of which the guards were to buy their uniforms.

Rules for prisoners were as repressive here as in all prisons of the time. A gray uniform was issued to each new prisoner, and later, subject to good behavior, it was exchanged for one of blue. The common black and white striped uniform was not worn, except by prisoners in the "third class": recaptured escapees and others under punishment. Prisoners could write a letter every two weeks; the government furnished the envelope and stamp. All mail was censored, of course. And "when approaching any officer or guard of the penitentiary to speak to him, caps must be removed, arms folded, and low tones and respectful language used." Among the items in a list of forty-three possible offenses were such vaguely defined crimes as "crookedness," "coat not buttoned when in use," "laughing and fooling." The list ended with a catch-all offense, "Unbecoming conduct not above mentioned."[11]

Spartan as the regimen sounds, Warden French was pleased with himself for having improved the amenities after he took over from the army. Within a few months he reported to his superior, Frank Strong, that the prisoners, previously given no pillows, now had muslin pillows stuffed with straw; previously without tobacco, prisoners were now being issued a quarter-pound of plug chewing tobacco weekly, though smoking still was not allowed. Bed time, previously 8:00 PM, was now 9:00 PM.[12]

The monumental building that French and his prisoners were constructing was designed by a St. Louis architectural firm, Eames and Young. This contract to design and superintend the construction of the new prison soon extended to a similar responsibility to design the Atlanta penitentiary. The contract marked the beginning of a relationship with the Department of Justice that lasted over many years. William S. Eames was constantly and personally involved and made frequent trips to both Washington and Leavenworth. In January 1897, Eames and Warden French visited other prisons, going to see Zebulon Brockway at Elmira, New York, and R. W. McClaughry at Pontiac, Illinois. Eames had an enthusiasm for the project which led him to urge that this "should be as impressive as other national institutions." He asserted that the approach should include monumental gateways at the entrance to the grounds, leading to well-planned, spacious park-like walkways.[13]

The successive attorneys general resisted many of Eames' proposed embellishments and urged plain and simple construction for the sake of economy and with respect to the somber character of the institution's purpose. But Eames, aided by cost savings due to using prisoner labor, managed to carry through a remarkably impressive construction. The central administration building was topped with an imposing rotunda and flanked by two cellblocks. The entrance was approached by a grand flight of steps. Eames avoided the elaborate medieval battlements then so popular in much state prison design, while he achieved a degree of tasteful grandeur—a little too much grandeur in the opinion of some. When Cecil Clay was appointed general agent in 1903, he visited the prison construction sites and later reported to the attorney general that the Leavenworth building had too much fine marble work in the corridors. Clay considered the building too elegant for criminals, but the work was too far along for him to order changes.

With its two main cellblocks in front, the prison presented a facade eight hundred feet from end to end. The main cellblocks and the two smaller ones angling out from behind the rotunda were built in the Auburn style, with back-to-back cells facing the outer walls. Eames advised, "The plan provides for 1200 cells because while some good state prisons put more than one convict in a cell, it is universally conceded to be better to have each in a separate cell."[14] He was right, of course, but he could not have guessed how seriously his plan would be violated by future crowding.

Attorney General Judson Harmon approved the plans, and by May 1897, French was able to report that twenty-five prisoners had been trained in stone cutting at the quarry on the reservation. Thereafter, year after year, the prisoners marched back and forth, every day, and worked in gangs, according to type of work or skill. One typical warden's report showed the daily division to be 60 or more prisoners working as stone cutters; about 200 as excavators; and about 130 as laborers. The situation presented a worrisome security problem; it was inevitable that a serious effort would be made to take advantage of the outside work site, where security depended on the constant alertness of the armed guards. The most serious break came in November 1901, when a former prisoner brought two pistols to the construction area at night and hid them under a hoist engine. The next day, prisoners who were part of the plan picked up the pistols and took hostages; twenty-six prisoners joined the escape. One guard was shot and killed and two others injured. One prisoner was killed during the break; two others were shot and killed the next day.[15]

In 1899, Warden French resigned under conditions that tell something about the general context in which all three federal prisons initially had to struggle for managerial integrity.

The federal Civil Service Commission had been established by the Pendleton Act, signed by President Chester A. Arthur in 1883, but such patronage plums as the wardens' jobs were, for a long time, exempt; wardens continued to be appointed politically and, of course, could be removed in the same way. French was a Democrat, appointed during the second Cleveland administration, and he knew that when McKinley and the Republicans captured the White House in 1897, he could be removed from his job. However, he was incensed when local politicians attacked him with innuendos of incompetence and malfeasance as their means of getting him out. Some of the opponents were Republicans, associated with the nearby Kansas Penitentiary at Lansing, who were obviously envious of job possibilities at the federal institution. They complained that some of the federal prison officials "took a prominent and offensive part in the campaign last fall." Other officials, they said, "infested saloons at night and abused Republicans and made themselves as offensive as possible." These critics also alleged that good discipline was lacking at the prison. "They say this is due largely to incompetent guards. Some of the guards are all that could be desired, while others get drunk nightly and are not fit for duty the next day." (The rule, previously mentioned, prohibiting guards from engaging in exciting discussion of politics, was instituted soon after this controversy.)

As for Warden French, he was said to be a "rampant free silver fusionist. He was extremely anxious for the election of Bryan and expected something 'high up' in the case of the boy orator's success. Warden French was a college chum and roommate of Bryan and he felt certain of getting something good."[16]

One particular sore point with his opponents was the effort French had made to put his operation under Civil Service, thus preventing the jobs from being available for patronage. Hit with a barrage of allegations, French prepared a carefully reasoned response directed to the new attorney general, Joseph McKenna. French admitted being a Democrat but insisted that when he was appointed by Attorney General Harmon, he had declared his intent to operate the institution on a nonpartisan basis—and he had done so.[17] In a separate response to his local critics, French gave a dignified, point-by-point refutation of all the accusations against him.[18] He remained in the job for another two years, then yielded to a Republican appointee, Robert W. McClaughry who then was serving a second time as warden of the Illinois State Penitentiary. One historian comments, "When McKinley and the Republicans took over the government, they cast about and selected the best Republican warden in the country—the veteran of Joliet."[19]

When he was appointed to Leavenworth on July 1, 1899, Mc-Claughry was sixty years old and had already had a lengthy career. He had been appointed warden of the Illinois Penitentiary in Joliet in 1874 and made an impressive reputation there. When the state of Pennsylvania built a new reformatory at Huntingdon, its board recruited McClaughry as the first warden, in February 1889. Two years later he returned to Illinois, to be chief of police in Chicago during the time of the Chicago World's Fair. Next McClaughry became superintendent of the new reformatory at Pontiac, Illinois, and in 1897 returned to the warden's job at Joliet. In 1899, his election as president of the National Prison Association enhanced his national prestige. McClaughry was well read in classical literature, including the Bible, and in some ways became the most significant warden at Leavenworth, serving longer than any warden since then. He was unusual in that he maintained a broad, nationwide—even international— perspective on correctional matters.

The advent of a new warden did not interrupt the daily plodding of several hundred prisoners to the construction site; the building grew with exasperating slowness, but it did grow. By 1903, enough space was under roof to permit the first prisoners to move in, although the old military prison also had to be used for three more years. Finally, on February 1, 1906, all prisoners had been transferred to the new building, and the War Department appreciatively accepted the return of its prison.

Construction at Leavenworth was well under way when planning for a prison in the southeast section of the country began. In April 1896, an appropriation bill was introduced in Congress that included funds for the second of the three authorized prisons. Competition between prospective sites quickly developed, but in Atlanta, when James G. Woodward took office as the new mayor in January 1899, he declared that acquisition of the prison would be a major goal for his administration. "One of the most important transactions that will confront us in the near future is the location of the proposed Federal prison in or near the city. This is an institution that, if secured, will be of great benefit to the city in many ways. The expenditure of $2,000,000 here means employment for our people and a corresponding benefit in every channel of trade. We should use every legitimate means at our command in the accomplishment of this purpose."[20]

Unlike Leavenworth, where land was obtained without cost by annexing it from a military reservation, choosing an Atlanta locale meant that a suitable tract would have to be purchased. But the city was sufficiently interested to make an attractive offer. Two areas on the edge of the city were considered; one of them, the "Dickey site," was selected on the recommendation of Mr. Eames, whose architectural firm would design the building. Attorney General John W. Griggs came to Atlanta to inspect the site and give it his approval.

Next, Mayor Woodward had to acquire the site and have it presented to the federal government. Knowing that the prison would be a steady, long-term source of business for the Southern Railway Company, Woodward approached company officials, and on September 5, 1899, the parcel of land was purchased with twenty-five thousand dollars from the city and thirty-five thousand dollars from the railroad. The delighted mayor immediately notified the attorney general that the deed to the land would be sent as soon as the legislature could confirm and approve the action. Only two days later, Eames mailed preliminary drawings for the building to the attorney general, noting that Warden McClaughry had consulted generously with him in details of the design.[21]

No prisoners were available for labor on this construction project, so the job was contracted to the local firm of Griffiths and Wells. The Dickey farmhouse, barn, and outhouses were repaired and made usable for construction offices and temporary staff housing. The railroad ran a spur to the site, and the city laid a six-inch water main as another part of its contribution. No sewage treatment plant was planned or initially built. A small nearby stream, Intrenchment Creek, already carried the untreated sewage from southeast Atlanta; now it would also carry the institution sewage.

From among various true blue Republicans who applied for the job, Walter H. Harrison was selected to be superintendent of construction. Site preparation began in early 1900, and by June, Harrison reported to the attorney general that the foundations had been poured. By then, too, both Harrison and Eames were writing to the attorney general with petty complaints about each other. Dealing with these and other details was the responsibility of the general agent, Frank Strong.[22]

The plans supplied by Eames and Young again called for a monumental, impressive building, and Georgia businessmen loudly demanded it be faced with Georgia limestone. Though the initial appropriation and the first contract called for 380 cells in two wings, to house 760 prisoners, the plant eventually was to have 1,200 cells in four wings. The contractors planned to have the first space ready by May 1, 1901, though it was not until early 1902 that Eames could pronounce that job done.[23] The certificate of inspection and acceptance was dated January 28, 1902, and just two days later, the first prisoners were admitted. By the middle of that year, the population reached 350. More construction was yet to be done, and the full job would take nearly two more decades.

Mayor Woodward was always pleased to call attention to the prison as one of the bright achievements of his administration, though his pride reflected no concern about good penology. He was interested only in the economics. A comment in his annual report for 1903 was typical. "Let us not forget the really magnificent Federal prison. While the inmates contribute nothing to society, yet are they the source of a large aggregate trade to the city."[24]

Eames and Young continued to superintend the construction job as successive phases were authorized and funded. In 1903, a handsome house for the warden was completed on one side of the prison entrance. Also that year, the first warden resigned after two unsatisfactory years in the job.

Samuel J. Hawk, a friend of President William McKinley, had been appointed warden on July 1, 1901, two months before the president was assassinated. Hawk had previously been warden at the West Virginia Penitentiary, a prison that had been used frequently to board federal prisoners. Unfortunately, another patronage appointment, made at the same time, pitted two incompatible people against each other. Bradford Dawson, the new deputy warden, came from the Ohio State Penitentiary where he had also been deputy warden. His appointment there, he claimed, came from McKinley when McKinley was the Ohio governor.

Hawk and Dawson were at odds with each other from the beginning. Competitive and mistrustful of one another, each sought the support of other staff members, thus extending their own animosities to factions among the employees. The feud festered so severely through 1902 that General Agent Strong sent an examiner, R. V. LaDow, to Atlanta to investigate. LaDow was dismayed; he noted in his report, "There exists between Warden and Deputy Warden Dawson avowed hostility. In the management of the prisoners each claims the credit for what is good and blames the other for all that is bad."[25]

Dawson was contemptuous of what he considered Hawk's lack of forcefulness. Hawk was down on anyone who favored Dawson, and he resented and mistrusted the several guards from Ohio who had followed Dawson to Atlanta. The men baited each other and behaved in a manner that was petty, immature, and without insight. The only possible solution was for both to leave, as they did in 1903. On July 1, a new warden reported for duty.

Attorney General Philander Knox had been impressed with the discreet competence of one of his department's special investigators, William H. Moyer, and though Moyer did not apply for the warden's job, Knox persuaded him to accept it. Warden McClaughry, asked to appraise the situation after Moyer's appointment, went to Atlanta in September, and in his report to the general agent he noted, "I found the discipline in as good shape as could be expected, taking into consideration the condition that must have prevailed prior to July 1st, 1903. That no mistake was made in the change that occurred on that date is evidenced by the conditions yet remaining." McClaughry noted that prisoners who had been pets of the former administration had been reduced to the same regimen as other prisoners, and did not like it. But he also saw that Hawk and Dawson had been severely handicapped by the unfinished physical plant and shortages in staff, so he urged that more guards be hired immediately. McClaughry saw a dangerous security problem in the location being well out from the city and with woods on all sides. "Until it is completely surrounded by a proper wall it presents a constant invitation to desperate outsiders who have friends imprisoned therein." McClaughry was alarmed that only two guards were on duty at night, and they could not watch the woods in all directions.[26]

Like McClaughry at Leavenworth, Moyer was dependable and competent, and he too stayed longer in the job than any of his successors—twelve years. Under his administration, construction went forward, and the management was relatively uneventful. But Atlanta would have other wardens and other crises.

Then there was to be a third prison, west of the Rocky Mountains. Did that prison start operation before the other two, or later? Simple as the question seems, the answer is not clear. The usual practice of letting each new state take over its formerly territorial prison did not work in the case of McNeil Island (known as McNeil's Island in its early years).[27] In 1899, on George Washington's birthday, Washington Territory became a state; something over a year later the attorney general directed Marshal Thomas R. Brown to transfer the prison. The marshal dutifully wrote to Governor Elisha Ferry in July 1890 to say that the prison was available for state take-over. But, breaking the usual pattern, the governor declined the offer.

Elisha Ferry had been the territorial governor some years earlier, when the prison was opened, and he had never been impressed with it. There was reason for his lack of enthusiasm; as he pointed out, the prison was small and insecure, and was located on inadequate acreage of very poor land.[28] Another factor in Ferry's decision was that Washington, not waiting for statehood, had built its own prison at Walla Walla. Thus, in 1889, the new state had no need to take over the unimpressive federal facility in Puget Sound.

When Governor Ferry rejected McNeil Island, his response was not quite clear and final. The governor said only that he was not authorized to accept the prison; the state legislature must make the decision. So the Department of Justice, through its marshal in Washington state, continued to operate the prison on a wait-and-see basis. The waiting was prolonged; the outcome was never decisive. The new state legislature, with much else to occupy its attention, did nothing about this issue. A year after Governor Ferry declined the offer, Congress passed the three-prison act, and that opened the question of what to do about a prison west of the Rocky Mountains. For the remainder of the century, nothing was decided about McNeil

Island, and the marshals continued to operate it for federal prisoners from that area.

This unusual prison was situated on a small corner of a beautifully wooded island, about four and one-half thousand acres in size, located twelve miles southwest of Tacoma and not quite three miles from its mainland contact point, the village of Steilacoom. When no other acceptable location could be found, a pair of logging partners donated twenty-seven acres near the shore of the island. Construction started on a stone cellblock building in 1871, and considering its diminutive size, the structure took far too long to build. It was an Auburn-style cellblock, three tiers high, with forty-two interior cells, each 6 feet by 8 feet. The prison finally opened in 1875, with no plumbing, no dining area, no bath facilities, and no industry or work program. More serious, the facility lacked any water source of its own and was dependent upon the sufferance of a neighbor who allowed the prison to obtain water from his spring. When the weather made outdoor work impossible—which was often—prisoners remained in the cellblock all day, with nothing to read, nothing at all to do. It is hardly surprising that Governor Ferry had low regard for the facility.

When the prison opened, it employed a total staff of three; the salary was seventy-five dollars per month. Each guard was given two and one-half days off per month to visit his family on the mainland, but otherwise he was on duty twenty four hours a day, seven days a week. Much of the time, the three staff on duty would be reduced to two, as it was necessary almost daily for one guard, assisted by one or two trusty prisoners, to take one of the sailboats and go to the dock at Steilacoom to obtain supplies, pick up and post mail, and perhaps bring back new prisoners. That people were willing to tolerate such demands speaks eloquently of the country's depressed economic conditions during much of the prison's first three decades. With all its drawbacks, the job at least brought a dependable paycheck in a depression-proof line of work.

The surrounding water of Puget Sound made escape difficult, but it also brought worrisome disadvantages. There was no telegraph to the island; in rough weather boats could not operate, and the staff could not even get newspapers. A prisoner badly in need of dental or medical attention might be taken to a doctor on the mainland in good weather, but in bad weather the only alternative was whatever home remedies the staff could contrive.

Rarely had any prison had such a tenuous hold on its site, or even its existence. The site selection had been ill-advised in the first place, and year after year, for the rest of that century, recurring proposals were made to move or to abolish the institution. During the 1890s, two unresolved questions hung over the prison. Would the new state government at some point take the facility over? Or would the three-prison act of 1891 in some way affect the institution's destiny? When the new century arrived, neither question had been resolved. The attorney general and his general agent by then had invested their interest, their time and their energies in the great building projects being undertaken in Leavenworth and Atlanta. Congress made no move to define and authorize the third prison. McNeil Island remained in limbo, unwanted by the state, unappreciated and neglected by its parent Department of Justice, but still serving a need by housing prisoners of the Northwest and Alaska.

One fiscal management aspect of McNeil Island was unique. As Leavenworth and Atlanta were built and became operational, they were recognized as discrete organizational entities with their own budgets; but McNeil Island, as a territorial prison, did not have this status. It was supported out of a general appropriation to the attorney general for the care of federal prisoners. The marshals always had to write supplicating letters to the attorney general in regard to any nonroutine expenditure, for instance, a few dollars to repair the boat or to buy some fertilizer. Invariably, the attorneys general not only were reluctant to spend money, they were also grossly ignorant of the realities of operating a primitive prison in a distant frontier area.

The uncertain status of McNeil Island was reflected in the fact that it operated for its first twenty years or so with no clearly designated or titled warden. Initially, the marshal for Washington Territory was responsible. Although he could be on the premises only infrequently, he was the one person clearly in charge. He hired the guards and was their immediate supervisor; they carried out the daily operations according to his written instructions. So that necessary decisions could be made in his absence, the marshal designated one of the guards as the "first guard."

This, then, was the administrative arrangement at the time the sixteen-year-old, and already obsolete, prison was offered to Governor Ferry. Because both state and federal governments were indecisive, the informal status of the prison continued on into the twentieth century. The men who successively filled the position of first guard gradually were referred to as "warden," and Gilbert Palmer, who took the job in 1893, was eventually remembered as the institution's first warden.

The general air of uncertainty about this institution was not dispelled until July 1, 1909, when it was officially recognized as a regular federal penitentiary; it was granted its own budget, and all its employees, except the warden, were reappointed to civil service status.

Neither Congress nor the Department of Justice ever formally declared McNeil Island to be the prison west of the Rocky Mountains authorized by the 1891 three-prison act. But in effect it happened, for now there were three penitentiaries, alike in official status, and one of these was west of the mountains. Although the prison had been unplanned, unintended, and even unwanted, it finally was a fait accompli.

4.

THE EXPERIENCE WITH PENITENTIARIES

As the new penitentiary at Leavenworth slowly took shape at the turn of the century, neither police agencies nor prisons were able reliably to identify individual suspects or prisoners. It would be here at this federal prison, under Warden McClaughry, that a significant start would be made in building a national criminal identification service.

McClaughry early became interested in the Bertillon system, a tedious and complex process of taking physical measurements, which was the only accepted identification system of the time. While he was still in his teens, Matthew McClaughry, the warden's son, had helped take Bertillon measurements at the Illinois State Penitentiary, where his father was then the warden.[1] The Bertillon system was also used at Leavenworth. Later, both McClaughrys visited Alphonse Bertillon in Paris and became friends with him. Fingerprinting, a far more efficient process, was known by this time, but people did not trust the system and it did not become popular until the middle 1890s when Mark Twain, in his novel *Pudd'nhead Wilson,* built a story around the technique and caught the public fancy.

In 1904, McClaughry attended the World's Fair in St. Louis where he met Sergeant John K. Ferrier, an officer from Scotland Yard, who was there to demonstrate the fingerprint system being used in London. McClaughry invited Ferrier to Leavenworth, and there they fingerprinted the entire prisoner population.

In the preceding year an uncanny event had dramatized the need for the improved system. A new black prisoner, Will West, had been received, and the admitting office staff seemed to remember that he had been admitted previously as William West. Though the prisoner stoutly denied ever having been there, the staff's impression seemed

51

confirmed by the Bertillon records. West's face matched the photo taken with the previous admission, the names were almost the same, and the new Bertillon measurements were essentially identical to the previous ones. The astonishing outcome was that Will West was right; he had not been in Leavenworth before. However, an unrelated William West was still there, serving a life sentence.[2] It was an incredible match and nothing could have made the case for fingerprints more forcefully. McClaughry's son, Matthew, set to work developing a central file of fingerprints, not only those of Leavenworth inmates, but also prints he invited from police departments and other prisons. McClaughry's breadth of interest was always global and he sought more avidly than anyone else in his day to establish a comprehensive criminal identification center for the country.

In 1906, the attorney general noted in his annual report that there were more than three thousand fingerprint records at Leavenworth, and he suggested that Congress authorize the Department of Justice to collect such criminal records, as a service to law enforcement officials generally. In the following year, the department centralized the files by moving all fingerprint records—more than twenty thousands by then—from Leavenworth, Atlanta, and McNeil Island to the headquarters in Washington. This central arrangement did not last; just a year later, in September 1908, the superintendent of prisons notified all cooperating state and federal agencies that the records had been returned to Leavenworth. No reason was given, but one is suggested by some relevant facts. The headquarters of the Justice Department was then in several rented houses, where space was severely restricted and security was poor; in addition, budgetary restrictions had forced staff lay-offs. So the penitentiary, with its better space and security and its generous supply of free inmate labor, resumed custody of the records under the care of Matthew McClaughry.

As a parallel service, the International Association of Chiefs of Police had also started keeping identification files. In 1921 the association offered its records to the Department of Justice, and in 1924 Congress provided an appropriation to take over the two collections. Once again, the Leavenworth files moved to Washington, this time in the new Bureau of Investigation. Its young director, J. Edgar Hoover, needed something more to do in those days, and he grasped the public relations opportunity in this kind of service. "Long after fingerprint identification had become thoroughly familiar to the public, Hoover continued to trumpet the Bureau's collection as its proudest achievement, even its trademark."[3]

Meanwhile, at Leavenworth, construction dragged on toward its eventual completion in about 1929. The cellblocks were completed by 1919, the shoe shops by 1926, a brush and broom factory in 1928, and, last of all, the administration offices and rotunda. During that time, the federal prisoners who were boarded in various state prisons were transferred gradually into Leavenworth. However, the practice of boarding out has never been completely discontinued. As space became available at the new prison, the superintendent of prisons sent his examiners to the various state prisons to select the federal prisoners who would be transferred. Various factors had to be considered in each case. As a matter of economy, the government should no longer pay board bills for prisoners in state institutions when the government now had its own prison. However, if some prisoners had limited time left to serve, it might be more economical to leave them where they were, rather than to incur the considerable transportation costs of taking them to Leavenworth. Sometimes humanitarian decisions were justified and prisoners were not moved away from useful prison programs or from areas where their families lived. In some cases examiners faced a morale problem; some prisoners were boarded where state law gave them the advantage of time reduction for good behavior, an advantage they would lose on transfer to the federal system.[4]

Leavenworth's vast size was never a surety against overcrowding, nor were its modern security features any surety against escapes or disturbances. By 1910, the prisoner count was more than one thousand, and ten years later it was about double that. Warden McClaughry was forced into uncomfortable economies and adjustments. Because there were so few staff positions far too many jobs were handled by inmates. Much of the time, the large inmate population and the low budget forced McClaughry to stretch the prison's supply of milk by diluting it with water.[5]

At the same time he had insufficient staff, McClaughry had to contend with hordes of visitors. The prison's size and advanced design caught the public's attention. Also that was a time when most prisons accepted the idea that they had to be on the regular tourist route. In 1910, in just one day, tour groups from Kansas City chartered four special railroad cars that brought about two hundred sightseers to the institution. With that, the warden decided that enough was enough, and in the following week he suspended all tours for the rest of the summer.[6]

In tune with the times, McClaughry accepted the practices of racial segregation, although he was not aggressive about it. When he testified at a congressional committee hearing in 1912, he reported that about half his prisoners were black, about one hundred were Indians, and the remainder were white. There was no racial segregation then, but under pressure from the committee chairman, Mc-Claughry agreed that it would be feasible to institute the practice when the new cell house was completed. He professed to disapprove of corporal punishment and described the milder measures he was using. In some cases, a prisoner was put in a segregation cell, wrists handcuffed to the bars at chest height, and left there during the working hours of the day. An inmate who refused to work was put in isolation and given a pile of stones and a hammer to break them with. The large stones had to be broken into pieces small enough to pass through a two-inch ring. If—and only if—he satisfactorily broke half the pile by noon, he would get lunch. If he broke the full pile by evening he would receive supper. This punishment would be continued until the prisoner was ready to return to work. Inmates no longer wore striped clothing, McClaughry reported, but an inmate's number was stamped on the pants legs and on the jacket of each solid color uniform. A trusty prisoner wore a white star on his jacket, and this served as a pass so he could move freely from building to building.[7]

His time at Leavenworth capped an impressive career for McClaughry. He was widely known and respected in the corrections field; his son Matthew served long as special agent in charge of the Bureau of Criminal Identification; another son, Charles, became the deputy warden at the Atlanta Penitentiary and later headed other correctional institutions. By 1913, McClaughry was seventy-four years old and apparently becoming less effective. According to a 1913 clipping (otherwise undated) from *The Kansas City Star,* McClaughry had resigned: "It does not appear on the surface that Major McClaughry was invited to resign, and in all probability he was not formally notified to do so. But for a long time the hungry politicians have had their eyes on this job at the federal prison and the veteran warden has been subjected to many and various annoyances to force his resignation."

With McClaughry's departure, the political process turned up an appointee with no corrections experience but with the necessary political attractiveness. He was T. W. Morgan, editor of a newspaper in the small Kansas town of Ottawa. Morgan's background in journalism may explain why the prisoner publication, *New Era,* was inaugurated during his first year at the prison. Within another year, Morgan had brought in a phonograph on which records could be played in the cell house, he acquired a moving picture machine; he allowed inmates to use plain paper for letter writing; and he started the practice of giving two hours free time for recreation in the prison yard, every Sunday afternoon. He instituted a radical innovation that allowed those prisoners in a good behavior status (first grade) to write one letter per week. The warden admitted to his superior that this was rather much, but he argued that the practice was becoming common, and he considered it reasonable.[8]

One immediate problem for the new warden was how to complete the unfinished east cellblock without the help of any construction company. The steel for it had been in the yard for several years.[9] Morgan was able to take advantage of an odd windfall to push the work along. Six months before Morgan came to Leavenworth a mass trial had ended in Indianapolis when thirty-four men, spoken of as "the dynamiters," were convicted. The ironworkers union had destroyed bridges and buildings nationwide in an effort to intimidate open shop construction companies. The crimes were said to have utilized one of the earliest applications of nitroglycerin and the alarm clock. The union managers were tried for conspiracy in what was reputed to be the largest criminal trial in the country until then. The president of the union, Frank M. Ryan, was sentenced to serve seven years; the other defendants were sentenced to terms that ranged from one to six years. On New Year's Eve, the day after the sentencing, the U.S. marshal and thirty-two temporary deputies brought the prisoner contingent by special train to Leavenworth.[10]

When Morgan became warden the following June (1913) he set the ironworkers to erecting steel for the cellblock. There really was no time to lose. Early the next year, 133 federal prisoners were transferred from the Minnesota State Prison, and a year later the population was up to 1,800. For many years following, he struggled with the increasing problem of overcrowding, while at the same time he tried to complete the construction. In addition to civilian offenders, wartime conditions brought the prison a large and difficult group of military prisoners. In 1918, Warden Morgan informed the superintendent of prisons that 551 military prisoners were on hand, "who in all probability belong to the very worst class of Army offenders."[11]

In 1925, FBI investigators probing charges of malfeasance at the prison were alarmed to find that 3,262 prisoners were housed in space intended for 1,400; many were required to "sleep in dark basements, the cots or beds being arranged in double rows along the corridors." So little work was available that more than two thousand of the inmates were completely idle.[12]

Congress had never faced the fact that the initial work prisoners performed in constructing the buildings would end. Other work would have to be developed by funding prison industries shops. At one point, Warden Morgan, looking at the example of the nearby Kansas penitentiary, urgently suggested developing a coal mine. He advised the superintendent of prisons that a twenty-two-inch vein of coal, 720 feet below the institution, could be mined profitably for many years.[13] The proposal was never acted upon.

The institution was so underfunded that one prominent prisoner who arrived there in 1918 reported that all clerks in the shops, record office, and administration offices were prisoners.[14] This condition continued for years and got even worse. The FBI investigation found that record keeping for the massive population was in the hands of one civilian chief clerk, and he had to rely on twenty-two inmate clerks to classify fingerprints and file prisoner records. In other ways, too, security was jeopardized; the outside patrol officers used horses, but these were "of age and have been in service for many years. They are lame and hardly able to meet an emergency such as running down a prisoner who has escaped."

The penitentiary depended on inmate workers to an extent that would be unthinkable in later years. For instance, the FBI inquiry revealed an ominous situation with the prison's electrical generating plant. The agents saw an urgent need for an independent back-up electrical source, "To supplant, in an emergency, any failure of the prison lighting system which is almost wholly in the control of inmates." Medical services were similarly vulnerable. Modern policy rules out use of prisoner doctors as physicians in prison hospitals, but in the 1920s and earlier, the practice was essential. The investigators found only one physician for the three thousand inmates, and they modestly suggested that an assistant be hired. But they observed also, "There are many physicians listed as inmates and there ought not to be any great difficulty to make a safe, sane, ambitious and learned selection of this number."[15]

The outstanding physician who served time at Leavenworth, and one of the most respected prisoners ever held there, was polar explorer Dr. Frederick Cook. Cook was assigned regularly to work as a doctor in the prison hospital, and sometimes he was in charge of the hospital on the night shift. According to Cook, he had reached the North Pole in 1908, a full year before Robert Peary's arrival there. But Cook was slow to make his claim and it was rejected in favor of Peary's more believable report. (Later Peary's claim was also challenged, though apparently validated when his records were reappraised.)[16] Cook had served as a fellow scientist and doctor on polar explorations with both Peary and Roald Amundsen; he was especially respected by Amundsen who, in 1911, was the first to reach the South Pole.

With his exploring days behind him, Cook founded an oil promotion company in Texas and in 1923 was charged with making false claims in his mail solicitation of prospective investors. He was convicted, fined, and sentenced to fourteen years in prison. Ironically, after his incarceration, the land Cook was charged with misrepresenting did indeed prove to be a productive oil field.

Cook spent five years in Leavenworth where, in addition to serving as a doctor, he edited the *New Era* and taught in the evening school. Invariably he was a cooperative, constructive inmate. One of the visitors he received in 1926 was his loyal friend Amundsen who visited the discredited Cook at some cost to his own prestige.[17] After Cook was paroled in 1930, he worked to clear his name, and three months before his death in 1940, he received a full pardon from President Roosevelt.

During the 1920s, the Leavenworth prisoners filled the dining room in three shifts for each meal. They sat at the typical bench and table combinations, all facing the same way; that arrangement was not changed until 1959. Inmate waiters, with trays hung by straps from their shoulders, ranged through the dining room, while an inmate band entertained. Presumably, some of the prisoners enjoyed the music, mostly jazz, but others found it hard to bear. One reminisced later that breakfast was the best meal of the day because the band did not play then and he could eat in peaceful quiet. There was always an inmate bugler; his reveille provided the wake-up call every morning, and taps announced bedtime every night.[18]

The list of unique and interesting individuals who served time at Leavenworth is far too long to include here, but two prisoners from the institution's history must be noted. The best known of these was Robert Stroud, popularized by author Thomas E. Gaddis as the "Birdman of Alcatraz."[19] Gaddis fostered the idea that Stroud was a brilliant researcher, mainly characterized by his highly useful contributions to the world's understanding of bird diseases, and that he was maligned and mistreated by a repressive Department of Justice.

Stroud became a federal prisoner in 1909 when, at age nineteen, he was received at McNeil Island Penitentiary for a murder committed in Alaska. He never again was out of prison. After he stabbed a fellow prisoner at McNeil Island, he was transferred to Leavenworth, where he continued to be unpredictably violent. In 1916 he stabbed and killed a guard in the penitentiary dining room, an act that led to three trials for murder, with the third conviction later upheld by the Supreme Court. In 1920, President Wilson commuted Stroud's death sentence to life imprisonment, and the attorney general ordered that Stroud thereafter be held under the tightest custody to prevent any further assaults. So it was here in Leavenworth, not Alcatraz, that Stroud raised and studied his birds. He did, indeed, become noted for his discoveries, and he wrote of them in two published books.[20] But for all his constructive research, Stroud continued to show deep hostility and constant potential for violence. In 1942, he was transferred to Alcatraz where, no longer allowed to raise birds, he spent part of his time writing about the prison system history, as he knew it.[21]

The other prisoner of note, now far less known, but more sinister, was Carl Panzram. He was one of the most dedicated criminals who ever roamed from one to another of this country's prisons. Born in 1891 in Minnesota, he started his succession of crimes and incarcerations when he was eleven. As his career ended he freely admitted to twenty-three murders and countless crimes of barely lesser sorts. Dr. Karl Menninger, who examined Panzram, noted, "He does not pretend to have had justification for these murders but says that he killed because he enjoyed killing. He might easily have gone on to many more murders. He outlined to me in detail a plan he had conceived for bringing about the destruction of the entire human race, a plan which was by no means absurd in its conception."[22]

Panzram came to Leavenworth with a twenty-five-year sentence, and it was in the prison's laundry that he committed his final murder on June 20, 1929. A minor reprimand from the laundry foreman was all the reason he needed to retaliate. Approaching the foreman from behind, Panzram brought a heavy iron bar down on the victim's head. He was sentenced to death. But Kansas had abolished capital punishment years before, and the state had no execution apparatus. The federal penitentiary officials had to build a gallows and carry out the execution themselves. When conducted to his hanging at 6:00 A.M. on September 5, 1930, Panzram was still in character; contemptuously insulting his hangman as inept and obscenely ordering the two ministers to go away, he walked quickly to the gallows, as a man eager for the occasion. "His execution was, in essence, a suicide, a direct accomplishment of what he had indirectly sought for all of his thirty-eight years."[23]

In Atlanta Warden Moyer had many of the same problems that McClaughry faced in Leavenworth. Moyer struggled with both population pressures and protracted construction. He contended with a guard force that was insufficient for the job and increasingly restive about the low pay and long hours.

In Atlanta, too, the problem of visitors reached dimensions that seem incredible today. Moyer once told an audience of other prison officials that when he arrived at Atlanta, "every day was visiting day and . . . indiscriminate visitors, sometimes to the number of three thousand, were admitted and shown through the prison in one day during business hours. Indeed, I found that engraved annual passes, similar to those used by railroads and other common carriers, had been prepared and issued to the number of several hundred, admitting the person named thereon to any part of the prison at any time during the year."[24] Moyer did not eliminate the practice altogether, but he did reduce the public sightseeing drastically.

The eight-hour day became a vital issue at Atlanta during the period from 1906 to 1908, and the staff at Leavenworth sympathetically echoed the same concern. McNeil Island, because of its remoteness and its unique insular location, was less affected. It is hardly surprising that the Atlanta guards were discontent with a work week of eighty-four hours! Superintendent of prisons, Cecil Clay, was none too sympathetic toward the guards, but in 1908 Clay retired. He was replaced by one of his examiners, R. V. LaDow, a vigorous and competent man who gave constant, detailed attention to the prison operations for many years. LaDow corresponded copiously with Moyer, McClaughry, and others, in trying to resolve the issue of working hours. He was sympathetic to the wish for lighter hours and was pleased when he could advise McClaughry that Congress had approved his request for enough positions so guards could cut their work weeks to seventy-two hours—six days of twelve hours each.[25]

McClaughry had mixed feelings about the matter. He worried that the eight-hour day would bring serious trouble because prisoners would be supervised by two different guards each day. He observed that prisoners were adept at playing one guard against another. "The result would be a paralysis of the institution."[26]

The issue was debated for most of two years. The ferment was greatest in Atlanta, where guards had caught the sympathy of their congressman, Leonidas F. Livingston, who was determined to push for more staff and shorter hours. Warden Moyer tended to appreciate the guards' view and noted that many other jobs in the Atlanta area offered easier work, fewer hours, and better pay. Moyer wished for an eight-hour day, but he, too, worried about having a shift change while inmates were out of their cells. He guessed the guards would accept a plan calling for the same long hours at a higher rate of pay, instead of fewer hours at the same pay. But when he canvassed them on this point, he was surprised to find all but one preferred to accept the current pay of seventy dollars per month with an eight-hour day. As one of the guards put it, "I am able to live on $70 a month, but I will not be able to live very long on twelve hours a day."[27]

Since the main impediment to the reform of working hours was the cost of hiring additional staff, legislators were painfully slow to resolve the problem. In the fall of 1909, both LaDow and the attorney general, George W. Wickersham, visited Atlanta and personally questioned guards about their feelings. Soon after that, the big change occurred. On December 4, LaDow gave Moyer and McClaughry authority to convert to three shifts per day. By March 1910, Moyer was able to report that the eight-hour day was in effect and working satisfactorily.[28]

Atlanta, no less than Leavenworth, had its share of unique prisoners; some of them over the years have been notable for their impact on institution policies. One of the first of these was a Wall Street financier whose imprisonment aggravated and embarrassed the attorney general. Charles W. Morse, convicted of embezzlement and admitted in January 1910, was accustomed to exercising power and did not easily accept any curtailment of his business activities. Moyer tried to treat Morse as he would any other prisoner, but that proved hardly possible. Morse was an aggressive manipulator, as was his wife, and together they besieged the prison and the Department of Justice with an unrelenting blizzard of efforts, both to conduct business from the prison and to accomplish early release. They were fairly successful on both counts. Morse was one of the first in a long succession of prisoners with outside business interests who posed a challenge for prison policy-makers. How could they curtail the inmates' business dealings without denying them the right to protect their necessary and proper legal affairs? Morse, among the most ebullient of such prisoners, was almost more than Warden Moyer could handle. Soon after his arrival, Morse persuaded the warden to let him send a telegram, in code, to authorize sale of some stock. Afterward, he informed Moyer that he had netted two thousand dollars on the deal and in gratitude he wished to give the warden half of it. Moyer considered that a bribe and refused it. Sometime later, Morse informed Moyer of his plans to buy a small railroad in that area and asked Moyer if he would like to be the president of it.[29]

Moyer needed help from headquarters to deal with this prisoner who was so demanding and who brought the institution to newspaper attention almost weekly. In response to Moyer's inquiry, the superintendent of prisons admonished him, "The private business affairs of prisoners should be reduced to a minimum. Under no circumstances should they be allowed to engage in speculation."[30] Sensible policy, but Morse had the inventiveness and spirit to defeat it much of the time. His ultimate weapon, which he used with brilliant effectiveness, was ill health.

In some manner, Morse contrived to develop symptoms of serious illness, so he would be put in the prison hospital. His wife visited and afterward gave a tearful interview in which she insisted that her husband could not live much longer if he remained in prison. That incident marked the start of a heavy bombardment to persuade both the attorney general and the White House to grant Morse a pardon. The attorney general was skeptical, but Morse managed to keep up the pressure, aided by responsive friends on the outside who signed petitions. President Taft could not ignore the highly publicized affair. He did not wish to forgive a man whom he believed was an unmitigated swindler; yet he did not want such a noted prisoner to die in custody. Taft called for an independent medical inquiry by a board of army doctors, and though the doctors did not agree that Morse's condition was life threatening, they did conclude that he was ill, probably with Bright's disease. Taft reluctantly commuted Morse's sentence; in February 1912, Morse left the prison and, with his wife, took the train to New York. A reporter who covered the departure was not impressed by the alleged illness. "The improvement in Morse's condition was evident. Three weeks ago reported to be dying, his face today did not indicate that he had ever been desperately ill."[31] Indeed, from all accounts, Morse underwent a miraculous recovery immediately following his release. Morse and his wife were soon reported to be enjoying an extended cruise in the Mediterranean. Although Morse previously claimed to be impoverished by the costs of defending his case, it was now revealed that he was paying an Atlanta law firm one hundred thousand dollars for their services in obtaining his commutation.[32] And the persistent rumors about his faked illness were confirmed when members of the army medical board realized, in retrospect, that Morse had not been severely ill but had been an exceptionally clever actor.[33] By that time, in good health, Morse was back in full swing at his business in New York.

Meanwhile, Moyer brought many improvements to penitentiary conditions. He instituted daily calisthenics, organized a thirty-piece orchestra that played at meals in the dining room, added a dentist and an oculist to the medical services, discontinued striped clothing in 1912, and—in an act that was courageous at that time—allowed talking at mealtime. He also removed the regimented dining room bench-tables that had faced all the prisoners the same direction. In 1911 it was necessary to replace the wooden dining room floor with concrete, so with this opportunity Moyer had the shops build eight-place tables, and he purchased nine hundred chairs to go with them. He completed the change many years, even decades, before prisons generally switched to this more informal and natural arrangement. (Photographs taken some years later suggest that some other warden restored the one-way benches to use for a time.)

Moyer opened a prison school, utilizing inmate teachers supervised by the chaplain, and he began a baseball program instituted with several teams of inmate players. Apparently Moyer had some help with the latter from an affluent inmate, Frederick A. Hyde, a Californian who came to Atlanta to serve a two-year term for land fraud. Hyde "laid out plans for an athletic field, which, with money furnished by him, was constructed by himself and his fellow prisoners."[34] As Hyde was leaving, newspaper accounts told of his remarkably constructive attitude toward his imprisonment. Hyde praised Moyer, and he spent his money freely, not only to buy recreation equipment for all prisoners, but also to provide funds for departing inmates who lacked sufficient resources to make a new start.

Another benefactor was Emma Neal Douglas, the widow of an Atlanta attorney. Her contribution was a motion picture projector that was first used about Christmastime in 1912. And one day in 1913, the inmates assembled to hear a song recital by an eminent visitor, Enrico Caruso.[35]

At odds with the various measures to improve prison life, racial segregation was practiced then and for many years to come. In fact, the inequities were far more pervasive than just segregation. In Atlanta, as in most prisons in the country, discrimination was common; black prisoners were given the most menial work and white inmates were given the office and skilled maintenance jobs. (An odd example of apparent differential treatment was in Puerto Rico, where U.S. prisoners were boarded in jails at a daily rate of twenty cents for blacks and twenty-six cents for whites.)[36]

Although Moyer pushed construction work forward for the twelve years of his tenure, the physical plant was still five years short of completion when he left the job in 1915. Over the next few years he was followed by a succession of undistinguished wardens who served shorter terms. The Moyer administration has to be rated as competent and honest, though it was not without its critics. One of the most articulate of these was the son of the famous poet, Nathaniel Hawthorne. In 1913, in New York, Julian Hawthorne was convicted of using the mails to defraud, and he was sentenced to prison for a year and a day. In a book he wrote about his Atlanta experience Hawthorne presented a scathing criticism of Moyer, whom he accused of hypocrisy for presenting to the outside world a facade of progressive, humane treatment of prisoners that hid the brutal realities of prison life. "Then there are the insults, the gibes and threats, the obscure forms of tyranny and outrage, the degradation of manhood—there are a hundred subtle ways of destroying and corrupting the spirit of a man." Part of the problem, he alleged, resulted from the low quality of the guard force, recruited mainly from among former soldiers. "With some shining exceptions, they are petty tyrants of the worst type, sulky, sneering, malignant, brutal, and liars and treacherous into the bargain." He described the punishment of the dark cells where, he said, men were chained, fed on bread and water, and left to sleep on the bare floor up to three weeks at a time.[37]

Hawthorne's account gained attention because of the brute force of his writing, and while there was undoubtedly some truth in the allegations, they were not documented, and their credibility was diminished by the lack of balance, the unrelieved anger on every page. Warden Moyer was obviously stung by the criticism. In 1915, Frederick Zerbst, deputy warden at Leavenworth, came to Atlanta to replace Moyer; he started by making a complete inspection tour of the prison, searching particularly for the dungeons described by Hawthorne. When he did not discover any, Moyer reminded Zerbst that he had always denied having the dungeons and had challenged his critics to find them.[38] (In the fall of 1916, the famed prison reformer, Thomas Mott Osborne, resigned as warden of New York's Sing Sing prison. After an interim warden served for two months, the post was offered to and accepted by Moyer.)

Although a contracted construction company had begun building the Atlanta Penitentiary, after 1902 when the first prisoners arrived, construction was continued primarily by inmate labor. In its earliest days, a special feature of the prison was an adjoining camp for tubercular inmates; it was said to house sixteen men in individual tents placed on wood floors. By 1912, with nearly one hundred prisoners inside, one cellblock, the dining room, and the house for the warden had been built. By 1917, the administration building, the hospital, and another cell wing were finished. The overall construction was essentially completed by 1920.

An issue that inevitably arose during these years was the perceived need for a federal parole law. Two factors forced attention to it: the prospect of easing the overloaded prisoner populations through parole releases, and the complications that occurred because many states had their own parole laws. Parole procedures varied from state to state, and federal prisoners boarded in state prisons were subject to the state law in each case. Thus the federal prisoners who were boarded out faced inconsistent release prospects, and at the same time, those in the new federal prisons had no parole privileges at all.

Through the first decade of the century, sentiment built up strongly for a federal parole act, and each year the attorney general called the attention of Congress to the need. Here again, the efforts of the attorney general were augmented by the work of private citizens, and in this case by one devoted person in particular, a New England Unitarian named Samuel June Barrows. Though he is now mostly forgotten, during the first decade of this century, Barrows was certainly one of the world's most respected advocates of prison reform. As a prominent minister in the Boston area, he was elected to Congress in 1896. He served one term in the House and during that time worked for a federal parole law. Though ostensibly he acomplished little at that time, his influence continued, and even increased, after he left office. Barrows soon became a leading figure in the Prison Association of New York and in the International Prison Association. Probably the most erudite and intellectual of the prison reform leaders, Barrows quietly but persistently influenced the move for federal parole, as well as for probation, and he stoutly defended the move by Warden French to put the Leavenworth Penitentiary staff under Civil Service. "He was made chairman of a committee chosen by the National Prison Association to bring the subject of parole for United States prisoners to the attention of Congress in

1900, and from that time he appeared before Congressional committees every winter till the battle was won."[39]

In 1905, as U.S. commissioner to the International Prison Congress in Budapest, Barrows was elected president of the congress
and arranged for its 1910 meeting to be in Washington, D.C. In the
meantime, he continued his work on behalf of a federal parole law,
with success that he did not live to see. He died suddenly in the
spring of 1909; the United States Congress passed his law in the
following year.[40]

In framing the new parole law, Congress had to find a compromise
between having a single parole board, with its great expense, that
traveled the country from end to end, or having separate boards,
with their resulting inconsistencies, for each institution. Legislators
resolved the problem, they hoped, by establishing a parole board
of three members at each institution. To provide uniformity, the
superintendent of prisons was to serve as chairman of each board,
and the warden and the chief medical officer of the institution comprised the other two members. To carry the parole process to board-
ed-out prisoners the superintendent of prisons traveled to the state
prisons and joined with state parole officials to act on those cases.

The parole law was signed by President Taft on June 25, 1910,
and by September, the attorney general had approved and published
the rules and regulations. The parole boards were to meet at each
institution three times a year; prisoners were eligible for consideration after they served one-third of their sentences, if they had been
"continuously in the first or highest grade for at least six months."
The legislation did not provide for any parole field services to meet
the need for follow-up supervision, so the wardens, with the superintendent of prisons, devised a plan to find a volunteer supervisor for
each case. Before an inmate could be released, a "first friend" in the
community would have to agree to keep in touch with the former
prisoner and submit monthly progress reports. The first federal
parolee was released on November 26, 1910; by the end of that fiscal
year, June 30, 1912, 345 parolees were released and nine paroles
were revoked.[41]

Though no field service was created, the parole law did authorize
a parole officer in each institution; that officer's duty was to prepare
cases for board consideration and to locate and engage the first friend

in the community. The institutional parole officers were hired at salaries of fifteen hundred dollars at Atlanta and Leavenworth, and twelve hundred dollars at McNeil Island.

The parole process gave rise to several problems and these quickly became apparent. First, life termers were not eligible, an oversight that particularly troubled Warden McClaughry. His response was to offer a concept of parole eligibility that would "have our life prisoners sentenced according to the expectancy of life as calculated by the great insurance companies, so that if, for instance, a man comes to this prison for life and he is say fifty years old, he shall be considered as imprisoned for twenty years and be permitted to earn 'good time' on that sentence. This gives him hope and some ambition, and a chance to live out his term."[42] Congress did not seriously consider McClaughry's imaginative plan, but in 1913 it did amend the law to provide parole eligibility to life termers after they had served fifteen years.

The more serious problem, one that persisted for twenty years, was in having the warden and chief medical officer at each institution serve as ex-officio board members. Despite his earlier advocacy of the arrangement, LaDow quickly saw that the procedure caused a serious problem in prison management, and he was blunt in saying so to Congress when he had the opportunity. A congressional committee chairman asked, "Do you think, Mr. LaDow, that these parole boards as now constituted are properly constituted?" LaDow's response was clear and simple: "I do not." He went on to read to the committee a previous statement from the attorney general (a statement he had no doubt written himself). "While the prisoners had no means of knowing exactly on what grounds an application for parole was denied, yet they easily inferred that such denial must have been with the vote of one or both of the prison officials on the board of parole, and they have not hesitated to show their resentment of the adverse action in their cases"[43]

LaDow saw the problem first hand, of course, but he also heard the fervent complaints from the wardens and doctors. Dr. A. F. Yohe at Leavenworth particularly protested that prisoners at sick call included all too many who were not sick at all, but came to pester him about their parole hopes.

The legislators were not sufficiently persuaded to correct the problem by providing the expensive alternative of a separate parole board. The wardens had to live with the problem.

In 1915, a new superintendent of prisons was appointed, and LaDow was transferred to the post of inspector of jails. The new superintendent, Francis H. Duehay, served only briefly and was followed by Denver S. Dickerson. Then President Warren G. Harding appointed his brother-in-law to the position. Heber H. Votaw had served twelve years as an Adventist missionary in India and then had worked awhile as Harding's asssistant secretary. Votaw, an unqualified patronage appointee, undertook a job he knew nothing about; he handled it without scandal, but also without distinction. Though his appointment brought him into an unfamilar field, he would serve long enough to witness its first steps toward professionalism.

More important to the accomplishments in prospect was Harding's appointment of a young, dynamic woman to the post of assistant attorney general. Californian Mabel Walker Willebrandt came to the job in 1921 at the age of thirty-two and remained for eight influential years. She was responsible for tax, prohibition, and prison matters. With so many and such widespread duties, the time she gave to prison matters was remarkable. The Atlanta penitentiary invited her attention more than any other, partly because her superintendent of prisons was so ineffectual. Observed one historian, "Sentimental and inefficient, knowing little of 'what it was all about,' as Mrs. Willebrandt put it, Votau [sic] made it easy for politicians to use the Bureau of Prisons [sic] for patronage."[44]

In 1923, Willebrandt's boss, Attorney General Harry M. Daugherty, appointed Albert E. Sartain as warden for Atlanta. Sartain had been a sheriff in Ohio and was active in Republican politics there. His conduct at the prison soon attracted suspicion, and an investigation uncovered a conspiracy between him and four notorious bootleggers who had been sentenced to serve terms there. In advance of their arrival at the prison, the bootleggers had arranged for Sartain to receive $10,500 in exchange for special living quarters, catered meals, and occasional weekend furloughs. One of them was assigned to be Sartain's chauffeur, and once Sartain took the men with him on a hunting trip.[45]

To investigate and correct the situation, Willebrandt borrowed a former Texas Ranger, T. B. White, from the FBI and appointed him temporary warden of the institution. Remaining less than a year, White completed his task and returned to his permanent job, but he was a man who would be important in other federal prison posts.

When the facts of his mischief were clearly established, Sartain was called to Washington; he resigned and was later convicted on charges of conspiracy to accept a bribe. On February 28, 1927, Sartain entered the Atlanta Penitentiary, no longer as its warden, but as prisoner #24207, with a sentence of eighteen months.[46]

During the 1920s, the Atlanta Penitentiary received many prohibition violators; one of them, George Remus, sentenced in 1923, took himself comfortably to Atlanta in his own private railroad car, and once there he too began to buy favors.[47] The testimony at Sartain's trial incidentally revealed bribes paid to several prison employees by Remus and other bootlegger prisoners.[48]

One insouciant inmate was the famous Broadway musical show producer, Earl Carroll, who had given a memorable party at his theatre in New York City. During the event one of his chorus girls, nude, settled cheerfully into a bathtub full of champagne while the appreciative guests dipped into the wine and sipped it. When the host was prosecuted for this violation of the prohibition law, he adopted a posture of amused innocence; in court he seemed to remember that the tub had been filled not with liquor, but with mixed fruit juices. Undoubtedly the court was highly entertained by Carroll's tongue-in-cheek testimony, but not diverted from its duty. He was convicted of perjury and sentenced to serve a year and a day. But Carroll was spared the usual marshal-escorted ride to the prison in handcuffs. In the style to which he was accustomed, he picked his own schedule, bought his own ticket, rode in comfort in his own train compartment to Atlanta, and presented himself at the prison entrance. Soon after his admission to the prison, however, it came to Willebrandt's attention that he, too, was getting special treatment. Rather than being assigned to a regular cell, Carroll was comfortably housed in an apartment over the garage at the warden's house; witnesses also alleged that one of his actresses visited him there, after which she was also entertained by the warden.[49]

Willebrandt was especially distressed by this case because a new warden had been appointed from whom better things were expected. Although John Snook was a patronage appointee, he had been picked also as an experienced prison expert. His selection reflected the way that Willebrandt's career involved a transition from the long-standing tradition of patronage appointments to a new appreciation of appointments based on professional qualifications. Willebrandt had been comfortably oriented to the patronage tradition, but now, responsible for running the prisons, she felt keenly the need to employ wardens of proven competence. Not surprisingly, at times she was frustrated by the difficulty of keeping the two considerations compatible. The Snook appointment was an example of the problem. Snook was an active Idaho Republican and a friend of Senator William Borah; but he was also an experienced professional. Snook had been a U.S. marshal and had served acceptably for several years as warden of the Idaho penitentiary. Nevertheless, the much larger Atlanta prison was beyond his capability. He proved to be inept in handling staff and was insensitive to the nuances of ethics.

The situation created prolonged stress for everyone involved as Willebrandt attempted to get the elusive but necessary facts by means of an undercover operator. At her request, in January 1928, the FBI supplied an agent from its Detroit office. The agent was sent to Atlanta as a prisoner, under the name Peter Hanson, with false commitment papers signed by a cooperative federal judge. Somehow, Snook soon learned of the "spy" and put him in solitary confinement. Willebrandt transfered her agent to Leavenworth, where he was then released. About the same time, a second undercover agent was sent in, but he remained only a few days.

Snook's reaction was one of wild indignation, and he proved to be a clever fighter. Much of the time, he managed to make Willebrandt look like she was the one at fault. The contest between them went on through the rest of that presidential election year while Willebrandt endured some uncertainty about what her position would be after the election. During the fall, and at election time, she sent several investigators to probe management problems at the prison. When Snook resisted and criticized the agents, Willebrandt lectured him for his uncooperative stance, while Snook protested that he was the very model of a cooperative administrator.

Snook's principal success was in persuading the public and some congressmen that Willebrandt's "spy system" was mean, unfair, and unsporting, and that she persecuted him only because he resisted that un-American device. Willebrandt seemed unable to get attention focused on the real issue of Snook's administrative incompetence. Senator William Borah accepted Snook's complaint about the undercover investigators, as did several others. Senator Walter F. George of Georgia exclaimed, "If such a practice has been introduced it is unAmerican, borders on czarism and will never be tolerated by the congress of the United States."[50]

Snook was unrestrained in criticizing his boss when he wrote frequent letters to Borah. Shortly before the election, Snook told the senator, "It would appear to me that from the standpoint of a republican interested in the success of the Republican party and the election of Mr. Hoover as President, that the time of this investigation is very inopportune, as the fact that I am being investigated will no doubt be used to advantage by the Democratic Party." He noted with alarm rumors that Willebrandt might be named attorney general under the next administration; if so, "the position of Warden of a Federal Prison would be intolerable."

As it was, Herbert Hoover was elected and was inaugurated on March 4, 1929. His new attorney general, William D. Mitchell, ordered an end to the undercover agents in the prisons. However, Mitchell did support Willebrandt's view of Snook as a poor manager, and just two weeks after the inauguration, Snook submitted his required resignation.

The Atlanta troubles were part and parcel of a larger pattern of administrative shortcomings that Willebrandt tackled throughout her time in office. While she contended with Snook, she also fretted about Warden W. I. Biddle, at Leavenworth. The previously mentioned inquiry there in 1925 resulted from extensive allegations of misfeasance. Investigators finally concluded that there was no proof of corruption, though some management procedures needed to be reformed. Nevertheless, Willebrandt still believed that Biddle was neither competent nor honest.[51] Again, the close ties between a warden and his congressional patron proved a frustrating obstacle to disciplinary action. After many months of painful effort Willebrandt won the battle; when Biddle resigned in November 1926, Willebrandt promptly replaced him, again enlisting the services of T. B. White, a man who brought ability, integrity, and a colorful style to a new career in federal prisons. (Serving as warden at three federal prisons,

White put in twenty-six years at these posts, longer than any other federal warden before or since.)

In the weeks that followed the Hoover inauguration, Willebrandt reviewed the frustrating, exhausting nature of her job and the many years she had given it. She received an attractive offer from the private sector, and it was too tempting to ignore; in June, President Hoover accepted her resignation and paid sincere tribute to her impressive record of government service.[52]

During their long periods of construction, the two giants, Leavenworth and Atlanta, absorbed the attention and energy of the successive superintendents of prisons; the McNeil Island institution existed in a persistent state of neglect. By 1910, a new cell house augmented the minimal original building, but another decade and more would pass before a dining room, a kitchen, or an administration building could be built. Progress was similarly slow in getting the usual utilities to the insular prison. Recurrent problems plagued the water supply from unreliable springs and wells; a modern water system was not developed until the late 1930s.

An electric generating plant was built in 1911, but no telephone service was yet available. In fact, it would then be another four years before the first transcontinental call would be placed to San Francisco. By 1923 a single telephone wire came across to the island, but telephone service remained inadequate until the 1950s. Through the 1920s prison officials communicated with the Department of Justice, in Washington, either by ordinary mail or by telegraph; thus they were required to travel first by boat across the three miles of water to post office or telegraph key in Steilacoom.

By 1922, a new cellblock and a dining room and kitchen were completed and the original primitive cellblock from 1875 was razed. A few more parcels of the privately held land were bought up gradually and by 1926 a prison farm was in operation. Throughout this period, the McNeil Island wardens, as those elsewhere, were patronage appointees, but in contrast to the wardens at Atlanta and Leavenworth, they were undistinguished either by special competence or by corrupt administration. Their service could best be characterized as quiet mediocrity. The first warden to bring some color to the job at McNeil Island was Finch Archer, appointed in 1922 under the patronage of Washington's Senator, Wesley L. Jones. Archer had been a county tax assessor, a state fisheries inspector, and a police chief. In many ways, his twelve-year administration typified the prison philosophies of his time; progressive new ideas were being introduced but existed alongside repressive practices of the past. Under Archer, a prisoner publication, *The Island Lantern*, was established, and over the next half century, it won frequent penal press awards. A music program and a basic educational program were started. Such accomplishments were noted respectfully by the press. One fulsome account read, "Archer transformed the crude prison in the savage wilderness to its present modern state."[53]

At the same time, however, prison discipline was peremptory and harsh. Prisoners could expect summary punishments, and staff members, too, could expect to be summarily fired if they incurred the warden's dislike. At times, Archer was remarkably naive in his appraisal of inmates. Any persons—staff members or inmates—who became his favorites were able to deceive him outrageously.[54]

Although new housing capacity was added during Archer's time, McNeil Island was no different than the other two penitentiaries in respect to being overcrowded. McNeil Island was never as large as Leavenworth or Atlanta, but it suffered proportionally. The number of inmates hit a high point in 1930, when more than thirteen hundred prisoners were housed there. Beginning in 1871, four years before the institution opened, critics agitated for its replacement or relocation. Even through the 1920s, when new construction was regularly going on, the Department of Justice was unenthusiastic and uncertain about the far away island prison. The department begrudged any improvements and it never granted the favor of bureaucratic appreciation and assurance of permanency. McNeil Island was indeed badly situated, insecure, and inadequately staffed and funded. But in many respects it became one of the best federal prisons—an outcome unlikely to be believed by those who knew it in its first half century.

5

PLACES FOR
WOMEN, PLACES
FOR YOUTH

J. Ellen Foster, special agent for the Department of Justice, made an inspection tour of the West Virginia penitentiary at Moundsville one day in 1910 and was dismayed to find that male and female prisoners were making surreptitious contact. The women took their daily outdoor walks in a yard where the male prisoners could observe them from the shop windows, and they were able to pass unseemly notes to each other. Foster feelingly reported the problem to the attorney general.

> The desire for companionship between the sexes is human and universal. God honors it in the family relation. Angels must weep to see it perverted. The hellish perversion of this heavenly gift is one of the problems which penologists have to deal with. . . . The knowledge that beyond a wall too thick to be broken through, too high to be climbed over, there are a lot of men of criminal character and rampant desire who accomplish their purpose if they could, this knowledge has a bad effect on the minds of women who are prone to do evil. . . . Prisoners are physically developed men and women; they are mentally children. God only knows what they are morally in his sight. . . . These considerations and many more have caused penologists to insist on separate prisons for women. They even declare that where possible a prison for women should be located in a town as far as possible from a prison for men.

The superintendent of prisons took up Foster's complaint and wrote a stiff letter of rebuke to J. E. Matthews, warden at Moundsville.

Dear Sir,
In the report of Mrs. J. Ellen Foster, a special agent of this Department . . . attention is called to certain features in connection with female prisoners. Mrs. Foster says that it is common practice, or at least an occasional practice, for small bags to be thrown over the prison wall from the men to the women, and the women to the men; the bags contain notes and various articles. This practice suggests possible contact between the sexes, and I write to admonish you of the care which should be extended in order that male and female United States prisoners may not be allowed to associate or mingle together.[1]

Whatever a more modern judgment of Foster's romantic moralizing might be, her protests were taken seriously since they were in accord with conventional views of that time and also because Foster was a woman of impressive credentials. For a short time during the first decade of this century, she was the government's one effective advocate for improved conditions for female prisoners.

Born in 1840 and orphaned as a child, Judith Ellen Horton remained loyal to the staunch beliefs and militant social concern of her abolitionist Methodist minister father. At age nineteen she married but later obtained a divorce, a move unconventionally bold for a young woman of pious family in that day. Her second marriage was to a young lawyer, Elijah Foster, whom she met while both were doing social service work in Chicago. After they moved to Clinton, Iowa, where her husband set up a law office, she, too, studied law and was admitted to the Iowa bar in 1872. But her interest was far broader than a small-town law practice. With her husband's wholehearted support Foster took up some of the great causes of the time. She became an active participant in developing the Women's Christian Temperance Union and played a major part in writing its constitution. She traveled the country on speaking and organizing assignments for the W.C.T.U. and the Republican party. As a board member of the Red Cross, she went with Clara Barton to attend its 1902 international conference in Russia. At the same time, she was active in Methodist church affairs and was raising several children.[2]

In 1888, when the Republican administration appointed Elijah to an office in the Department of Justice, the Fosters moved to Washington.

After Theodore Roosevelt became President, Ellen Foster was assigned to survey labor conditions affecting women and children in the South. Though her husband died while she was in the midst of that task, she did not slacken her pace, and when she finished her report to the President in 1907, she was appointed to the Department of Justice as an examiner, under the general agent, the position later titled superintendent of prisons.

Foster applied the same energy and devotion to her new mission that she had put into all her other interests; the job called for her to travel country-wide, visiting prisons wherever there were federal boarders. Though she evaluated and reported on prison conditions for men as well as women, Foster showed a special concern for the women and was realistic enough to know that the ideal of separate prisons in separate cities would have to yield to the attainable. Her letter to the attorney general, quoted above, ended with this kind of compromise. "There are so few female federal prisoners that I have felt justified in asking the Department to make provision for the few for whom the Department is responsible in a cell house to be built for this purpose at the Leavenworth prison." This request undoubtedly reflected the enormous respect she held for Warden McClaughry.

In occasional instances, circumstances forced federal prisons to take female prisoners. Before Leavenworth penitentiary was built, the Fort Leavenworth facility had contended with the problem briefly. After Warden French took over the facility in 1896, he wrote to the attorney general, "I now have 3 female convicts confined in this prison and am advised of 2 more that will soon be here. I respectfully suggest that a Matron should be appointed by you to care for these unfortunate creatures. I have them in a building apart from the men and will employ them in making convict clothing."

When French received the requested authorization, he hired his mother-in-law as matron at forty dollars per month and soon was surprisingly content with the arrangement. He informed the attorney general that the building used for the women had space for ten, and it could just as well be filled. The women were making clothing and were an asset to the institution. Late the next year, however, when the women were long gone and their space converted to other uses, one new female prisoner was brought in; French protested that he could not operate a female unit on the basis of one or two occasional cases.[3]

Other than these prisoners, no females were ever incarcerated at Leavenworth or Atlanta, but Foster was aware that females had been accepted occasionally at McNeil Island. That institution was intended as an all-male facility also, but because of its remote location and the absence of any other accommodations for females in the upper northwest, females were sometimes lodged there as a necessary expedient. In one case, a husband and wife were admitted; in another case, an Eskimo woman with a one-year sentence died there before completing it. With no separate cell space available for women, the usual recourse was to use a hospital room. In one such instance, in 1905, the warden was accused of enjoying closed-door visits to the prisoner's room, a charge that was investigated, but not conclusively proven.[4]

Foster's suggestion for a female cellblock at Leavenworth was in fact, acted upon, spurred by the Justice Department's increasing problems in finding space for females. In May 1910, the attorney general approved construction of a separate cellblock for females on the penitentiary grounds. Foster studied McClaughry's suggested design for the building and scaled it down from the proposed forty-eight cells to thirty, a figure that reflected more accurately the number of women then on hand. Foster did not live to see the acquisition of any federal cells for females. On August 11, she died suddenly at age 69. She had served as a prison examiner only three years, but her involvement in prison issues was phenomenal. Though her occasional moralizing now seems naive, she was unique and greatly respected for her deeply caring approach to a wide range of social problems.

After Foster's death, the construction project at Leavenworth lost momentum and eventually was given up. The foundation and the walls for the women's unit were built but the inadequate records suggest that the roof was never added. During a congressional hearing some years later, one committee member recalled the situation of that time. "Originally Congress's plan provided a place for the incarceration of federal women offenders and there was built at the Leavenworth penitentiary a small inclosure. A wall was built around this and a women's prison was supposed to be built there. Later it was thought inadvisable to build a women's institution as a mere annex to a man's penitentiary for a number of reasons. The whole body of penologists have gotten away from that and that plan was abandoned."[5]

Another factor involved in the story of the projected women's building, was the problem of one particular prisoner. When the superintendent of prisons, R. V. LaDow, approached McClaughry about putting up such a building there was nagging pressure from the case of a District of Columbia woman, Ada Cross, who was being boarded intermittently at Moundsville. As LaDow explained, "We are still sending male prisoners to Moundsville where their terms do not exceed two years, and also all females from the District regardless of length of term."[6]

In 1904, Ada Cross was sent to Moundsville with a twenty-year sentence for housebreaking. Later, while working in the prison sewing room, she attacked and killed another prisoner by stabbing her with a pair of scissors. Cross became one of those inmates who flit between prison and mental hospital without being welcome in either. She was judged insane and sent to St. Elizabeth's Hospital in Washington in April 1907. The following October, she was declared to be sane and was readied for return to Moundsville. However, the warden there protested that, medical opinion notwithstanding, Cross was a "fiend incarnate"; she was indeed insane and should not return to his prison.

Cross remained at the hospital and LaDow wrote to various other prisons in search of a place that would take her. They all declined, but eventually the warden at Moundsville died, and the prison board agreed to accept Cross again. She returned to the West Virginia institution in January 1910; only four months later, the new warden, J. E. Matthews, reported that Cross was insane again. The St. Elizabeth's Hospital superintendent countered that Cross actually was not insane and probably never was. The unfortunate prisoner was kept at Moundsville, but she was confined by herself in a windowless room, on the ground floor of a stone guard tower situated at a corner of the perimeter wall. As Foster reported, her moaning and screaming could be heard at all hours and was unbearable.

Because of this case LaDow urged the Leavenworth warden to plan a cellblock for women. The need was so urgent that in the spring of 1910 he wrote to McClaughry, "It would be wise to go ahead and build a small building in which to confine Ada Cross as soon as it was finished without waiting for the erection of general quarters for all female prisoners."[7]

For some temporary relief of the problem, McClaughry turned to the nearby Kansas penitentiary at Lansing. The warden there, who already had several federal female prisoners, was reluctant, but assured that Leavenworth would take over the female prisoners as soon as its new building was finished, he agreed to take Cross for the interim. However, instead of expediting action, this move only relieved the pressure; construction slowed down and eventually stopped. Even Ada Cross helped relieve the pressure by making an unexpected improvement. Foster visited Cross at Lansing and found that the change of setting had somehow reduced her anger; she was doing well in the general prisoner population and said it was the best place she had been.

Fortunately, at that time there were few federal female prisoners; in a letter to McClaughry in May 1910, LaDow noted that altogether they then had just twenty-six females. During the previous century, there were far fewer. Marshals had always placed the rare female prisoners in women's units at the same state prisons where male prisoners were kept. These accomodations were always minimal, in every respect.

An example of the problem was the Virginia State Penitentiary. Although that prison was close enough to Washington to be convenient for federal prisoners from that area, it was virtually never used. It had a good separate building for females, but the population was usually about 95 percent black, and the treatment of the women tended to reflect their low social status. Joseph Fishman, a Department of Justice agent, explained why he could not deal with the Virginia Penitentiary warden when he visited there in about 1910, seeking space for women. "In questioning the officials concerning various matters of administration I learned about the whipping of women. But the warden positively declined to discontinue this practice when I told him I would not under any circumstances recommend the use of the institution unless it were stopped."[8]

The accommodations for female prisoners continued to be little short of degenerate well into the twentieth century. Poignant evidence of this was seen during World War I. Two federal female prisoners, anarchist Emma Goldman and socialist Kate Richards

O'Hare (chapter 7), were so articulate that they became embarrassing as they exposed demoralizing conditions in the Missouri penitentiary where they were boarded. O'Hare's book, *In Prison*, was published in 1923, two years after Mabel Walker Willebrandt became assistant attorney general, with responsibility for prisons. Doubtless, Willebrandt was aware of O'Hare's experience and her book; there is also indication that she heard Foster speak some years before on the prison subject.[9] In any event, after she got to Washington, Willebrandt was quick to take up the issue. She clearly enunciated three major goals to be accomplished in respect to prisons: (1) employment for federal prisoners, (2) a reformatory for young men, and, (3) an industrial farm prison for female prisoners.[10]

The figure of thirty or so prisoners that Foster planned for in 1910 grew rapidly. In the annual report of the attorney general for 1920, the superintendent of prisons told of having 150 female prisoners and of being forced to use many substandard facilities for them. By 1924, Willebrandt reported the figure to be 300, while the number of jails or prisons willing to take female prisoners was shrinking alarmingly.

In her aggressive move to acquire the necessary new institution, Willebrandt initially made a tactical error that set the project back for a few months. Before getting an authorizing bill through Congress Willebrandt found a site that seemed suitable, so she prepared legislation with language that specified the selected location. An abandoned weather observation post in northern Virginia, Mt. Weather, offered the advantages of being immediately available, being owned by the government, and being rural but not too far from Washington. However, the authorizing bill, introduced in January 1923, was defeated in the face of vigorous opposition from residents near the site. A new bill was introduced the following December, this time with no site specified and with a prearranged massive show of support.

Proponents wanted a pastoral setting, a feature that perhaps reflected the ideas of J. Ellen Foster, who once glowingly decreed, "An ideal prison for women should be a reformatory located in the country several miles distant from a city or town. It should be in the midst of arable and timber land and with health giving and beautiful natural surroundings. . . . The sun and the wind, the dew of the morning, the heat of mid-day, the frost of nightfall." When Foster wrote that, she was also preparing a report on the women's section of the District of Columbia jail where, she was discouraged to find, "The feet of these women do not touch the sod, the sand or the rocks of Mother Earth from the day they enter to the day they leave the jail"[11] Foster would have been highly pleased with the site finally chosen for the women's prison.

Willebrandt's reworked enabling act, finally passed in June 1924, authorized site selection by a committee of three cabinet officers: the attorney general and the secretaries of Labor and Interior. Ostensibly this took the decision out of Willebrandt's hands—but only ostensibly.

To insure passage of the act this time, Willebrandt marshaled some impressive backing, exploiting the political strength of women's groups and other national organizations that would naturally be sympathetic to the cause. Representatives of twenty-one such groups met in Washington in September 1923, in a conference sponsored by the General Federation of Women's clubs. A few of the organizations, such as the Republican and Democratic national committees and the American Prison Association, were not women's groups as such; but many were, including the Daughters of the American Revolution, the National Council of Jewish Women, and the politically potent Women's Christian Temperance Union. The delegates, impressed by speeches from Votaw and Willebrandt as well as from many prominent women who were involved with state institutions, gave resounding support to the idea of a new federal facility for women. The momentum was unstoppable.

Meanwhile, residents of the small town of Alderson, West Virginia, decided they wanted the institution and launched an energetic campaign that included offering the government 202 acres of land bordering the nearby Greenbrier River and the Chesapeake Railroad. Willebrandt, who had invested herself emotionally in the Mt. Weather site, was unenthusiastic about Alderson but agreed with it to avoid more delay. Now, with a site selection committee composed of cabinet members who had much more urgent (to them) issues for their attention, Willebrandt had to educate, encourage, and prod them into the desired action. Her thinking, her method, and her problem with her indecisive boss are suggested in a memo to Harlan F. Stone, then the attorney general.

I do not care about the Alderson site particularly, but it is disheartening to undergo further delay. After all it is the Attorney General's office which has the real responsibility in erecting this institution and maintaining it. Why should two secretaries merely called in to join with the Department, who will not have the permanent responsibility, hold the thing up?

May I respectfully suggest that the real judgement in this matter is yours, just as the actual responsibility falls permanently on this Department. I believe as quickly as you are sure in your own mind you can by a firm stand get the other two secretaries to join with you. They will be ashamed to take the responsibility of preventing you doing what you feel is safe, especially as they will never have any future connection with the institution. [12]

Six days after that memo was written, the attorney general and the two secretaries sent to Congress their certification of Alderson as their choice, and within a few weeks, in March 1925, the first construction money was appropriated.

With that accomplished, Willebrandt turned to the selecting of the woman she wanted to be the superintendent. (The law at that time required that the superintendent be a woman.) Within that same month of March, Dr. Mary Belle Harris was offered the job, accepted it, was appointed by Attorney General Stone, and made her first inspection of the site where she was to build the new institution.

Her education and early experiences were hardly the sort to point Mary B. Harris in the direction of a corrections career. Her father was the long-time president of Bucknell University, an ordained minister, and a scholar in classical languages and literature. Mary Harris fell easily into the same interests, earning a Ph.D. in Sanskrit from the University of Chicago, and then teaching Latin at Bryn Mawr. At the same time, she pursued musical studies and was an accomplished singer and organist. In 1912 and 1913 her interest in numismatics led her to take an extensive trip to Europe, where she studied and wrote about Roman history and coinage.

While at the University of Chicago, Harris had met a fellow doctoral student, Katharine B. Davis, who later became the commissioner of corrections for New York City. When she returned from Europe in 1914, Harris visited Davis who persuaded her to become superintendent of the Women's Workhouse on Blackwell's Island. Harris' four years there were followed by war work on problems with "camp followers," and then by five years as superintendent of the New Jersey State Home for Girls. Then, at age fifty-one, she was ready to accept appointment as head of the as yet nonexistent, but urgently needed, federal prison.[13]

During most of her first two years as warden at Alderson (she much preferred the title superintendent), Harris worked from an office at the Department of Justice in Washington, planning the construction, equipping, and staffing of the institution. In addition to the land supplied by the town of Alderson the government bought an adjoining farm, bringing the total holding to 515 acres. Adapting to a natural slope, the "campus" was built with two groups of residence buildings, one around an upper level rectangle and a similar one nearby on a lower level. Construction was completed by a contracted builder, but a great amount of site preparation, road building, and continuing grounds work was done by prisoner labor. About two hundred minimum custody male prisoners were transferred in from other facilities, mainly Atlanta, and lodged in a temporary camp on the grounds.

By 1927, one residence building was sufficiently finished to be usable, and on April 30, it received the first prisoners—three women transferred from the women's prison in Vermont. A few more soon came in from Rhode Island and Kentucky institutions and worked to prepare the facility for full use. The formal opening took place on November 24, 1928, the attorney general, John G. Sargent, Mabel Walker Willebrandt, and many other officials gathered for the ceremonies. By the end of that year, the new prison had more than two hundred inmates in its beautiful, open, campus-like setting.

By Harris' account, her institution was initially planned with fifteen residence buildings, a hospital, school building, industries building, laundry, power plant, and superintendent's residence. A food services building came only many years later as the first plan was to have food prepared and eaten in the cottages.

Nine years before, Kate Richards O'Hare had started her federal prison term under conditions which both physically and managerially were degrading and degenerate, but nevertheless typical for women prisoners. Now Alderson suddenly changed the confinement conditions for federal women dramatically to a level of decency previously unheard of. When Heber H. Votaw had first presented the original bill to authorize the institution he had used carefully reassuring language to allay any suspicion that it would be other than a real prison. "No novel, fanciful, or idealistic theories of reformation have been invoked, neither are any drastic or reactionary measures contemplated."[14] To some conservative critics, however, the final result was in fact more idealistic than punitive. "Women were housed in cottages complete with private dining rooms with tablecloths, living rooms with curtains, and a scattering of vases with fresh flowers from the gardens."[15]

Though Alderson was radically comfortable compared with the usual prisons, the objectors were few compared with the many who admired its humane decency. The institution, without a surrounding fence or other obvious custodial physical features, bore no outward resemblance to a conventional prison. Though Mary Belle Harris was to some extent unrealistic in her determination to reclaim her prisoners by the gentle force of treating them like ladies, her new domain was nobility itself in its brave, civilized departure from the kind of experience common to women prisoners until then.

The juveniles, too, needed attention. The idea of treating children as children was a long time coming.

In most states, through most of the nineteenth century, juvenile offenders simply went into the same prisons used for adults. Though a few specialized refuges were developed in mid-century (most notably in New York City, Boston, and Philadelphia), these facilities were available for only a fraction of the potential cases. And considering their coldly rigid character, it may have been just as well.[16]

Juveniles seem to have been a rarity in federal courts previous to the twentieth century; typical federal crimes, such as postal violations, counterfeiting, treason, or assaults on the high seas, were ordinarily the province of adults. Juveniles as federal offenders began to be seen in greater numbers only much later, after there were automobiles to be stolen and driven across state lines, or when the Volstead Act made moonshining a crime. Agents who raided the illicit backwoods stills often caught the younger family members at work.

Throughout their history, most federal courts had no resources at hand for sentenced juveniles if the local authorities did not elect to take them into their own state courts. The few federal juveniles received by the Department of Justice during the nineteenth century were usually placed in certain of the same institutions as adults were. One facility that was particularly favored was the Detroit House of Correction. Because of Zebulon Brockway's enlightened administration, the operation there was well regarded, even long after he had left.

Gradually, during the last two decades of the nineteenth century, the general agent made more use of the growing number of state-operated juvenile "reform schools," and by the first decade in the new century, it was the regular practice to use these. In 1907, in a memo to the attorney general, LaDow explained that they were using the Reform School at Grafton, West Virginia, for federal juveniles from that state. At another time, he noted that boys from areas farther west were placed in the Missouri Training School at Booneville. Its superintendent was Charles C. McClaughry, who had been appointed there after serving as deputy warden at the Atlanta Penitentiary. At about the same time, J. Ellen Foster was placing federally committed girls in the Illinois juvenile facility at Geneva.

A reform school for boys, in Washington, D.C., was the first specialized institution for juveniles that could be classed as federal. In 1866, Congress appropriated twelve hundred dollars and authorized incorporation of the trustees for a "House of Correction" for boys. The first location, upriver from Georgetown, was unsatisfactory, so a new appropriation was obtained to move the school to Fort Lincoln, a disused Civil War fort on Bladensburg Road, at the Maryland line. Fifty boys were transferred there when it opened in 1872, and a substantial and extensive institution was gradually developed. Fire destroyed the original main building in 1905, but it was shortly replaced by a new administration building. In 1908, Congress changed the name of the facility to the National Training School for Boys (NTSB), a name that better recognized its broad federal commitment. "It defines the scope of the school and at the same time indicates the nature of the work which it is trying to do for its boys."[17]

The boys were housed in several so-called cottages, bulky, high-ceilinged buildings of sixty or more beds each. In accord with the practice of the times, the buildings were designed to discourage escapes; the dressing area, with showers and closets, was on the first level, while the sleeping area was an enormous dormitory on the third level. Its windows were high above ground and all clothing was locked up two floors below. Each dormitory had a raised balcony on one side where a staff member sat all night to oversee the sleepers and prevent any escape attempts or other mischief.

Through most of its existence, the institution was a hybrid of a sort—part federal, part District of Columbia—governed by a board created by Congress. E. C. Wines noted in 1880 that it was presumably under the supervision of the U.S. attorney general, although the administrative arrangement did not give him clear authority or control over it.[18] When Cecil Clay was superintendent of prisons he was, ex officio, a member of the school's board; the president appointed the board, while the attorney general appointed staff and approved salaries.[19]

Once it was well started, the school was available to two different categories of boys, both technically federal: those committed from District of Columbia courts and boys sent by federal courts from any other U.S. jurisdictions. The attorney general's annual report for 1883–84 discussing the reform school as a federal resource, reads: "Upon favorable reports to officers of the Department of Justice as to its management during the last year, it has been designated as the place of confinement of all juvenile convicts from convenient states."

Far too many boys still went to jail, however, instead of to the juvenile facility; the fact that a reform school was available was not enough to cause judges to break from their accustomed practice of using the jails. In 1899, the Washington, D.C., jail warden reported, "There were 362 boys between the ages of 8 and 17 years committed to the jail by the courts of the District during the last fiscal year, while only 55 under 16 years of age were committed to the reform school during the same period." It was a source of worry for the warden who transferred boys to the reform school whenever possible.[20]

In 1897, the average daily population of the school was 219, and 69 percent of these were from the District of Columbia courts. Three decades later this distribution had changed considerably; the 1926 figures show 103 boys from District of Columbia courts and 247 from other federal courts. This change came despite the effort of the superintendent of prisons to divert cases to other facilities. Three of the state institutions had then been designated for boarding of federal juveniles; the training schools at Golden, Colorado, Monroe, Washington, and St. Anthony, Idaho.[21] By 1933, the attorney general had designated fifteen institutions where federal juveniles could be boarded. These included the private coeducational Children's Village at Dobbs Ferry, New York, and the coeducational state and county institutions in Ogden, Utah, and Louisville, Kentucky. For girls, the reformatory at York, Nebraska, and the institution at Peakes Turnout, Virginia, were designated. For boys, the state training schools or reformatories in Colorado, Georgia, Idaho, Illinois, Minnesota, New Jersey, New York, and Washington could be used.

A major factor behind the increased federal commitments was the effect of two laws that defined federal crimes. The Volstead Act of 1918 brought in the era of prohibition, and the Dyer Act of 1919 gave federal status to the interstate transportation of stolen cars. The dash and excitement of quickly moving stolen cars to other areas for disposal was profitable and highly appealing to many teenagers. The "illicit distillers" were a rather different type; they tended to be cultural law breakers as distinguished from criminals. Many of these boys, often from Appalachian areas, were brought into the NTSB, and as a group they were the most tractable and least troublesome of any. Typically, they were illiterate and mainly needed educational programs and basic health services.

The regime at the National Training School tended to be harsh; before 1940, racial segregation and summary corporal punishment were unquestioned practices, though these were common to most such schools. Military drill was instituted in 1901 and continued as a daily activity for many years. This, too, was a common feature of juvenile institutions then. At the NTSB, where the boys drilled with blank cartridges in Springfield rifles, the superintendent insisted, "The military department is indispensable in schools of this character, as it makes discipline easy and teaches self-control and obedience to authority."[22]

The two legal categories of boys—those from District of Columbia courts and those from other federal courts—were handled alike in the institution, but procedures for their release were different. An Act of February 26, 1909, confirmed and defined the practices generally followed until then: boys committed from District of Columbia courts were paroled on the decision of the board of trustees, while boys from other federal courts were released by the authority of the attorney general.

It was not surprising that having a school for boys awakened interest in having a similar facility for girls, nor was it surprising that the concept was shaped along lines that would now be considered inexcusably sexist. In 1881, the trustees for the boys' school opened the subject, with a view to making their institution coeducational, as were many of the state institutions of that time. "It is found to be of very great advantage to have the girls do all the washing and ironing as well as the making of clothing for the boys in addition to their own, thus giving a large number of girls work which will be of advantage to them in the future, as well as relieving the boys of that work, and permitting a large number of them to follow such other pursuits and trades as would be to their future benefit."[23]

However, Congress preferred separate institutions for the sexes. In 1888, a Reform School for Girls was authorized; in 1893, an appropriation of thirty-five thousand dollars was granted for construction, and in November of that year, the institution opened—taking black girls only. The new school was located on Loughborough Road and Conduit Road (changed to MacArthur Boulevard during World War II), on a site now occupied by Sibley Hospital. Another building was completed by 1901, making it possible for the school to accept white girls, although very few were admitted. Most of the white girls were sent to Houses of the Good Shepherd, in either Washington or Baltimore.

In most respects, the administrative structure for the girls' school duplicated the difficult arrangement of dual responsibility borne by the other school; it had its own board; it accepted mainly District of Columbia girls, with others admitted at the direction of the attorney general. One difference was that the boys' school accepted boys up to age sixteen, while the girls' school took girls up to age eighteen. In 1912, Congress changed the name of the school to the National Training School for Girls (NTSG), and in the next few years the board increasingly agitated for a new site. The institution was badly crowded and situated on limited acreage, and the board was never comfortable with having black girls and white girls in such close proximity. In 1923 Congress authorized purchase of a site at Muirkirk, in nearby

Maryland; finally, in 1926, the girls (including seven from federal courts) were moved to the new campus where the 30 white girls and 115 black girls were housed in widely separated buildings.[24] At that time, the superintendent was Fannie French Morse, respected for her work both there and previously as superintendent of the girls' training school at Sauk Centre, Minnesota. When Mabel Walker Willebrandt attempted to persuade Congress to adopt the Mt. Weather site for the proposed prison for women, she enlisted Morse to inspect the site and testify in favor of it at a congressional committee hearing. In the 1930s, the girl's school closed; it was succeeded by new juvenile facilities operated by the District of Columbia near Laurel, Maryland, a short distance from the former Muirkirk site.

During the 1920s, the boys' institution, like the adult prisons, was crowded, and at the same time its deteriorating physical plant made it difficult to manage. Its location gradually became a handicap as the city crowded around it, with the result that "boys must be regimented within the confines of the school to a degree which is contrary to accepted principles of good training school administration."[25]

Little could be done about the institution while responsibility was divided among the attorney general, the District of Columbia commissioners, and the school's board. The assistant attorney general, Mabel Walker Willebrandt, neglected it while she focused instead on the need for an institution for slightly older offenders. Willebrandt and superintendent of prisons, Heber H. Votaw, campaigned vigorously for a reformatory for young first-time prisoners at the same time they made an equal effort to get the institution for women. The result was that Congress authorized the reformatory for young men in January 1925.

To get the institution in the fastest way, "Willebrandt asked the War Department to provide a list of all its properties of more than a thousand acres suitable for the reformatory."[26] She chose an abandoned military site, Camp Sherman, near Chillicothe, Ohio. One year after Congress authorized the institution, the property was acquired; the old barracks buildings were made habitable, and a group of prisoners was brought in to help build the permanent institution. The need for the facility was quickly demonstrated by the rapid growth of its population. In 1930, before construction was completed, the population had risen to more than fifteen hundred, and the attorney general advised the federal courts that no more prisoners would be accepted for the time being.

Although the Department of Justice provided poorly for the juveniles in its custody and would soon discontinue any service to that category, it was committed to provide quality programs for young men in their late teens and early twenties. At Chillicothe, by 1930, about four hundred prisoners attended a strong academic school. For the first time, a federal prison employed a full-time professional librarian. The former army warehouses had been converted to vocational training shops where seven instructors taught masonry, plumbing, sheet metal, and electrical work. There was also a large farming program.

The Alderson Reformatory for Women and the Chillicothe Reformatory for young men easily represented the high points of three decades of operations under a superintendent of prisons. But at the end of those three decades, the need for expansion was evident, and the task would be much too taxing for the severely limited capability of the superintendent's office. It was clear to the attorney general and his overworked assistant, Willebrandt, that it was time for a bureaucracy.

6

BUREAUCRACY
ACHIEVED

The attorney general took a minimal step toward a bureaucracy in 1907 when he created the position of superintendent of prisons, within the Department of Justice. For some years the department had employed a "general agent" and one or two subordinate "examiners" who were responsible for overseeing the conditions of federal prisoners in various state facilities. However, the general agent was ineffectual; he had no resources for keeping statistics or other records, and no authority for enforcing quality services. The work of initially placing prisoners was ordinarily handled by the marshals, while the general agent arranged subsequent transfers when necesssary, or attempted to mediate in other individual case problems.

The first person appointed to the position of superintendent of prisons was Robert V, LaDow, a man of impeccable integrity and proven competence in prison matters. He had served as an examiner since 1898, first under Frank Strong, the general agent, and subsequently under Strong's successor, Cecil Clay. When Clay died in 1907, the title of general agent was abolished, and LaDow was promoted to the new position of superintendent of prisons.[1]

By that time, in addition to the old McNeil Island facility, the two giants, Leavenworth and Atlanta, were being built. Both were in use, although they were unfinished; their construction was to demand LaDow's constant attention through his seven years in office.

As already noted, LaDow was followed by a succession of politically appointed superintendents, the best qualified of whom was Albert H. Conner, appointed in 1927 with the political backing of Idaho's Senator William Borah. Conner's previous experience included three terms in the Idaho state legislature and two terms as the Idaho attorney general. After he was appointed superintendent of prisons, it was Conner who prepared the original draft of the bill that would soon establish the Bureau of Prisons.

The time had come for new administrative strength in handling federal prisoners. The reasons were set out in a rational, well-crafted report prepared in 1928 by James V. Bennett, an agent of the U.S. Bureau of Efficiency.[2] The most impelling factor was the deteriorating condition of the prisons caused by gross overcrowding. The three federal penitentiaries could not meet the need, or even a substantial portion of it. Bennett pointed to three federal legislative actions that had driven up the volume of cases since 1920: the Prohibition Act, the Harrison Narcotic Act, and the Automobile Theft (Dyer) Act. And while federal cases were increasing, the states were having their own upsurge of criminal convictions. And this meant they had much less space available to lease to the federal government.

Bennett reported that Leavenworth was at double its capacity, with prisoners sleeping in basements, activity rooms, and even offices. The conditions at Atlanta were similarly alarming. And while McNeil Island was too small to help much, it, also, was overloaded. Bennett stoutly rejected the idea of increasing the size of the existing penitentiaries. Not only were they already too large for effective control by one warden, there also was the problem of long-distance transportation. To avoid the expense of taking prisoners so far, the government needed a scattering of smaller prisons in various regions of the country. He pointed out that in the case of a person sentenced to serve only one year, transportation was likely to be the major part of the cost of incarceration.

Bennett did not spell out the next logical step—instituting central headquarters control. He did not need to. An obvious reason he might have argued for it was the very reason it could have been self-defeating to do so. Until then, wardens were political appointees and their loyalties were given first to their political patrons. This was a sensitive topic—one that could not easily be broached in a public report. But it was a problem that had to be corrected if progress were to be made.

Various concurrent moves in Congress to authorize new federal prisons or to investigate the existing ones fomented increased concern.[3] These actions occurred in the context of increased public awareness of federal prison problems. The contention between the assistant attorney general, Mabel Walker Willebrandt, and the Atlanta wardens, Sartain and Snook, was highly visible. Willebrandt of course supported the move to establish a new bureau.

In 1929, the House Special Committee on Federal Penal and Reformatory Institutions held hearings under Chairman John G. Cooper of Ohio. The Cooper committee found that congestion in the prisons defeated any proper classification and care of prisoners; a new central bureau was needed to administer the prisons.[4] Many other recommendations were included to upgrade and expand federal corrections. The committee's report was well received, and before that year was over, legislation was drafted to establish a bureau of prisons within the Department of Justice. And thanks to the efforts of Willebrandt, the person to fill the director's job was already at hand.

Well in advance of the final enactment, the advent of the Bureau had been anticipated, and there had been considerable speculation about who its director should be. One name put forward was that of Hastings H. Hart, the widely respected consultant on penology for the Russell Sage Foundation. Hart had been secretary of the State Board of Charities and Corrections in Minnesota for many years, and then served as secretary of the Illinois Children's Home and Aid Society. His final post, with the Russell Sage Foundation, gave him national visibility that he used vigorously to promote better corrections programs throughout the country. Reputedly, the Cooper committee was created largely as the result of Hart's lobbying. Hart was imbued with much the same concern about federal prisoners that earlier had motivated Roeliff Brinkerhoff.[5]

In testifying before the Cooper committee, Hart spoke with good natured sarcasm about the impossible task faced by Willebrandt who "at the present time has a sinecure. She has nothing to do except to enforce the revenue laws, the immigration laws, the Volstead Act, and the drug act. In her leisure moments she attends to the minor duty of being the responsible head of the prison system." He also pointed out the load carried by the superintendent of prisons. "No Federal officer is entitled to more ardent sympathy and consideration. He is loaded down with a multitude of responsibilities, enough to break the back of any ordinary man."[6]

It was natural and even obvious to think of Hart as a prospect for the directorship of the anticipated new bureau, but he was in his late seventies and had no recent experience in actual prison system administration. So Willebrandt looked elsewhere, nor did she wait for the new bureau actually to be in existence. Her choice was the Massachusetts commissioner of corrections, Sanford Bates.

Bates did not seek the job, nor did he originally mean to work in the corrections field. He intended to pursue a career as a lawyer. The events that changed his plan started with his election to the Massachusetts State Senate in 1915 (after serving three years in the lower house) and his consequent acquaintance there with a fellow senator, Calvin Coolidge. Both men served only briefly in the state senate before going on to other jobs; Coolidge went to the governorship, while Bates was soon recruited by the Boston mayor to be the city's commissioner of penal institutions. Though he had no experience in such work, he handled it brilliantly. Less than two years later Governor Coolidge called him to become state commissioner of corrections. Bates accepted and served nine years before being enticed to Washington.

Correctional service appointments in Massachusetts were political, and Bates himself was politically experienced after twice running successfully for the state legislature. It is natural to assume he would bring to Washington an easy acceptance of political patronage practices; but surprisingly, he took federal prisons out of politics. The explanation for this seeming anomaly apparently is that while Bates had worked within a politically driven system, he was never primarily a politically partisan bureaucrat. Bates was recruited for the Boston correctional post; he did not seek the job. Indeed, he hoped the job would be temporary and he could return to practicing law. In such a context, Bates felt free to take bold, innovative measures without worrying about job security. His basic sense, his management skill, and his fresh administrative approach were just what that stagnant agency needed. His success there of course led directly to the offer from Coolidge.

In administering the state agency, Bates' legislative experience enabled him to work effectively with key politicians. He was a political realist, but again, because he did not ask for his job or engage in any political bargaining to obtain it, he was free to put sound management practices ahead of most political accommodations.[7]

It was not easy for Willebrandt to entice Bates to Washington. She first tried to hire him in 1926, when the incumbent superintendent of prisons, Luther C. White, died. White, formerly head of the prison industries at Sing Sing, had been appointed after Heber H. Votaw resigned in 1925; but after only a few months in the job White got sick and quickly died while visiting McNeil Island. Willebrandt left the job open awhile, hoping to persuade Bates to take it, but he declined because of unattractive salary and because his wife and daughter wanted to remain in Boston.

Willebrandt was persistent. She wrote to one helpful Massachusetts official that she "would go pretty far to get Mr. Bates' vigor, knowledge and zeal enlisted in the interests of the Federal Penal System." She pursued the salary issue in a memo to the attorney general, noting that the salary of six thousand dollars was the same as Bates' Massachusetts salary. She argued that the federal government should at least match the $7,500 salary paid J. Edgar Hoover.[8]

Bates firmly refused the position of superintendent of prisons, and A. H. Conner was finally appointed. But later, as momentum built up to create the new bureau, Willebrandt, aided by attorney general William D. Mitchell, renewed her offer to Bates. After a lengthy Saturday interview with Mitchell and further reflection at home, Bates prepared a letter to the attorney general in which he presented a thorough and cogent outline of the philosophy he would expect to follow if he were to organize the new bureau. He explained, "I have had the somewhat unfortunate experience in the past of working for a chief who was not whole heartedly in sympathy with my own ideas. This has not only interfered with the full working out of our program, but it has rendered the job rather uncomfortable."

The thoughtful letter revealed that Bates held a realistic view of criminals. "Punishment must be promptly inflicted but it must not be so severe as to defeat its own ends or degrade a community." Bates stressed that he was not a sentimentalist, but he saw a need for scientific study of the individual, to the end that reformation of the prisoner would be the best protection for society. He saw the proffered job as a great opportunity for constructive public service and asked for assurance that the administration would resolutely support his efforts. "I should realize, as I have continuously, the important part which the representatives of the people in Congress and elsewhere have in the general picture, but I should confidently expect the backing of my superiors in withstanding that happily infrequent kind of pressure which comes sometimes from the unreasonable demands of persons whose chief aim in life is political."[9]

The attorney general's response was satisfactory, and two weeks later Bates telegraphed his acceptance of the offer. Conner was transferred to another assignment, and President Herbert Hoover appointed Bates as superintendent of prisons at a salary of eight thousand dollars, effective June 1, 1929. (Other staff later remembered that Conner accepted his transfer and demotion gracefully and remained as a useful, gentlemanly member of the staff for many years.) The Bates appointment was one of Willebrandt's last satisfying accomplishments. Only days after Bates' appointment she left office after eight hectic years.

As Bates arrived, the movement toward creating a bureau was well underway. Bates and his staff kept up the momentum from the Cooper committee's work, as they helped to write and move the legislation along. The bill for a bureau of prisons, principally written by Conner, was approved by Congress, and on May 14, 1930, it was signed by President Hoover. Bates was immediately appointed director of the Bureau of Prisons, at a salary of ten thousand dollars.

The first leader of a new program or organization is especially important. That person may set the philosophy and quality of the operation and may establish a pattern to persist long after his or her own service ends. For that reason, Sanford Bates was a fortunate choice. He could be as articulate and courageous as necessary in confrontations or decision making, while personally he remained affable. He was both intelligent and scholarly, but without conceit. His wide-ranging personal interests included an appreciation of opera, a substantial acquaintance with Shakespeare, a sense of humor, and charming skill as a raconteur. He did not need to be the fount of all the ideas or decisions, so he was able to bring in some of the brightest and most progressive people available to fill managerial jobs at headquarters.

Three assistant directors were hired. James V. Bennett was one of these; his well-crafted report in 1928 was basic to the effort to get the Bureau created. "Austin MacCormick was in charge of academic and vocational training and the formulation of prison discipline reforms. William T. Hammack administered fiscal affairs and the recruitment and training of a new career service for prison personnel."[10] Bates, appreciating the management skill and vision these men possessed, gave them responsibility, backing, and the encouragement of his own eminently sensible ideas.

Both the records and the memories of those involved indicate that the first few years of the Bureau's development were ones of vibrant action, of stimulating intellectual ferment. Bates' talented headquarters staff tackled their jobs with optimism and enthusiasm, all the more impressive in view of the system's entrenched mediocrity. MacCormick brought a fresh vision of correctional programming, and for his time, he had a unique sense of the human needs of the prisoner population. Hammack, an attorney who had worked for the Library of Congress, took the lead in forging responsible and competent financial accounting services at the new Bureau. He is best remembered for his efforts in promoting a career civil service system and professionalized staff training. Others who joined the system during the Bates years included F. Lovell Bixby, who distinguished himself in the Bureau and later in New Jersey as a creative corrections innovator, and Dr. Benjamin Frank, a highly intellectual educator who served the Bureau for many years in a variety of influential posts.

In view of the sparkling quality of the top management Bates brought in, the first few wardens appointed under Bureau direction were disappointing. Reacting strongly against the previous tradition of political patronage, Bates and his team were determined to put the wardens on a merit basis. They started filling vacancies for wardens by Civil Service selection and appointment. The people hired in this way had solid experience elsewhere in prison administration, but too often they also had temperamental idiosyncrasies that put them at odds with the Bureau philosophy. Edwin A. Swope, who first came to the Bureau as warden at McNeil Island, was a strong, incorruptible manager, but he had a talent for alienating everyone who dealt with him. Henry C. Hill, the first warden at Lewisburg, was experienced but obsessed with his own ego needs, requiring all staff to wear uniforms and to salute him whenever he and his two great danes passed by. A few such experiences made it obvious that the Bureau would have to develop its own wardens and promote from within.

At Chillicothe, Warden Albert McDonald, who was there when the

Bureau was created, experienced increasing problems and finally resigned in 1933. Austin MacCormick was sent there as acting warden to get the institution into better order. He took with him as assistant warden a newcomer to the system, Joseph W. Sanford, who quickly proved to be a person of special competence. MacCormick resigned after less than six months to accept appointment by Mayor LaGuardia as commissioner of corrections for New York City. Sanford moved up to the warden's job and later spent a decade as warden at Atlanta, where his service justified the idea of merit promotions from within the system. A later director of the Bureau remembered Sanford as one of the best in the Bureau's history. "Aggressive, likeable, ruthless in dealing with those who crossed him, he produced change unlike any other in his day. He roamed through his institution making changes first hand." He also "broke down forever the old ingrained concept that the deputy warden ruled everything back of the second gate."[11] If ruthless methods seem not to suggest good management, it must be remembered that tradition-bound Atlanta was then so resistant to fresh ideas that only a resolute approach could accomplish the necessary changes.

At the same time Congress created the Bureau of Prisons, it authorized an impressive expansion of institutional facilities, including a new penitentiary (Lewisburg, Pennsylvania), a prison hospital (Springfield, Missouri), several regional jails, and several camps. Since many in the glut of prisoners then were "illicit distillers" caught by the prohibition law and serving short sentences, it seemed feasible to use inexpensive open facilities for them. The new headquarters team scouted for federal parks or military sites that could be adapted quickly as prison camps; six of these camps opened before the end of 1930, and three more were added within two years. In his annual report of 1933, the attorney general asserted that nine thousand prisoners had been transferred out of the overcrowded prisons and into the camps. (This figure does not represent the population of the camps at any one time; it is, rather, a total figure that represents the turnover of these short-term prisoners.)

The camps had only the most basic physical facilities, with barracks-type dormitories and virtually no custodial features. The inmates selected for them were stable, short-term prisoners who could adapt to an outdoor work program and not be likely to attempt escape.

Some educational programs were offered in several camps, but these were were at an elementary level. The work in some locations (Mill point, West Virginia; Kooskia, Idaho; and Tucson, Arizona) involved primarily road construction. Elsewhere (Montgomery, Alabama, and DuPont, Washington), the camps were associated with military bases, and the prisoners performed various grounds-keeping or construction jobs around the reservations. The relaxed operation of these open camps is nicely suggested by the camp at Kooskia, in the Nez Perce National Forest. After a day of working in the woods, the prisoners sometimes spent their recreational time panning for gold.

The camps could be acquired and activated quickly, and they could be closed quickly as circumstances might require. Three camps that opened in 1930 were closed the following year, though the closings do not suggest that the camps failed. Others were closed later, when the work in their areas ran out or when the locations were needed by the military. The camp idea proved to be viable as well as essential. It was a workable way to house a large population, with minimal cost and in living situations that offered little of the negative aspects of the prison culture.[12] Few of the original camps became permanent; the pattern that emerged was for minimum security camps to be established as adjuncts to regular correctional facilities.

The new Bureau management was also concerned about the population of short-term jail prisoners, many of whom were boarded in local jails that were substandard, to say the least. The Bureau needed to develop some federally controlled facilities for prisoners who were serving jail sentences of a year or less. One jail was developed hurriedly in New York City; another jail was acquired in New Orleans in 1930 by adapting the old United States Mint; and new facilities for jail prisoners were built in La Tuna, Texas, and Milan, Michigan. The New Orleans jail was closed after thirteen years of use; the jails at La Tuna and Milan eventually became regular correctional institutions.

By 1933, these facilities plus the new major penitentiary at Lewisburg, Pennsylvania, had been opened. First known as Northeastern Penitentiary the new prison reflected a hurried, but innovative, effort to obtain a large prison of significant new design. Bates worked closely with the architect, Alfred Hopkins, to create an institution that would hold serious offenders in a secure physical plant designed to accommodate the new elements of prisoner management, classification, and treatment. To this end Lewisburg provided a mix of housing formats, some small cellblocks, some dormitories, though at times the architect's enthusiasm for the artistic appearance of the whole interfered with its practicality. "Perfection of the Italian Renaissance architectural style was at times allowed to override the most desirable design."[13]

Another new institution of a specialized type was also under construction and opened in September 1933. This was the "hospital prison" at Springfield, Missouri, for prisoners with chronic or serious health problems, including psychiatric cases. Until this facility became available, the Bureau was wearing out its welcome at overloaded St. Elizabeth's Hospital in Washington, D.C. The new hospital facility represented an unusual linkage between the Bureau of Prisons and the United States Public Health Service (USPHS). When the Bureau was created, the USPHS was authorized to furnish the medical services in the prisons, but in this one institution, the USPHS was also the administering agency. The first several of its superintendents were psychiatrists. In its first year of operation, Springfield admitted 297 prisoners, including 151 with mental diseases, 19 with organic nervous diseases, 72 with tuberculosis, and 55 with other medical problems.

For youthful prisoners, the Chillicothe reformatory was recognized as an important asset, to be favored with the best possible programming. Some of the Bureau's brightest brains were routed to it, to insure a rehabilitative quality of care. The attitude was, "Education is the center around which all other services should operate."[14] Beginning in 1940, in addition to a rich academic curriculum, the reformatory developed the most sophisticated vocational training program anywhere in the system—an aircraft mechanics course. In a large shop, splendidly equipped with a variety of aircraft engines, instructors conducted a thorough two-year course. The program was especially appreciated during World War II. The Bureau later claimed to have placed more than 350 men in civilian air mechanic's jobs during the war.

The reformatory was located on two thousand acres, and in addition to the educational programs, it operated a dairy farm and orchard plus several industrial shops.

The Bureau management saw the need for a similar institution that could take youthful prisoners from the western half of the country, leaving Chillicothe to serve the East. So, among the several new institutions authorized in 1930 was a reformatory at El Reno, Oklahoma. That location was picked, just as Chillicothe was, because land could be made available by the army; a one thousand-acre section of Fort Reno was transferred to the Bureau, and the new institution opened in April 1933. Like Chillicothe, El Reno had rich academic and vocational education programs, augmented by agricultural work when its farm center opened in 1934. The first warden was Henry L. Merry, whose unusual background and approach to his work tells something of the freewheeling operations during the Bureau's early days. Merry had been president of the Mayflower Hotel Company in Washington, but after he developed an alcohol problem, he resigned and went to live in an isolated retreat in the New Hampshire woods. Some months later he emerged, with his alcoholism under control, now a theosophist and a vegetarian. Merry was ready to bring to his next work a belief in the importance of basic, back-to-nature living. His friend Bates was intrigued by Merry's ideas for rehabilitation of prisoners and gave him his chance to test them at El Reno. Merry obtained a number of oxen to use as draft animals; inmates learned to drive them for the heavier farm work (though horses and mules were used for plowing), and even the daily mail run to town was by oxen-drawn wagon. Merry's unorthodox methods were never proved to be more successful than other methods, but his work was acceptable enough that after six years at El Reno, he went on to serve four years more at other federal prisons.

While El Reno was being built, still another facility for young men was under construction on a parcel of land given by the Fort Lee army base, near Petersburg, Virginia. This facility started as a reformatory camp that housed about one hundred prisoners in dormitories, and it underwent various changes in character and function through its subsequent history. At first it accepted young men, mostly bootleggers, who were transfered from Atlanta. With that type of short-term, non-violent offender, the facility operated with only moderate security. By 1935, the Bureau reported, "The Reformatory Camp at Petersburg is now nearing its maximum population of 600. We regard this institution as an outstanding model in the way of a minimum security penal institution."[15] Eventually, however, Petersburg evolved into a fully custodial correctional institution, with several changes in types of population.

The frenetic pace of adding new institution beds went on while a variety of problems competed for attention. On August 1, 1929, a few weeks after Bates' appointment as superintendent of prisons, a riot erupted at Leavenworth. MacCormick reported for work that day, so on his second day on the job, Bates sent him to Leavenworth to investigate the problem. The disturbance was analyzed as sponta-neous, triggered by an unpalatable meal, but more importantly, it reflected the tensions of severe crowding and lack of work, exacer-bated by a severe heat wave. One prisoner was killed, but otherwise the consequences were slight. The situation seems to have been well handled by Willebrandt's appointee, Warden T. B. White.[16]

Bates capitalized on this highly visible event to focus attention on the enormous problem of overcrowding, with some useful and quick results. After the riot, the army was again persuaded to give up its Fort Leavenworth Disciplinary Barracks, and the Department of Justice opened it on September 1 as another regular corrections facility. Though the institution was referred to as the Leavenworth Annex, the Bureau operated it as a separate facility with its own warden. The arrangement lasted ten years; the Annex was returned to the army in October 1940.

The first execution during Bates' tenure took place on a specially made gallows at Leavenworth, on September 5, 1930, when Carl Panzram (chapter 4) was hung for murdering a Leavenworth em-ployee just three weeks after Bates became superintendent of prisons.[17]

While a riot, a murder, and an execution added unwanted spice to Bates' introduction to his new responsibilities, he had other problems of a more subtle sort; politically appointed wardens, accustomed to enjoying their independence, exhibited some natural resistance to the new headquarters team.

They were not just annoyed at having to take administrative direc-tion from Washington, they resented equally the new philosophical directions being imposed. Wardens and second-level custodians had pursued traditional prison methods; they had rarely been held ac-countable for the sometimes heavy-handed actions that now were proscribed by the new regime. Staff training had been nonexistent and now it would be centrally instituted. Old-time officers were scornful and let the new experts know it. Classification procedures, casework, and other social services were quite threatening to custodians who had been accustomed to using physical measures whenever they wanted to assert their authority. As Bates' new breed of professionals—especially the young, entry-level people, joined the institution staffs, they invariably met cynical interference.

The concept of objective and individualized handling of prisoners was a key element in Bates' overall program. In his portion of the attorney general's annual report for 1932, Bates showed obvious pride when he noted, "The social service units established to promote individualism of treatment have been extended during the past year. There are now units of 3 warden's assistants each at Atlanta, Leavenworth and Chillicothe, a unit of 2 at Leavenworth Annex, and one warden's assistant each at McNeil Island and Alderson. . . . The routine of making brief social histories of all incoming prisoners has now been established."

This was a profound new development—more so than most of the people involved realized, for the warden's assistants who brought a social service function into prison management represented the entering wedge of the new philosophy. Bates was honest in his report in 1932, but he did not describe the shock and resistance the social service personnel encountered. One of the first of the warden's assistants was Myrl Alexander, assigned to Atlanta's Warden A. C. Aderhold in 1931. Many years later Alexander described the frosty welcome, when the uncomprehending warden sent him to the deputy warden to find something to do. The deputy "sat behind a desk in a resplendent uniform with velvet braid and service insignia on his sleeve. I was instructed to stand on a small green carpet in front of his desk. . . . 'We got word from some of those new guys in Washington that you fellows will be coming down here to be warden's assistants and social workers. I want you to know that I'm the only warden's assistant around here.' "

Years later, young men of that time, remembering their first experiences, commented, "We were not accepted too well by the old-time officers who considered us to be school boys." Warden Aderhold at Atlanta was typical of the old wardens who "believed that a warden's job was to preside over the administrative officers 'up front,' conceding all territory back of the second gate to the deputy warden. Under his philosophy, all control of fiscal affairs was within the domain of the chief clerk. The result: change was discouraged because it might 'upset the boat.' The deputy warden and the chief clerk became czars of their respective territories."[18]

As Bates and his team took over, their key instrument to advance the new techniques and philosophy was a staff training program instituted at the hastily contrived federal jail in New York City. Bates acquired this first modern federal jail in 1929 when he adapted a warehouse on West Street, in lower Manhattan. Steel partitioned cells with grill fronts were placed into its three floors, making a crude but serviceable jail that remained in use until 1975. For three years, it was the center of a germinal, hopeful new program for staff training.

When Bates arrived in Washington he quickly enlisted the help of his friend, Hastings Hart, to plan the staff training curriculum. Hart and Bates had learned about the just-opened British staff training school at Wakefield when they attended the 1925 International Prison Congress in London. In 1929, at the same time he asked Hart's assistance with training plans, Bates selected Jesse O. Stutsman to serve as superintendent for the new program. Stutsman had served as superintendent of three different prisons and demonstrated an interest in the professional quality of corrections work. He and Hart, both of whom started their careers as ministers, now worked enthusiastically together to develop the staff training curriculum. Stutsman was appointed to be superintendent of the federal jail at the same time, and it was there at "West Street," in January 1930, that the first group of twenty-eight correctional officer trainees convened.[19]

The basis of the training curriculum was an emphasis on broad behavioral science themes rather than daily custodial practicalities. Stutsman and Hart wanted the training to impart an understanding of causes of crime and ways to reduce deviant behavior. "Emphasis was placed on methods of controlling men by intelligence and leadership rather than by force."[20] This factor certainly contributed to the scorn with which the "school boys" were greeted by older officers at the institutions.

Stutsman's training program was an impressive start, but only a start—and a brief one. Stutsman died in 1933. At the same time the program faced problems with funding and was terminated. For some years afterward, the training was conducted instead at various institutions, and the unwanted result was that the quality declined.

Another example of resistance to the new Bureau management was in a class by itself, in regard to both its character and its persistence. Mary Belle Harris, warden at Alderson, possessed an intransigent, independent spirit. Hers was not the resistance of the traditionalist opposed to change; she felt nothing in common with other wardens and their methods. Of all the wardens, Harris was the most difficult to bring into a team relationship with headquarters. She considered her task in such elegant, progressive terms that she believed she should not be constrained by the prosaic character of conventional prison management. This spirit of elitism comprised her independence, her resistance.

"Dr. Harris . . . believed that from the vantage point of her high ethical, moral, and intellectual standards, unfortunate women could be led to change their lives and become constructive productive women."[21] She was determined to treat her prisoners like ladies and presumed they would change accordingly. Though there was much that was decent and valid in this view, Harris was handicapped by a two-fold problem. First, she did not understand and was not interested in the extensive engineering and maintenance issues to be dealt with in operating a large physical plant; and, second, she did not understand the inmates' basic needs. Her personal background—her cultured, academic family and professional life—was so different from the background of her prisoners that, for all its humaneness and decency, the program too often was unrealistic.

Inevitably, Harris chafed under bureaucratic requirements, and she believed that the headquarters managers did not appreciate her special institution. She was a woman, working with women, and she resented being bossed by male bureaucrats.

The Alderson institution was unique in that it had an advisory board, authorized and defined by statute, that included some influential, nationally known members. The board tended to be persuaded by Harris' concepts, and this support undoubtedly prolonged her resistance to Bureau control. In any event, the resistance persisted for most of the years that Harris was at Alderson. A typical issue was the relative importance of having inmates work at maintenance or industries tasks, or having them involved in cultural and educational programs to which Harris gave priority. Bates naturally expected the industrial "power sewing room" to be run on the same cost-effective principles required of shops in all the other prisons. He was frustrated to see that women often were pulled away from their production work for such activities as "supervised reading, candy making, table services and painting." When Harris protested that she must train her charges to be homemakers, Bates replied, as reassuringly as possible, that he sympathized with her goals and was proud of her institution, but, "men and women outside have to spend an average of eight hours in labor, which interferes with their cultural development. In other words I do not agree with you that the industry prohibits the proper training of a large group. I insist that it is an essential element in their proper training."[22]

On such points, Harris continued to be a difficult pupil, and her blind eye for proper physical plant operation continued to frustrate the central office managers. Even after six years of Bureau control, Bates found it necessary to write to Harris a letter which was a classic in delivering a stern, point-by-point reprimand at the same time that it was balanced and dignified. The occasion was the visit of the Bureau's agriculture expert who found that the Alderson farm was wastefully managed and said so in a blunt way which Harris found too ungentlemanly for her taste. When she complained to Bates, he responded firmly.

> We did not send Mr. Foristall into the field simply to be polite or to tell you only the things which he found were satisfactory. . . . The question with me now is not what he said or how he said it, but whether the things he said were true and whether they should be remedied. I cannot understand, to take one example, what kind of farm supervision you could have had to permit a feed trough to exist in such a state of repair that the feed ran out of and over it into the manure pile.

Bates reminded Harris that there had also been some previous problems.

> You will recall that your per capita cost at the time that central cost supervision from this office was established was $1.25 and that today it is about 78 cents. It would be difficult to convince the

Committee on Appropriations or any impartial person that Government supervision in your case has not been beneficial. I recall the mess which was uncovered when Mr. Butterworth first went to your institution. Leaky steam pipes; high cost of power; inefficient boiler room operations; buildings heated way beyond any necessity; polluted water being used, and many other evidences of lax and inefficient management in this regard.[23]

In 1933, a specialized type of alternative placement was developed for a few women. Gangsterism was rife, and the female prison population included some gangsters' wives or confederates who were potentially dangerous or likely escape risks. As the attorney general explained, "We have set aside a portion of the Federal detention farm at Milan, Michigan for the housing of a small group of female prisoners. Here they can be adequately guarded by armed officers and housed in the more traditional type of steel cells. A matron and a number of warders have been appointed to assist the Superintendent in guarding these women, who are entirely segregated from the male portion of the institution."[24] The unit was maintained until 1939, when the women were transferred out and Milan was made a correctional facility for male narcotic offenders.

When Mary B. Harris retired in 1941, she was replaced by Helen Hironimus, who, according to the then director, was "an equally considerate leader but more practical and aware of the facts of life."[25] Hironimus, with a degree in law, had gained virtually all her work experience in the Bureau, including some years at Alderson and a brief stint at another of the new institutions. By the mid 1930s a second institution for females was needed, especially for women from further west. The result was the construction in a moderate art deco design of a reformatory for women at Seagoville, near Dallas. Hironimus was picked to be the warden and went there in 1939 to prepare for the opening in October 1940. A prominent psychiatrist, Dr. Amy Stannard, was selected to be associate warden. (Dr. Stannard later became a member of the U.S. Board of Parole.)

Hironimus had little more than gotten the new institution off to a good start before being called back to take over Alderson, but Seagoville was about due for a change anyway. Under pressure of wartime need it was turned over to the Immigration and Naturalization Service in June 1942, for detention of aliens. When the Bureau of Prisons took it back three years later, they needed less western space for females, so Seagoville became a minimum security facility for men. Hironimus was succeeded at Alderson in 1949 by Nina Kinsella, a talented woman Bates had brought from Massachusetts to be on his central office managerial team.

Alderson demands this disproportionate amount of attention for several reasons. First, its leadership was unique and many of the management details tell of the times and of the philosophical strain in the institution's relationship with headquarters. Alderson was special, too, because of its long-held status as a model prison for women.

Though Harris' successors approached the inmates with more realism, her philosophy persisted for some years. In retrospect, it suffers after close inspection of some aspects of the daily treatment of inmates. It can be argued that Harris' unquestioning acceptance of racial discrimination was only the pattern of the times (and not materially different from the practices in the mens' prisons), but it also can be argued that, even in that context, it was needlessly insensitive. For instance, the prison complex was divided into an upper campus and a lower campus; a sidewalk, with a flight of sixty-four steps, connected the two. That route, "the 64s" as inmates called it, was for white inmates only. Black inmates had to walk in the street. Inmates lived in cottages, separated by race; white inmates held the office jobs, while black inmates worked in the laundry or piggery. Desegregation was accomplished in the 1950s, under Kinsella.[26]

Curiously, in her the zeal to treat inmates like ladies, Harris seems to have had some blind spots in regard to clothing. Records reveal that for the first three decades or so, Alderson inmates were not allowed to wear their own clothes, and the institution clothing policy showed an insensitivity to inmates' femininity. Staff were expected to wear nylon stockings, but inmates were restricted to bobby sox. In a letter to headquarters in January 1951, Kinsella noted that the prison was not supplying ready made underwear. "Due to the shortage of funds in the last year these garments for institution wear were made from cotton mattress covers. The heavy twill cotton cover was used for brassiers. . . . We are making the slips and pants for institution wear out of nylon parachutes. . . . We have a supply of

the parachutes which are ripped up by some of the semi-invalids."
Similarly, inmates were not allowed to choose their own shoes, but
were supplied with shoes made at Leavenworth.

Dr. Harris, who never married, was adamant in insisting that the
institution was to be run by women; staff positions for men were as
few and were at as low a level as possible.[27] This attitude dominated
for decades. Male staff members usually were allowed to speak to
inmates only if an escort were present. Virginia McLaughlin, the fifth
superintendent, promoted to the post in 1969, introduced a much
more open attitude in many respects. She was the first married
woman in the job, and she brought to it a modern appreciation for
having institutional life conform more closely to normal social living.
From then on, although Alderson departed substantially from the
more repressive principles defended so resolutely by Harris, it did
not lose its zeal to be elite among prisons.

Four of the five superintendents who followed McLaughlin were
men; in 1973 the protective advisory board, no longer effective or
important, ceased to exist. The institution, no less committed to
quality care, was finally comfortable as a member of the Bureau team.
(The Bureau's new willingness to employ men to head institutions
for women was soon paralleled by its willingness to appoint women
as wardens of prisons for men.)

Stories of prison escapes are legion and cannot possibly be cata-
logued here except for the very few that lend some touch of historical
significance. One that meets this requirement occurred early in the
Bureau's experience, at Leavenworth in the time of Warden T. B.
White. The institution's shoe factory regularly needed a paste that
came in barrels from a supplier in St. Louis. Several inmates arranged
for outside contacts to obtain a barrel of the paste and bury in it a
package of weapons. The package, sealed in a section of inner tube,
was a weapons bonanza. It included five pistols, a rifle, a sawed-off
shotgun, plenty of ammunition, and fifteen sticks of dynamite with
the necessary caps and fuse. When the barrel was delivered to the
prison, as if from the supplier, the inmates sequestered it and removed the contraband; two weeks later, they made their escape.

A well-armed group of seven prisoners picked up several hostages
as they approached Warden White's office on the morning of Decem-

ber 11, 1931. White was taken hostage at gunpoint and the escapees demanded that he order the guards to open the front gates. White did as he was told, and the guards, in turn, obeyed him.

Eventually it became, and still is, well-known Bureau policy that a warden, or any other staff person, taken hostage immediately loses all authority; no other staff is to accept any orders from him. However, such policy was not in place in 1931.

When the group reached the outside they released all the hostages except White. They intended to take the warden's car, but White had thrown his keys under his desk. Instead, the men commandeered a passing car and drove off, taking White with them. In the course of the next several hours, the men stopped at a farm house and took another hostage, a young woman named Elizabeth Phillips. They forced her to walk with them across a plowed field and through a barbed wire fence, to a road where they flagged another car. At that point, White seized what looked like a good opportunity and attempted to take a gun from the man guarding him. However, his arm caught in the car door and, during the brief delay, he got a shotgun blast in his arm and side. Mrs. Phillips dropped on the ground and rolled into the ditch. The escapees abandoned the hostages and continued their wild flight, finally taking refuge in a farmhouse where they were surrounded. During the subsequent shooting, one was killed, two committed suicide, and four escaped but were soon recaptured.

Warden White, though seriously injured, did recover, and the appreciative Bureau assigned him to a less pressured post. The new prison at La Tuna, Texas, was being built and White went there as its first warden, remaining until he retired nineteen years later. Elizabeth Phillips survived with some damage to her nerves and her clothing. Her Congressman petitioned on her behalf, requesting reimbursement of her expenses to a total of $55.50, including $45.00 for doctor's bills and medicine, $4.00 for the loss of her slippers, and $1.50 to replace her ruined stockings. Congress in its wisdom considered the request and granted it in full, along with grants to a guard whose car engine needed major repairs after the strenuous chase ($63.30), and another guard who had to replace his car window after it had been shot out in the gun battle ($4.95).[28]

The most visible and controversial new thrust during the early Bates regime was development, for high risk offenders, of the specialized institution on Alcatraz Island. It is a subject that deserves its separate discussion—chapter 9.

A far less visible unit that required some upgrading was the one institution for juveniles, the National Training School for Boys. When Bates was appointed superintendent of prisons he was also appointed by President Hoover to the board of trustees for the Training School, the president of the board then being Francis H. Duehay, a former superintendent of prisons. Though the awkward administrative arrangement left the Bureau of Prisons in a weak position in regard to the institution's management, Bates made what efforts he could to redefine its mission. Mainly he wanted the Bureau to withdraw from involvement with juvenile cases and for these to be diverted instead to state courts. Because juveniles were tied closely to their homes, Bates disliked having boys brought in from all parts of the country to an institution in Washington. Too often it blocked them from the family contacts they needed.

In his first few months on the board of trustees, Bates asked for a survey of the institution, to be undertaken by an outside expert, Harrison Dobbs, then at the University of Chicago. Bates enlisted the sympathetic help of the U.S. Children's Bureau which told Dobbs, Bates "is very anxious to have legislation taking children under 16 or 17 entirely out of Federal Court jurisdiction and he says that the Attorney General would support such a proposition."[29]

The Children's Bureau arranged for the requested survey and started a cooperative record keeping process to achieve more accountability in juvenile cases. Congress passed the requested legislation in June 1932, permitting federal courts to divert juveniles to local or state jurisdictions. Also, the active involvement of the federal probation service was enlisted to intervene in juvenile cases and arrange for the diversion.[30] No basic change in administrative format or function was accomplished at the National Training School during Bates' tenure. Nevertheless, change would come without too much further delay; the institution's time was running short.

Though Bates did not accomplish all he desired in regard to juvenile services in his eight years, he did succeed in building a central management system that remained firmly in control. He gave the agency a solid start toward a professional career service with a progressive philosophy well enough rooted to have promise of permanence. Proving the nonpartisan quality of his administration, Bates and his team survived in office through the change from a Republican president, Herbert Hoover, to a Democratic president, Franklin Roosevelt.

Perhaps Bates is best remembered for introducing a newly humane attitude toward prisoners as people. A clue to his beliefs on the subject is found in a paper he once wrote, mingling his interest in criminal justice and his interest in Shakespeare. Bates referred to a scene where Hamlet, dismissing a group of actors after a rehearsal, asked Polonius to take good care of them. Polonius replied, "My lord, I will use them according to their desert."

In Hamlet's quick response Sanford Bates obviously found an appealing philosophy for a prison administrator. "God's bodykins, man, much better; use every man after his desert and who should 'scape whipping? Use them after your own honor and dignity; the less they deserve, the more merit is in your bounty."[31]

George Washington Cable. (National Portrait Gallery, Smithsonian Institution)

Roeliff Brinkerhoff. (Ohio Historical Society)

Warden R. W. McClaughry (first row, center) *and guard force, Leavenworth, Kansas. (Bureau of Prisons)*

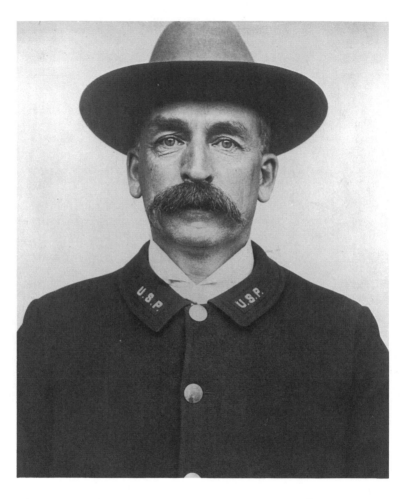

Warden Gilbert L. Palmer, McNeil Island, Washington. (Bureau of Prisons)

Aerial view of U.S. Penitentiary, Leavenworth, Kansas.
(Bureau of Prisons)

Warden William H. Moyer, Atlanta, Georgia. (Bureau of Prisons)

Samuel June Barrows. (By permission of the Houghton Library, Harvard University)

Mabel Walker Willebrandt. (District of Columbia Public Library)

J. Ellen Foster. (Courtesy of the Library of Congress)

Warden Mary Belle Harris, Alderson, West Virginia.
(Bureau of Prisons)

Hastings H. Hart. (Rockefeller Archive Center)

Sanford Bates. (Bureau of Prisons)

John Joy Edson. (Copyright, Washington Post; reprinted by permission of the District of Columbia Public Library)

Myrl E. Alexander. (Courtesy, National Archives)

(Left to right) *Sanford Bates, James V. Bennett, Myrl E. Alexander, and Norman A. Carlson, on the occasion of Carlson's swearing in as director of the Bureau of Prisons. (Bureau of Prisons)*

James V. Bennett. (Bureau of Prisons)

Norman A. Carlson. (Bureau of Prisons)

The first federal jail, "West Street," New York, opened 1929. (Bureau of Prisons)

A federal jail opened forty-five years later: Metropolitan Correctional Center, San Diego, California. (Bureau of Prisons)

J. Michael Quinlan. (Bureau of Prisons)

7

DISSENTER
PRISONERS

In the spring of 1920 twelve respected attorneys from several U.S. cities issued a remarkable monograph. Though workmanlike and temperate, the document was nonetheless a scathing indictment that accused the U.S. Department of Justice of wholesale violations of law and defiance of Constitutional principles.[1] Particularly prestigious among the several authors were the dean of Harvard University Law School, Roscoe Pound, and future justice of the Supreme Court, Felix Frankfurter. The attorney general, they asserted, had "committed continual illegal acts. Wholesale arrests both of aliens and citizens have been made without warrant or any process of law . . . homes have been entered without search warrant and property seized and removed; other property has been wantonly destroyed." To back up these and other accusations the authors went on to give detailed examples.

The occasion for the complaint was the so called Palmer Raids of 1919, a draconian response by Attorney General A. Mitchell Palmer to widespread activities of radicals who seemed bent on disrupting the public peace and security. The raids provided a classic example of the triumph of raw emotion over the rational rule of law. The offenders who seemed so threatening just then were the passionate, impulsive sort who have appeared periodically as federal prisoners from the beginning of the Republic, although they were never so feared as during the "Red Scare" that followed the First World War. It is a type that at times has been common, and even numerous, in federal prisons, but ordinarily not seen in state prisons.

Although some true criminals are swept into the fervor of a dissident activity, many dissenters escape being called criminalistic because they do not act out of greed, or for selfish gain, or from desire to hurt. They are motivated by a desire to correct a social or governmental fault, as they see it, and their sense of mission often makes them unique as prisoners; sometimes they are helpful and cooperative; sometimes they resist rules and remain unaffected by the usual control measures in the prison. The story of federal imprisonment is not complete without due notice to some of these iconoclasts, including anarchists, a type that was prominently active for a few years in both the United States and Europe, engaging in highly visible acts of violence, and causing enormous apprehension among the public—as they intended.

In 1919, Attorney General Palmer had a legitimate concern; the disruptive activities he sought to stop were indeed dangerous, but in his overreaction, he abandoned the principles of the Bill of Rights— a document that he, of all people, was duty-bound to uphold—so his raids were counterproductive. As the twelve attorneys observed, "No organization of radicals acting through propaganda over the last six months could have created as much revolutionary sentiment in America as has been created by the Department of Justice itself."

During the spring of 1919, anarchists or similar militants resorted to dramatic use of explosives; nearly forty bombs were mailed to various public officials. In June, Palmer himself was a target. "One of the bombs blew in the front of Palmer's house in Washington, D.C., just as he was getting ready for bed. It had evidently gone off prematurely, because parts of the bomber's body were scattered in all directions."[2]

With that, Palmer ordered his Bureau of Investigation to arrest suspected Reds everywhere. The raids began on November 7 and in the next few weeks more than six thousand people had been arrested in thirty-three cities. Most of the arrestees were soon released, but at Christmas time, 1919, an old military transport ship, the *Buford,* left Ellis Island with 249 of them aboard. They were deported to Russia.

As an incidental point of interest, Palmer's intense reaction to the bombing at his house introduced to public prominence a twenty-four-year-old Department of Justice employee who had the luck to be in the right place to take on an important new assignment. "It was this blast, never solved, that provoked the Justice Department's 1919 drive against radicals and launched the FBI career of J. Edgar Hoover."[3] During the war Hoover had operated the Department's Alien Enemy Bureau and was familiar with the country's radicals and their activities. He was the logical person to round up this apparent new wave of terrorists. Hoover carried out the task zealously, though he later realized, and learned from, the mistakes he made in the excitement of the massive sweep.

The Palmer raids marked a high point in the nation's frightened reaction to radical dissidence, but revolutionary movements had been brewing for many years, fed by painful social conditions that sharply polarized the haves and the have-nots. The enormous wealth of the industrial tycoons was not so provocative in itself; more provocative was their arrogant disregard of the human needs of the armies of workers they depended upon. The fact that a concept so utterly unrealistic as anarchism could gain such strength is ample testimony to the extreme degree and extent of social injustice that existed. Anarchism called for eliminating all government in the simple belief that the natural virtues of humankind would prevail and bring about equal opportunities for all. In Europe, the idea had such powerful appeal "that six heads of state were assassinated for its sake in the twenty years before 1914."[4]

Although the issues varied, and the different radical groups followed their own defined goals, at times they merged in their related concerns. In their great efforts toward trade unionism, the militants frequently became violent, and at different times the socialism and anarchism movements joined ranks with labor to exploit worker discontent.

The general campaign for women's rights constituted a parallel movement, with its sub-issues of woman suffrage, abortion, and birth control. These separate currents of dissent each produced its hero leaders, many of whom gained luster and visibility during their ordeals as federal prisoners. Some were far from being terrorists; instead they were loyal Americans, impulsively trying in unconventional ways to make their government more sensitive to the hardships of the times. One of the more unlikely of these leaders was Jacob S. Coxey, who advocated nothing more radical than governmental help in stimulating jobs for people who needed work. His brief campaign resulted in federal jail terms for more hundreds of followers than any other leader could ever boast.

The occasion was the panic of 1893. Widespread unemployment and the lack of any economic cushion, such as unemployment insurance, caused grievous suffering among families, and even whole communities. Coxey, an Ohio industrialist, was the hero of all discouraged, jobless workers. He was a naive, dedicated idealist who briefly became one of the most visible of federal offenders even though he committed one of the slightest of offenses. In May 1894, in Washington, D.C., he was indicted for a violation of federal law in that he did "unlawfully enter the grounds of the United States Capitol, and did then and there step upon certain plants, shrubs, and turf then and there being and growing, against the form of the statute in such case made and provided."[5] As can easily can be guessed, the charge was hardly more than a pretext—an excuse for arresting a troublesome leader and dampening the effect of a troublesome uprising.

When Coxey organized his march on Washington, sensible people knew the effort was impractical and useless, and yet, surprisingly, thousands of hungry, frustrated men responded eagerly and followed Coxey on foot or in wagons, railroad boxcars, or boats. Only a few hundred actually reached Washington with Coxey in April 1894, but great numbers of others were still struggling to get there from various parts of the west. These people wrote a chapter in the history of federal imprisonment that had a surreal quality, almost hilarious in retrospect. Never had federal imprisonment been so improvisational or half-hearted.

In the western states, the would-be Coxeyites (usually referred to as Commonwealers, after Coxey's proclaimed designation of the movement as the Commonwealth of Christ) faced the daunting problem of how to finance the travel, lodging, and food, all the way across the country, for many hundreds of men who had no money at all. Their spontaneous, but none too effective, solution in many cases was to steal trains.[6] Among the thousands of unemployed men were many who had been railroad workers, including brakemen, firemen, and engineers. With such men in the Commonwealer ranks, it was not at all difficult to appropriate idle trains for the great march to Washington. Typically, a small army of three hundred or so Commonwealers would invade a railroad yard, help themselves to any handy engine and boxcars, warn the dispatchers down the line that they were coming through, and then steam eastward, hoping for the best.

The marshals' duty was to apprehend and arrest such groups, but for one marshal to apprehend several hundred determined men on a speeding train posed a challenge that no one was prepared for. One of the marshals, William McDermott in Butte, Montana, was overwhelmed by the problem and begged the attorney general for some help. McDermott had no army of deputies at his command, nor did he have funds to pay for temporary help at five dollars per day plus expenses. It would be difficult to find enough deputies anyway, as the public was generally sympathetic toward the Coxeyites. McDermott's telegram to the attorney general asked, "Have I authority to call on militia or regulars or am I authorized to employ a great many deputies at large pay? Excitement runs high and I request some positive instructions by wire and will obey to the letter."[7]

The attorney general advised McDermott to hire the deputies necessary. But then what should he do when several hundred men were arrested, convicted of stealing trains, and sentenced to jail? More telegrams went to Washington. The only solution McDermott could work out was to rent the racetrack at the county fairgrounds at twenty-five dollars per day and hire enough deputies to guard the sentenced prisoners there. Of course, a contract also had to be made with a local supplier to feed the prisoners and the deputies.

Variations on the same problems and solutions occurred elsewhere, and often the courts ordered most of the prisoners to serve only a month, or less, gradually releasing them in small groups so that they would not be so likely to reassemble. Probably as many as fifteen hundred of Coxey's followers served federal sentences during the summer of 1894, under conditions so primitive that only the shortness of the sentences made them tolerable. In the western part of the country, the only ones who served their sentences in a regular prison were about sixty men who were sentenced to serve ninety days each in the McNeil Island Penitentiary.

At that time the big corporations strongly opposed unionism or any measures for job protection. But the employers were beginning to be met by a current of radicalism that would bring a variety of activists into federal prisons over the next two decades. Two of the most prominent and colorful of these were sometime lovers Alexander Berkman and Emma Goldman. They were young revolutionaries, immigrants from Russia who shared a bare subsistence in New York

City. Berkman, a highly intelligent but impulsive anarchist, was raised in a privileged family in Russia and had the advantage of good education. However, after he came to the United States, he identified himself with groups that were radicalized by the dismal poverty of the unskilled workers and by the unconcern of the industrialists. Berkman made his first dramatic gesture at the time of a strike against the Carnegie Steel Company in Homestead, Pennsylvania.

The manager at the Homestead plant, the aggressive and truculent Henry Clay Frick, was determined to keep the plant operating and to break the union. On July 5, 1892, masses of union men collided in a miniature but violent war against the hired Pinkerton strikebreakers. Both sides were armed and determined; in that dramatic clash, ten men were killed and many more wounded. Berkman saw his chance to dramatize the cause of anarchism by using the national stage of this moment for a blow against capitalism. With gun in pocket, he took the train to Homestead and with a ruse managed to get admitted to Frick's office. In his excitement Berkman's aim was poor and his shot did not kill the manager. Frick, though seriously wounded, recovered. He kept his iron grip on the management and eventually defeated the union. Berkman was sent to Pennsylvania's Western State Penitentiary for sixteen years.[8]

It was much later that Berkman became a federal prisoner. After he was released from the Pennsylvania penitentiary he was just as committed to radicalism as before, although the issues by then had changed. He and Emma Goldman intermittently joined again in common concerns and became active opponents to American involvement in World War I. Their impassioned speaking against the draft was exactly the type of activity proscribed by the Espionage Act of 1917 and the amended act of 1918. Both of these laws made it illegal to engage in activities intended to cause disloyalty or refusal of military duty, to obstruct the sale of U.S. bonds, to utter or print abusive language about the government or its allies, or otherwise to incite opposition to the government in time of war. Both Goldman and Berkman were convicted of violating the espionage law and each was sentenced to two years in prison. Berkman served his time inconspicuously in the Atlanta Penitentiary. His prison writings dealt only with his previous time in the Pennsylvania penitentiary; he wrote no book about Atlanta since he was immediately deported on the *Buford* after his release.

Emma Goldman's career was a parallel study in turmoil; her two-year federal sentence, the last of many jailings, was served in the Missouri State Penitentiary, beginning in February 1917.

Goldman, born to a Jewish family in Russia, came to the United States in 1886 as a teenager. She became a passionate advocate of various radical causes and made herself effective by her energy, the contagious force of her conviction, and her dynamic speaking ability. Her enthusiasm for social reform was so prodigious that it encompassed labor unionism, anarchism, women's suffrage, free love, birth control, and opposition to war. Margaret Sanger, the best known promoter of birth control, was an admirer. One historian describes Goldman as "Sanger's major tutor in radicalism."[9] A more sinister example of Goldman's influence was her alleged effect upon Leon Czolgosz, who assassinated President McKinley in 1901. It would be too simple to say that Goldman's speaking was the only thing that influenced the assassin, but the confused, young Czolgosz did attend at least one of Goldman's lectures and later said in his confession that her teachings had given him the idea for assassination.[10]

Though she was a vibrant supporter of women's causes, Goldman's outspoken rejection of the family and of religion made the feminists uncomfortable. Her scornful appraisal of society's attitude toward women was that women were expected "to keep their mouths shut and their wombs open." Her commitment to radical causes made her indifferent to personal consequences; as one biographer comments, she "was arrested so often that she never spoke in public without taking along a book to read in jail."[11]

Goldman and Berkman achieved such notoriety that they were useful to young J. Edgar Hoover when he sought national publicity for their deportations in 1919. As these anarchists were released from their prison sentences, Hoover had them rearrested as aliens. When they were put aboard the *Buford*, Hoover himself went on board to be sure they departed amid suitable attention from the press.[12]

Anarchists, as such, had no single dedicated organization. Instead, as individuals they often drifted in and out of various other radical groups, one of the strongest of which was the Industrial Workers of the World (IWW), familiarly known as the Wobblies. Originally a western group that grew from a Montana miners' union, the IWW held its founding convention in 1905. The organization drew heated resistance from industrialists, partly because it went beyond the usual concept of a trade union and adopted the ideal of "syndicalism"; its goal was to encompass all workers, of every kind in one big union. Dismayed employers imagined the fearful power such a comprehensive union could wield.

The Wobblies were imbued with an aggressive sense of mission, of dedication combined with pugnacious energy. Wherever governments in one city or state tried to suppress an IWW activity, their posts in other states would quickly send in their members to overwhelm the opposition. The clashes were bloody, with beatings and killings on both sides. Bill Haywood, a muscular and imposing brawler, headed the general organization. Haywood inevitably became a federal prisoner, along with a large contingent of his membership. Most IWW members were not imprisoned as a result of their battles with industries, but instead because of the resolute antiwar stance of the organization. The Wobblies did not just refuse to accept conscription, as soon as World War I began they loudly campaigned against it with speeches and handbills.

In three different locations in the country, large numbers of Wobblies were arrested for violating the Espionage Act; their trials were held in a general atmosphere of intense public anger. The largest group was tried in Chicago, before colorful Judge Kenesaw Mountain Landis, a man whose alleged strong prejudice against the defendants has not been denied by historians. The trial began on April 1, 1918, and lasted five months. Haywood and ninety-two others were convicted and sentenced to federal prison. During the same year, two similar trials were held; in Wichita, Kansas, where thirty-one were convicted, and in Sacramento where thirty-nine were convicted.

Haywood and more than a hundred of his members were sent to Leavenworth to serve sentences that ranged from one year to as high as thirty-eight years. Some were difficult prisoners. They were idealists, passionate about their mission and opposed to any correctional procedure that, in their view, would imply they were guilty of crime. For this reason, most of them refused to apply for pardons or paroles. Many of them were educated and articulate; at one time more than thirty of them were teachers.[13] Unwilling to be subservient, these prisoners often insisted on being more independent than a good prisoner is supposed to be. The IWWs were a type of prisoner outside the usual experience of Leavenworth warden A. V. Anderson, and he was frustrated in his attempts to deal with them. Plaintively, Anderson invited advice from headquarters in Washington, but headquarters had no useful answers either.[14]

One of the Wobblies, a skilled artist, was surprised to find Anderson "affable." The warden approached the prisoner, Ralph Chaplin, and encouraged him to carry on his painting while in prison. Chaplin later wrote, "Warden Anderson was a young former Congressman. He was about to marry and wanted to hang the oil paintings in his new house."[15]

The Fort Leavenworth Disciplinary Barracks and other military prisons are not included in the scope of this history, but, as already seen, at some points their histories touch significantly on the stories of the civilian prisons and so call for some notice here. World War I was the first war during which the U.S. government operated prisons of its own for civilians, and the government had not yet developed a thoughtful policy about incarceration for war resisters. Were these protesters military prisoners or civilian prisoners? For the most part, they were treated as military prisoners, though there were many exceptions, and the reasons for these exceptions were not well defined. Several military posts around the country were utilized to hold conscientious objectors, including Alcatraz, Fort Jay, on Governor's Island in New York, and Fort Douglas, near Salt Lake City.

In retrospect, the most basic problem this presented seems all too obvious. Prisoners who were regular army soldiers, serving time for assault, theft or other such crimes, nevertheless saw themselves as patriots. Their scorn for men who had refused to be drafted was immense. To put several hundred war resisters in the huge, terribly overcrowded Fort Leavenworth prison, among hundreds of army prisoners was to ask for trouble. During 1919, amid overcrowding so extreme that the disciplinary barracks population at times went as high as thirty-six hundred, prisoners engaged in strikes and repetitive disturbances that made the prison essentially unmanageable.[16]

As the country came to its unwilling involvement in the First World

War, the Socialists, a group more organized and less rabid than the Wobblies, became more vocal. As a political movement, socialism had developed slowly for several decades before it found its effective format under the leadership of Eugene V. Debs in 1897. Debs was a federal jail prisoner when he developed his commitment to socialism; later, during an era when the party was strong enough to elect mayors in thirty-three U.S. cities, he ran several times as the Socialist candidate for president. Debs began his work career as a locomotive fireman; he became nationally prominent when he organized the strike against the Pullman Car Company in 1894, the same year that Coxey marched on Washington. In effect, the Pullman strike became a strike against all railroads that hauled Pullman cars, and it violated a federal court injunction against interference with the rails. Debs was aware of the risk and was prepared to take the consequences. When the strike ended in the spring of 1895, Debs and several colleagues were convicted of contempt of court for violating the court injunction. Debs was sentenced to six months, and the marshal arranged for this to be served in the McHenry County jail in Woodstock, about fifty miles from Chicago.

Countless numbers of federal offenders had been boarded in local jails under the most dismal conditions, but the jail in Woodstock turned out to be a happy exception. Like so many of its time, it was small and in the same building with the sheriff's home. In this case the sheriff was a genial, flexible sort who saw no need to make things worse than necessary. Debs and his co-defendants wore their own clothes, ate their meals with the sheriff and his wife, and spent their mornings reading or tending to union business. They were allowed ample time for recreation, and this often was a matter of playing football in the adjoining street. The prisoners moved about freely and were locked in their cells only at night.[17]

Just five years later, Debs was the Socialist party candidate for the presidency, and in that election he drew eighty-seven thousand votes. Then, with steadily increasing portions of the vote, he ran in the elections of 1904, 1908, and 1912. However, World War I brought painful new issues, and eventually Debs appeared again before a federal court, charged with violating the Espionage Act. An anti-war speech, given in Canton, Ohio, led to his prosecution, conviction, and ten-year sentence.

Debs, then age sixty-three, was first placed at the Moundsville, West Virginia, prison, but after two months, on June 13, 1919, he was transferred to Atlanta Penitentiary. Debs' quality as a truly caring person had endeared him to union members and political radicals; that same simple quality of caring now assured his affectionate acceptance by the Atlanta inmates. He gave up his own use of tobacco, for instance, so he could give his ration to inmates who had none. And the inmates, with their instinctive sense of what was honest and what was not, knew that Debs' gestures were genuine and not just for effect. Always, too, Debs respected staff and accepted the rules. His only noted failure to cooperate was when he refused, after one experience with Sunday services, to attend chapel. Chapel attendance was required then, but Debs protested to warden Fred Zerbst that the club-wielding guards standing about quenched any true religious mood. The warden did not contest the point and Debs' protest reputedly led to the rule being changed. [18]

Both staff and inmates were fascinated in 1920 when the Socialist party convention once more nominated Debs for president. When the notification committee arrived, Warden Zerbst had them use his office to meet with Debs, who of course accepted the nomination. Zerbst also permitted Debs to prepare and send out weekly statements during the campaign. [19] When election day came, Debs again used the warden's office to tally the returns as they came in by telephone. He made his best showing yet, with nearly a million votes.

At various times, Debs entertained famous visitors. On one occasion, for instance, Clarence Darrow sat for several hours, chatting about national issues with Debs, Zerbst, and other prisoners. Throughout Debs' time in Atlanta his outside colleagues kept pressure on President Wilson to grant Debs a pardon, pressure which Wilson stoutly resisted. However, Warren G. Harding's election brought a new mood. It was time for "normalcy"—a return to peacetime conditions. That mood had elected Harding then made it feasible for him to consider amnesty for many war resisters in prisons. During his time in office, Harding reviewed these cases and generally ordered release of those who had not actually committed criminal or destructive acts. [20]

In Debs' case, a preliminary interview was arranged with Attorney General Harry Daugherty only a few days after Harding's inauguration in March 1921. Debs was given an unescorted furlough; he took the train to Washington, met for three hours with Daugherty, then returned to Atlanta, leaving Daugherty favorably impressed.[21] Many people urged Debs' release, although many others opposed it (including Mrs. Harding). It took a few months to resolve the issue, but an eventual commutation was inevitable. "Harding had been elected to restore peace and return the nation to tranquillity. The release of Debs was symbolic of Harding's sincere pursuit of that goal."[22] On Christmas eve, 1921, a presidential order freed Debs and twenty-three other political prisoners.

At that point James Dyche had just replaced Fred Zerbst as warden at Atlanta, and he permitted the inmates a highly unusual general gathering in the main cellblock, to cheer their friend's departure. And cheer they did. No prisoner ever left Atlanta with such an outpouring of good wishes following him, even beyond the front doors. "When the grated doors swung closed behind the socialist chieftan and he walked down the steps and toward the outer gates between Warden J. E. Dyche and deputy warden J. J. Fletcher, a roar of cheers swept out from the prisoners. Debs raised his hat in one hand and his cane in the other and waved back at them."[23] He had gained the respect of fellow prisoners just as he had won the respect of union members or Socialist followers. "His disarming innocence was, in a curious way, Debs' greatest strength. In a world full of wolves and tigers, of ambitious manipulators and fierce rivals for power, his simplicity of spirit was irresistible."[24]

One more bit of ceremony was scheduled. President Harding had made a point of wanting to meet his recent opponent, so Debs again took the train to Washington. There at the White House he and President Harding enjoyed a warmly friendly visit, after which Debs left for his home and a tumultuous welcome in Indiana.

In the same month that Debs started his Atlanta confinement another opponent of the war began to serve a federal sentence under different and far worse conditions. Kate Richards O'Hare was a dynamic woman, and though she did not have the national visibility Debs had, she was his equal in fortitude, intellect, and the quality of caring. At that time, in the absence of any federal prison for women, female prisoners were boarded at several state prisons. O'Hare was assigned to the women's building at the Missouri penitentiary in Jefferson City.

Kate O'Hare was a native Kansan, an aggressively active Socialist, as was her husband, Frank O'Hare. The fact that they and their four children were a close-knit family was of immeasurable help to O'Hare in turning her prison term from merely a ghastly experience to a constructive one. In 1913, O'Hare was the International Secretary of the Socialist party, a friend of Debs, and a tireless speaker for the party or for various labor union issues. However, she tended to be a moderate in many respects and did not support the IWW. With the advent of the war, she took up the Socialists' antiwar stance and made frequent speeches, one of which, in Bowman, North Dakota, resulted in her arrest.

With her good education and great mental energy, O'Hare quickly resolved to make good use of her prison time to pursue some sociological study. To get support for the project in advance of her incarceration, she visited the governor of Missouri and asked his permission to interview female inmates and to develop sociological profiles on them during her anticipated confinement. The governor consented, and O'Hare designed a schedule of questions to be explored with all the female prisoners.[25]

While the survey proved a disappointment, O'Hare left her mark on the institution by bringing about some substantive and badly needed improvements. When she was admitted on April 15, 1919, this woman of good family and middle-class respectability was profoundly shocked by the gross indecency of the living conditions. She was not shocked by those things that are necessarily inherent in prison operation, but rather by the quite unnecessary elements of unsanitary facilities, bleak and depressing surroundings, neglect of buildings and equipment, badly prepared food served cold, and the callous insensitivity of staff. With a ready and facile pen O'Hare began to expose these conditions, often with successful results. When her husband came from their home in St. Louis to visit every week, he took away her written accounts, and he was effective in getting these printed and publicized.

Less than two months after she was admitted, O'Hare wrote, "The whitewash crew has been with us the past week, and the walls of the cell house are beautifully clean and white. The shower baths are almost finished now, and we are hoping the management will realize that 'cleanliness is next to Godliness' and allow us two baths a week at least."[26] After another two months she reported, "We have a real dining room now . . . beautifully decorated in green and white. . . . There has been an improvement in our food also, no more meatless days. . . . Our food is coming over nice and hot."[27]

Allied with O'Hare in her campaign for improvement was Emma Goldman, the anarchist, who was already there when O'Hare arrived. They were not a natural pair: O'Hare, a family-oriented woman from conventional middle America, and Goldman, the Russian immigrant who remained an unmarried advocate of free love. But as occupants of adjoining cells, subjected to the same debasing conditions, they became friends. Much later, thousands of miles apart, the two women wrote their separate but like impressions.

By Goldman:

> Mrs. O'Hare looked rather forbidding. Of tall stature, she carried herself with hauteur, her expression appearing more rigid because of her steel-grey hair. . . . Had we met on the outside, we should have probably argued furiously and have remained strangers for the rest of our lives. In prison we soon found common ground. . . . We quickly became friends and my fondness for her increased in proportion as her personality unfolded itself to me.[28]

By O'Hare:

> Emma is an anarchist and I a political Socialist, and I presume that the two theories are as far apart as the poles, but somehow theories don't seem very important here. The brutal naked tragedies of life crush them out.[29]

> Thwarted in physical motherhood, Emma poured out her whole soul in vicarious motherhood of all the sad and sorrowful, the wronged and oppressed, the bitter and rebellious. . . . The women here worshipped her with an idolatrous worship. I am lawyer, priest and physician, but I do not, and never can, fill Emma's place in their hearts.[30]

Mrs. O'Hare spent fourteen months in this penitentiary, leaving it when she received presidential commutation. She had the satisfaction of knowing how much she and her husband did to improve the place, but she was entirely thwarted in her sociological studies. She did conduct the interviews she had planned, but despite the governor's assurance, her completed records were confiscated and destroyed before she departed.

Kate Richards O'Hare's subsequent career was just as full and interesting as her life to that point. In 1928 she divorced and remarried, after which she and her new husband moved to California. As Mrs. Kate Cunningham, older and more moderate in her views, she added to her social concerns a new interest in prison reform. In 1938, California Governor Culbert L. Olson recognized that his state had an antiquated and ineffectual penal system. "Olson appointed John Gee Clark [to be] director of the Department of Penology. Clark selected as his assistant the famed penologist, Kate Richards O'Hare [*sic*], and the two of them set out to reform the state's prison system."[31] Among their accomplishments was the selection of Clinton T. Duffy to be the reform warden at San Quentin.

Another opponent of the First World War was a man named Roger Baldwin. Unlike Debs and O'Hare, Baldwin was unknown at the time of his conviction in 1918 in the U.S. District Court in New York City. He was a lawyer and had previously served as chief probation officer of the juvenile court in St. Louis; his notable career as founder and respected long-time director of the American Civil Liberties Union was yet ahead of him.

Both Baldwin and Debs held principles in opposition to the government's war policies, but where Debs had offended by making a speech, Baldwin, a young man of draft age, was arrested for refusing to be drafted. His was not so much opposition to the war as to the government's assumption of a right to conscript its citizens. As was characteristic through his long career, Baldwin was calmly and resolutely principled. His conduct in court was a model of restraint and dignity, a fact the judge noted appreciatively.

In his trial, Baldwin explained, "I am before you as a deliberate violator of the draft act. On October 9, when ordered to take a physical examination I notified my local board that I declined to do so, and instead presented myself to the United States Attorney for prosecution." When his trial concluded, Baldwin was conscientious about courtesies due. "And by the way, may I take this occasion your honor . . . to express my thanks for the courtesy of every officer of this court, and of the Department of Justice, through these trying weeks. It has been exceptional." Finally he said, "I ask the court for no favor. I could do no other than what I have done, whatever the court's decree I have no bitterness or hate in my heart for any man. Whatever the penalty I shall endure it."

Judge Julius M. Mayer (who also had sentenced Emma Goldman) complimented Baldwin on his forthright conduct and then was just as sincerely forthright himself. "I have not any question at all in my mind that the position which you have announced as being held by you is honestly and conscientiously held. . . . The maximum penalty, as I understand it, is one year in the penitentiary. You have already spent twenty days in imprisonment. You ask for no compromise. You will get no compromise. You are sentenced to the penitentiary for eleven months and ten days."[32] The marshals escorted Baldwin across the Hudson to Newark, New Jersey, where he was lodged in the Essex County Jail; later he was transferred and boarded for the bulk of his time in the nearby County Penitentiary at Caldwell.

While the above individuals stand out among violators of the Espionage Act, "There were nearly two thousand prosecutions and nine hundred convictions under the combined espionage acts."[33] All too short a time later, World War II erupted, and, again, the prisoners of conscience appeared. Alfred Hassler was a young man much like Roger Baldwin. Hassler, editor of a religious journal, entered federal prison in 1944. He refused conscription, with assignment to civilian war service, and chose to go to prison instead. During the time he spent in the Lewisburg Penitentiary, he was a cooperative inmate and an astute observer of the human interactions characteristic of prison life. His book about the experience serves as one of the most perceptive accounts any prisoner has written about the quality of life in a prison.[34]

Prisoners such as Hassler, Debs, or Baldwin were among those who had committed no acts of ordinary criminality. "These men were punished for refusing to accommodate their political, religious or moral beliefs to the duties of allegiance owed to their government.

Their criminality lay not in any affirmative deed against the government but rather in refusing to act in accordance with the demands of the authorities."[35] By the same token these men were usually cooperative prisoners who felt no need to be disruptive; like citizens generally, they recognized the necessity of prisons.

The dissenters who appeared following World War II were often of a more contentious stripe. Passive refusal to be enlisted was no longer an effective, or even available, avenue of dissent; the times required something more dramatic in order for them to gain personal satisfaction. A few of these later dissenters used forms of opposition that were, in fact, very affirmative, and they followed their offenses by employing resistive tactics in prison, too. Examples were the brothers Philip and Daniel Berrigan who were convicted in 1968 for destroying draft records in Catonsville, Maryland. They simply walked into the draft offices during working hours, emptied out four file drawers of records, and burned them, outside in a parking lot. At the same time, Philip Berrigan awaited sentencing for raiding a draft board office in Baltimore and pouring blood on its files. A news account at the time stated, "The Berrigans are beyond doubt the most revolutionary priests that the Catholic Church in the U.S. has yet produced. . . . In opposing the Viet Nam war the brothers have openly violated the law out of conviction that other means of dissent have been exhausted."[36]

The two priests had a talent for infecting disillusioned people with their radicalism, especially during this time when the country was heavily affected by disturbing social issues. In prison, completely consistent with the militancy of their offenses, the Berrigans retained their high profile by continually testing the limits of administrative patience. In August 1971, when they were denied parole, they and several other prisoners in the Danbury (Connecticut) Correctional Institution went on a hunger strike. Outside supporters quickly picked up the issue and picketed the prison. Philip and several other hunger strikers were moved to the prison hospital at Springfield, Missouri.[37]

The priests, unrepentant and feisty, continued their occasional rebellious behavior after they were released from prison. Philip, for instance, defied his church by marrying, and his wife, a former nun, conducted her own rebellious activities and was consequently imprisoned at Alderson. Philip was convicted of depredation of U.S. property in 1978 and went to the Prison Camp at Allenwood, Pennsylvania, to serve a six-month sentence.

Not directly related to war, but coinciding in time with World War I, numbers of women engaged in a militant brand of dissent by insisting that they should be allowed to vote. The male establishment found the idea preposterous, and uncompromising officials who had to deal with the young suffragists treated them with callous contempt.

The idea of votes for women had been around for a long time, with spasmodic outbreaks of activity, but during World War I, the suffrage issue came to a boil, particularly in Washington, D.C., where a large number of idealistic and courageous young women tried for maximum visibility by picketing the White House. As some of them later remembered, they picketed in groups of four, and as soon as one group was arrested, another four were deployed to picket in their place.[38] President Wilson was impervious to such nonsense, and the police and courts were severe. At that time federal female offenders in the District of Columbia were held either in the D.C. Jail or the workhouse at Occoquan, in nearby Fairfax County, Virginia. During 1917, workhouse officials had their hands full with the suffragists, a group they held in much scorn and found virtually unmanageable. The courage that led the women to picket and face arrest gave them the determination to assert themselves when they became prisoners.

Usually the women received light sentences. Thirty-day jail terms were typical, but jail conditions made the punishment onerous. In July, sixteen suffragists in the workhouse found that their treatment was deliberately humiliating, the food was bad and the officials were hostile.[39] As part of their defiant insistence on the rightness of their cause and the injustice of their imprisonment, the suffragists refused to work. When they were sent to the sewing room with the other women, they sat quietly, hands in their laps, and did nothing. In return, they had to bear petty harassment, such as having their mail privileges cut off. The superintendent knew he was only echoing popular sentiment when he declared, "I consider the letters and telegrams these prisoners get are treasonable. They cannot have them."[40]

It was the privilege of the Department of Justice to monitor the management of its prisoners in such facilities and to require humane, even-handed treatment, but the Department's available staff of agents for this purpose was minuscule and ineffective. Furthermore, when so few places accepted female prisoners, the Department of Justice had no leverage to enforce desired conditions. Another decade would pass before this deficit was remedied.

Altogether, during 1917, at least one hundred federally sentenced suffragists were held for varying times in the Occoquan Workhouse.[41] But despite the hostility they faced, the time had come for change; just three years later, the Nineteenth Amendment was ratified and women had their vote.

Another and rather different subject of dissent occupied the eastern federal courts off and on during the last two decades of the nineteenth century and for some years into the twentieth century. This was the struggle to define and prosecute public indecency. The focus of concern included obscene literature, art works, or anything not in accord with completely conventional family morality. The fluid, amorphous area of contention at times encompassed the related issues of free love and birth control.

The nature of the controversy is well personified in the case of one federal prisoner who served his thirteen-month sentence at the Albany, New York, penitentiary in 1879–80. New York book dealer and publisher DeRobigne M. Bennett was an agnostic, a liberal, and a stubborn advocate of freedom of the press; but he certainly was not a pornographer. His experience illustrates how public perceptions of decency evolve. The Bennett case would not have been a case at all were it not for a formidable, single-minded crusader named Anthony Comstock. Many prisoners at Albany, and at various jails, owed their incarceration to this remarkable man.

Comstock was an intensely religious young man when he was mustered out of the Union army at the end of the Civil War. After a short time as a dry goods salesman in New York City, he found his calling in the fight against purveyors of indecent books and pictures. The rest of his life was a personal crusade to suppress such materials. Most of that time, his only official status was as director of the New York Society for the Suppression of Vice. However, he gained strong additional leverage by his lobbying in Congress for laws to prohibit use of the U.S. mails to distribute obscene materials. In 1873, Comstock was instrumental in getting legislation passed to amend and tighten a previous statute on transmission of improper books and pictures. The amended statute, often spoken of as the Comstock law, made it a crime to mail obscene materials, including anything related to the prevention of conception. The law's potential for unfairness was in its failure to define obscenity; it simply became anything that the prudish Comstock said it was.

Once the legislation was enacted, Comstock persuaded the postmaster general to issue him a pass to ride on the railroads and give him a commission as an unpaid postal inspector so he could enforce the obscenity statute.[42] Armed with these, Comstock ruthlessly pursued the producers and distributors of indecent materials. He operated on the principle "that any material that discussed matters pertaining to sex in any but the most indirect and evasive terms was, prima facie, obscene."[43] He confiscated tons of printed materials and sought out and destroyed printing plates and other equipment used to produce them. He took an eager delight in personally arresting any miscreants he considered guilty.

From a later, more mature viewpoint, it is apparent that the materials Comstock confiscated presented the dullest, mildest form of indecency, if they were indecent at all; but worse, his methods violated principles now held to be basic in protecting defendants' rights. Comstock often persuaded courts that a piece of literature was illegal in its entirety, even if only a minuscule fraction of it contained suggestive references. And though the federal courts sometimes disagreed with Comstock, to his intense indignation, he freely made arrests and jailed offenders on the basis of his own personal bias.

It might be supposed that any injustice would be countered by the rigors of the trial process, but Comstock had a way of describing confiscated materials in indignant, but vague, generalities that were often accepted uncritically by the courts. In a jury trial, sometimes the jurors would have no opportunity to evaluate the supposedly indecent literature; the court, at Comstock's prodding, would agree that the material was too vile to be shown to them.

Comstock regularly employed the technique of entrapment; he made it an art. Whenever he got a hint that some person might supply improper books or pictures, or might give advice on preventing conception, he would write and request the materials or advice, using a fictitious address and signature. In this way, he caught and arrested many people, including doctors who meant only to give needed medical advice. Comstock was especially gratified when he cast his net and caught DeRobigne M. Bennett.

Bennett was an elderly, free-thinking publisher who attracted Comstock's disapproving attention with his unconventional religious and moral views. He published a radical paper, *The Truth Seeker,* and made the mistake of editorializing about the unfairness of the "Comstock laws." Bennett had also published a book, *Champions of the Church: Their Crimes and Persecutions,* a cynical book that simply debunked some of the revered figures in religious history.[44]

Comstock first prosecuted Bennett for selling two tracts, *An Open Letter to Jesus Christ,* and a sizzling item entitled *How Do Marsupials Propagate Their Kind?* The famous attorney, Robert G. Ingersoll, represented Bennett and the case was dismissed. The following year Comstock tried again. This time he persuaded Bennett to sell him a copy of a small tract called *Cupid's Yokes,* "a dull little sociological treatise, filled with antiquated phrases about 'legalized prostitution' and 'relics of barbarism.' "[45] Again, Ingersoll took up the issue, but Bennett was convicted and received a thirteen-month prison sentence.

It was a time when attitudes of severe prudery and vibrant defiance of convention polarized in a dramatic contest. Prudery usually prevailed, at least in court decisions, but a persistent, excited interest evolved—an interest in the new ideas about emancipation of women, the use of birth control, the right to free love, and the right to print and to read materials about such subjects.

The man who had published *Cupid's Yokes* in 1875 was a free-thinking Presbyterian minister, Ezra Heywood. Comstock had Heywood arrested in 1877 for mailing a tract that advocated the abolition of marriage; Heywood was convicted, fined, and given a two-year prison sentence. When President Rutherford B. Hayes was petitioned to commute Heywood's sentence he considered the case with much care and granted a reprieve on the grounds that Heywood had not intended to violate the law and that the pamphlet was not actually obscene.[46]

Less than a year later, Hayes again confronted this unwelcome issue of alleged indecency; Ingersoll gave him petitions with thousands of signatures that asked for a similar reprieve for Bennett.

When Hayes approached this case, however, he felt the sting of the adverse public reaction to Heywood's reprieve. Hayes also found passages in *Cupid's Yokes* that he thought were spicy beyond what was necessary to its basic argument. He took his time in coming to a decision, but he finally resolved to let Bennett's sentence stand. "In the last year of his life, Hayes admitted that he had failed to pardon Bennett largely because the main current of judicial opinion in 1879 held that *Cupid's Yokes* was obscene and that he simply followed the opinion of the judges. He was never satisfied, however, with the correctness of this view."[47] Bennett served his full sentence, and, being a writer, he improved his time by keeping a diary of his experiences in the Albany prison. His description of the physical plant and the daily activities there is the best that survives.[48]

Anthony Comstock continued his crusade well past the turn of the century; he lost a few cases, but frequently he gained convictions. And riding the general momentum of his crusade, prosecutors pursued other cases without Comstock's direct involvement. Reputedly J. B. Wise, a Kansas man, made the mistake of trying to spoof Comstockian prudery by referring to some of the racier portions of the Bible. When Wise mailed a postcard with a selected verse from Isaiah written on it, he was arrested and held for four months in Leavenworth Penitentiary. Finally, he was tried, convicted of mailing obscene material, and fined fifty dollars.[49]

During Comstock's life, his rigid views of morality were generally sustained by court decisions and majority public attitudes. But toward the end of his career, signs of drastic change were evident, though not to him. He lived long enough to be a serious threat to young Margaret Sanger, who was just beginning her life-long mission to make birth control available to women. Sanger managed to avoid Comstock's prosecution only by making a strategic trip to England, though her husband was prosecuted and sentenced by a federal court to a month in jail. In that same year, 1915, Comstock died; Sanger's career was well underway and the country was ready to progress steadily toward a new life style and freedom of public expression that would directly contradict all that Anthony Comstock had so assiduously personified.

8

A PERIOD
OF GROWTH

I n 1933, Sanford Bates noted with pleasure that there was a modest decrease in the total number of federal prisoners; the figure was down by 1,126 from the year before. He attributed the decrease to several factors, including the repeal of the prohibition law and "the measures taken by the Congress to reduce the prison population by extending the probation system to practically every Federal district court."[1]

Both the parole and probation laws were helpful, though not everyone was pleased. J. Edgar Hoover trumpeted the FBI attitude, asserting that "parole today is becoming one of the major menaces of America. . . . The records show 3,576 members of this desperate criminal group have at some time felt the angelic mercy of parole or probation or pardon, or some other form of sob-sister clemency."[2]

By the 1930s, Hoover's fulminations notwithstanding, the federal probation and parole services were solidly established and becoming more accepted and essential as countermeasures to prison crowding. But probation practice in the federal courts had a lot of catching up to do; the probation law had been late in coming, delayed by strident objections from many of the people who should have been the most supportive.

Early in the century Hastings Hart and Samuel June Barrows had called for a federal probation law, as did Attorney General George W. Wickersham. Over the next two decades, numerous individuals and groups, particularly the National Probation Association, aggressively campaigned for a federal probation system. However, some federal judges opposed the legislation, believing it would erode respect for their courts. One influential staffer in the attorney general's office, the one who always was delegated to provide official reaction

155

to the legislative proposals, viewed the probation idea as "all a part of a wave of maudlin rot of misplaced sympathy for criminals that is going on over the country."[3]

Another source of effective opposition was Minnesota Congressman Andrew J. Volstead, author and fierce protector of the Prohibition Act. Volstead and other supporters of prohibition were afraid that moonshiners and bootleggers would take advantge of probation in the federal courts, thus diminishing the deterrent effect of the prohibition law. As chairman of the House Judiciary Committee, Volstead was able to prevail. However, in 1923, Volstead left Congress. The need for federal probation legislation was becoming more apparent; thirty of the states had probation laws, some for several decades. Amid heated controversy the federal law to creat a probation system was passed and was signed on March 4, 1925, by President Coolidge, whose home state, Massachusetts, had started the probation practice more than half a century earlier.

When Sanford Bates was recruited in 1929, the probation services had no central directorship. Any supervision was carried out only by the superintendent of prisons. This was corrected in 1930 when the act was amended to give the attorney general authority to set standards and administer the combined probation and parole services. The attorney general delegated this responsibility to the director of the Bureau of Prisons, and Bates in turn hired Colonel Joel R. Moore to be supervisor of probation and parole. Moore had built an impressive reputation on the basis of his probation work in the recorders court in Detroit, and now he effectively persuaded the federal judiciary to utilize this new tool.

The same legislation that authorized federal probation also created the Bureau of Prisons. At the same time, the institutional parole boards were abolished and replaced by a full-time U.S. Board of Parole, with three members. For administrative purposes the board was placed in the new Bureau.

Moore resigned in 1937 to become warden of the Michigan State Prison at Jackson, and he was replaced by Richard A. Chappell, the chief federal probation officer for the Northern District of Georgia. Chappell remained with the federal probation and parole services and served in several capacities throughout a full and distinguished career. The Bureau of Prisons administered the probation and parole system for just one decade, then, on July 1, 1940, the system was placed under the administrative office of the U.S. Courts.

Federal involovement with jails was mainly concerned with promoting basic standards for any jails in which federal prisoners might be placed. Actual operation of jails by the Department of Justice was, until recent years, limited to certain jails in the territories. The most notorious of these was the one in Fort Smith, Arkansas, where a colorful judge, Isaac Parker, resolutely restrained the lawless opportunists who ran wild in the adjoining Indian Territory. Judge Parker kept his primitive jail well filled and frequently used the permanent gallows that stood in front of it. A few statistics suggest the enormity of the law and order problem that his court faced.

During his twenty-one years at Fort Smith, beginning in 1875, Judge Parker appointed two hundred marshals; sixty-five of whom were killed. The jail, two large rooms in the basement of the old log building where his court was housed, was always packed. When the 1885 term of court opened, more than two hundred prisoners were on hand and more than sixty of them were charged with capital crimes. The gallows out in front were built to hang as many as twelve men simultaneously, though the largest number ever hanged at once was six. In his time at Fort Smith, Parker handed out more than 160 death sentences, at least half of which were carried out.[4]

After the United States acquired the Territory of Alaska in 1867, U.S. marshals operated various small jails there, serving under the most difficult conditions possible The climate, as well as the sparse population and the vast distances were serious handicaps. In addition, Congress was disinterested and persistently neglected the area, giving no proper attention to the problem for more than eighty-five years. The marshals worked against insuperable odds to maintain a barely effective jail service. Finally, on July 1, 1953, six years before Alaska became a state, the Department of Justice established the Alaska Jail System, and gave responsibility for the jails to the Bureau of Prisons. Over the next seven years, a superintendent of jails in Alaska worked valiantly to overcome enormous logistical problems and improve the deplorable physical facilities.[5] When Alaska became a state in 1959, a gradual transition began; as the new state built its bureaucracy and proved its competence, it was able to take over and operate the jails as state facilities.

For Washington, D.C., the Organic Act of 1801 created the District and authorized the U.S. marshal to enforce laws and to operate a jail. The first small jail was built in 1804, followed by a succession of larger ones through the remainder of the century. Eventually, under Department of Justice management, the District Jail was nearly always overcrowded and deteriorating. In 1907 Theodore Roosevelt asked J. Ellen Foster to investigate the jail. Because of the dismal conditions she found, the president appointed a three-man commission to develop recommendations for improving the jail and other corrections services in the District.

The chairman of the commission was a prestigious Washington businessman, John Joy Edson, a civic-minded leader who for some decades influenced almost every worthwhile movement in the District.[6] Serving with him were Justice Wendell P. Stafford of the D.C. Supreme Court, and R. V. LaDow, the one corrections professional on the commission. In their scathing report, commission members criticized the jail and insisted that other facilities should be provided to relieve the load. They also recommended instituting a probation system and establishing a reformatory and a separate workhouse for misdemeanants. Their report soon led to construction of the new D.C. correctional facilities at Lorton and Occoquan, in nearby Virginia.[7]

When the Bureau of Prisons was created, the general problem with jails was hardly less serious than it had ever been. The law gave the Bureau the duty and authority to "provide suitable quarters for the safe-keeping, care and subsistence of all persons convicted of offenses against the United States or held as witnesses or otherwise." Also the Bureau was authorized to contract with state or local governments to use their jails. The problem was that many jails provided abominable conditions and management, but the Bureau was given no effective leverage to require improvements.

Bates put Nina Kinsella in charge of the Bureau's work with jails. She was a talented woman who had served with him in a secretarial capacity in Massachusetts. Although Kinsella lacked a college degree and had no special training, she did possess natural leadership ability and became an effective member of the management team. Her task was to establish standards for jails and to deploy the few jail inspectors to the multitude of jails throughout the country. In 1932, Kinsella informed a study committee that the federal government was paying state and local governments to board about 11,500 prisoners. Of these, 65 percent were serving short sentences and the others had not yet been tried. The volume of turnover in this population was suggested by the fact that, in just one year, 95,000 federal prisoners were admitted to jails. In an effort to achieve some measure of quality control for this deluge of prisoners, Kinsella's inspectors made 1,146 jail inspections in the second year after the inspection service was organized.[8]

The statistics cannot impart the flavor of life within the jails. The Bureau developed an objective system to rate each jail with a score between zero and one hundred. In her annual report for 1936, Kinsella asserted that among all jails inspected, 1,884 had ranked below 50; 900 between 50 and 60; and only 129 above 60.[9]

Two years later, Kinsella's findings were still gloomier. Reporting on the inspections of 2,067 jails she complained that "689 jails rated under 50 percent—some rated practically nothing." At the other end of the spectrum, only 15 jails rated 80 percent or higher. "It is evident that the largest group of prisoners held in custody are housed in filthy, insanitary, vermin-infested, over-crowded jails lacking in segregation and abounding in kangaroo court abuses and other vicious practices." She added that 1,944 jails were "wholly unfit for the custody of a Federal prisoner even for one brief hour."[10]

Problems of this sort kept alive the question of whether the federal government should have its own jails, just as it had its own prisons. While jails owned and controlled by the Bureau of Prisons would be extremely desirable and were truly needed, they also would be extremely costly. The Bureau would need a prohibitive number of jails, or else the jails would have to be regional, and thus at inconvenient distances from the courts they served. However, jail populations include not only pre-trial prisoners, but also those serving short jail sentences for misdemeanors. The new Bureau management considered it practical to have a few specialized facilities for convicted misdemeanants, and so they acquired institutions such as Milan, discussed previously.

The need for jail space was real and extensive. Even after several jail facilities had been acquired, the other federal institutions still were called on to accommodate such prisoners, along with the felon populations. The table[11] below compares the number of felons and misdemeanants confined in several of the prisons during the year ending June 30, 1941.

Institution	Number of felons	Number of misdemeanants
Ashland, Ky.	428	340
Danbury, Conn.	274	428
El Paso, Tex.	241	600
Milan, Mich.	298	90
Sandstone, Minn.	128	126
Tallahassee, Fla.	287	559
Texarkana, Tex.	224	30

During the Roosevelt administration, public works projects designed to stimulate the economy accomplished a modicum of improvement in the condition of county jails. In the 1930s, many counties nationwide applied for and received funds from the Public Works Administration to repair their jails or to build new ones. The Bureau of Prisons also tapped this source of funds to help with new prison construction; indeed, without it the Bureau could not have met the need for new prison capacity. PWA grants financed the planning or construction of six new prisons in the mid-1930s. Later in the decade similar funds paid for still more prison space.[12]

As the new Bureau took shape, it introduced classification as a major prisoner management tool. Until then, the few institutions carried out only the most rudimentary classification of prisoners. As far as possible, Alderson accepted all the women, Chillicothe received the males who were young first-time prisoners, and the three penitentiaries took all other categories, more or less on a regional basis. Before the Bureau was established, the three penitentiaries separately developed different custody categories, and inmates were assigned to these without reference to objective written guidelines. Staff relied on hunches and informal judgements, mainly those of the deputy warden. While he was superintendent of prisons, R. V. LaDow instituted uniform groupings to be used in the several institutions. As he reported it,

> There are three grades of prisoners: first, second and third. The
> first and highest grade carries with it certain privileges. A prisoner's

conduct determines his grade; for misconduct he may be reduced from the first to the second, or even to the third grade for a serious infraction of the rules; for each grade lost there is an accompanying loss of privileges. For good conduct a prisoner in the lower grades may earn his way back to the highest grade. Part of the punishment of the third grade man is to wear stripes.[13]

The concept of classification had hardly progressed beyond this level when the Bureau was created, but Sanford Bates was convinced that prisoners should be studied as scientifically as possible, and that individualized placement and programming should be carried out, case by case. Soon, the acquisition of new institutions enhanced the potential for classification, and the varied design of the new facilities permitted a degree of specialization. By the mid-1930s, a new range of institutional choices was available. Tractable, low-risk offenders were sent to the open, non-custodial camps. Serious felons were housed at Leavenworth and Atlanta, institutions that offered close custody and operated with industrial and school programs. Felons who would benefit from education and farm programs in a medium security setting, went to McNeil Island. Felons who needed a secure setting but were considered more amenable were assigned to Lewisburg. Springfield was reserved for those prisoners who suffered from physical and mental health problems.[14]

The next step in the process was to classify prisoners to assure appropriate program assignment and custodial handling within each institution. This procedure entailed a more subtle process and was much harder to implement. Many staff neither understood nor appreciated a process that seemed to repudiate the direct, summary judgments they had previously exercised without challenge.

At Bureau headquarters, Frank Loveland carried major responsibility for creating and implementing the new classification system. Loveland, a scholarly, respected professional, had helped develop classification systems in both Massachusetts and Texas. He found that designing the new procedures was, perhaps, easier than implementing them in the face of resistance at the institutions. Following Loveland's concept, the Bureau's first step was to create the position of assistant warden. These new professionals had to develop detailed case history for each inmate—the basic data necessary for sound case planning. In addition, the Bureau established an initial thirty-day orientation program for new inmates, during which clinical personnel systematically studied each prisoner.

With case data eventually in hand, the institution managers could organize their own classification committees. The new procedure would then work well if everyone involved regarded it favorably; otherwise it would be virtually useless. The strategy employed by the Bureau managers was to have the wardens chair the classification committees. This promoted the necessary management support in each institution by requiring the wardens to leave their front offices and become intimately involved with the process. Additionally, the planners believed that membership on the committees would, in itself, be educational, so at first the committees were large. A variety of staff members served on each, partly so they could contribute to the classification process, partly so they could be indoctrinated in the new concept.

As the idea of classification gradually became accepted, the committee size could be reduced. But, as wider varieties of work and educational programs developed, the committees had to make more significant kinds of decisions.[15]

The Bureau was in a period of rapid expansion, still in its first decade, when the first change of leadership occurred. Bates seemed to enjoy his directorship, and his superiors, colleagues, and Congress held him in high regard. However, Bates' basic commitment was to a public service career in a general sense, rather than to the Bureau of Prisons exclusively.

In early 1937, Herbert Hoover, who had approved Bates' selection in 1929, asked him to be the executive director of the Boys Clubs of America. Hoover was the chairman of that board. Bates liked the salary Hoover offered—it was 50 percent higher than Bates then earned—but he also liked the idea of administering services to younger people. He believed he had accomplished much of what he was hired to do and was ready to turn the prisons job over to a highly qualified successor.

Bates departed at the end of January 1937. After serving briefly with the Boys Clubs—a job he found disappointing—he went to New York as state parole commissioner, then, in 1945, to New Jersey as head of that state's corrections system. When he resigned from the

Bureau of Prisons Bates also resigned from the board of the National Training School for Boys. However, he continued to serve as a member of the board of the Federal Prison Industries until his death in 1972.

On February 1, 1937, James V. Bennett became director of the Bureau of Prisons in a transition that preserved the continuity of the agency's general philosophy. The changeover was eased by the managerial compatibility of the two men and their good personal relationship. They were long-time close friends, both in the office and on the golf course.

Unlike Bates, Bennett was essentially a Washington bureaucrat. He had graduated from Brown University, served in the Army Air Corps, and then, joined the U.S. Bureau of Efficiency. His assignment to investigate the federal prisons in 1928 led directly to his being hired by Bates. Having joined the prison service in 1929 Bennett apparently felt no temptation to leave it for the remainder of his career.[16]

Just as Bates had taken new initiatives, Bennett also faced new challenges. Even while custodial staffs were becoming accustomed to classification as a more modern method of prisoner management, they had to learn various other new practices, no matter how reluctantly. In the penitentiaries, guards had always carried billy clubs, and most of them assumed these to be essential—for aggressive use on some occasions and as intimidating symbols of authority at all times. Sometime during the 1030s, the practice changed. One source asserts, "Guards were relieved of their clubs in 1938. Many protested they were without personal protection. The clubs were never missed, however, and the relationship between staff and inmates was put on a sounder basis."[17]

Recollections vary about whether Bates or Bennett abolished the clubs, but the date is not really important. The important point is that both men opposed controlling prisoners just by brute force, and either one would have made this change as soon as it was feasible. It is enough to know that the billies were laid aside in the Bureau's first few years.

In the first month after Bennett's promotion, all Bureau personnel finally became part of the civil service, a process that started with an act passed more than half a century earlier. Custodial staff at

Leavenworth had been brought under civil service before the turn of the century, an anomaly that was due to the initiative of the warden of that time. But finally, "on February 11, 1937 all employees in the Federal Prison system, with the exception of the director, three assistant directors, the parole board and the chaplains, were placed under the Federal Civil Service."[18] This accomplishment was largely the result of efforts by W. T. Hammack, an assistant director who was responsible for personnel matters including staff training and professionalization.

Because the Bureau was late in becoming part of the civil service, some have supposed that Bennett was the one responsible for the move away from political patronage, toward appointments on merit. However, the Bates administration was a transition period during which, for the first time, patronage was resolutely avoided in staff selection, even though Bates retained the privilege of taking summary personnel actions as needed. In fact, because he needed to reorganize and upgrade his operation expeditiously, he used the freedom he had to take peremptory personnel action. More than likely, Bates was ready for the civil service process to be fully implemented and probably had taken the necessary steps to start this with the eager help of his assistant director, W. T. Hammack, who was determined to make the Bureau into a true career service. The full civil service coverage went into effect less than two weeks after Bates departed.

Another personnel policy that took shape under Bennett's administration was to tie promotions to transfers. During the late 1940s, personnel at the assistant director level realized that the institutions were much too provincial. Promotions were always from within; the institutional operation was not tempered or enriched by ideas or viewpoints from elsewhere in the system. Thus, the policies and philosophy of the top administration were resisted, and a uniform system-wide approach to prison management was defeated. Bennett recognized the problem and agreed to staff recommendations that (1) promotion to supervisory- or administrative-level jobs would mean transfer to some other institution, and (2) the Bureau should "replace random visits to institutions by Bureau individual staffers with a plan of team visits, with representatives of principal control areas, usually custodial, personnel, accounting, food, farms, classification, education, industries."[19]

Predictably, institution personnel resisted the plan of required transfers; some individuals turned down promotions rather than move. Institution staff members took at least two years to be reconciled to the idea, but the plan did take hold and it did have the desired effect. In time, the transfers and the team visits converted a group of highly individual institutions into a coordinated system. In later years, the scheme's effectiveness was evident: although an institution might get a new warden every two or three years, the procedure was generally acccomplished without lost motion or damage to staff morale. The practice was well accepted and the institution staffs knew that any new warden would come with similar training, experience, and philosophy as the previous one.

In the 1980s the Bureau retained a consultant in public administration who made a significant appraisal of the management. He was impressed with the quality of this bureaucracy, he reported, because "when I went out in the field, I saw people who are 'cosmopolitan', who are moving up through the system and one day will end up at headquarters or as wardens; and the locals, who will stay at Lewisburg or wherever they are. The locals and the cosmopolitans have tremendous respect for each other. In many organizations, the high flyers going through the system and the locals treat each other as enemies. But in the bureau, I saw a camaraderie that I hadn't experienced in other organizations."[20]

Although staff rotation benefited the Bureau, the practice sometimes interfered with family life; wives and children repeatedly had to get accustomed to new neighborhoods, new friends, and new schools—and sometimes in localities they would not have chosen. However, few people complained, since the policy was understood by everyone joining the organization.

Among the more massive problems that faced the Bureau during the administrations of both Bates and Bennett were prisoner idleness and the controversial issue of industrial production by prisoners. During the 1920s, Mabel Walker Willebrandt proclaimed that prisoner idleness was one of three main problems that required attention. In 1924, in the course of promoting legislation to authorize an industries operation at Leavenworth, statistics were compiled that showed 5,510 prisoners were incarcerated in the three federal penitentiaries, and, of these, 4,060 were idle.[21] The bill, authorizing a shoe factory, was passed, but that one industry still left great numbers of idle prisoners as a challenge for the new Bureau.

Both manufacturers and labor unions opposed prison-made products, especially during the depression years. In 1934, with 30 percent or more of the country's work force unemployed, Congress passed the Hawes-Cooper Act, and a year later, the Ashurst-Sumners Act. The two acts divested prison-made products of their status in interstate commerce and encouraged states to prohibit their entry. These federal laws, and the state laws they spawned, exerted an enormously depressing effect on industries in state and federal prisons.

At that time, the few production shops in the federal prisons attracted intense opposition, especially the cotton duck mill at Atlanta, the most profitable of the industries. The Leavenworth brush and broom factory was another vulnerable target, opposed by New York brush manufacturers who enlisted the aid of Representative Fiorello LaGuardia. An amendment that LaGuardia appended to an appropriation bill cut off funding to the Bureau of Prisons for that type of manufacturing.[22]

Finding an antidote to this type of opposition was the task of James Bennett, then an assistant director who was responsibile for operating the prison industries. Bennett's solution was to write legislation that would create a separate corporate entity, with its own board and its own capitalization, to operate the industries. The strategy was brilliant and over the succeeding decades it proved to be one of Bennett's outstanding accomplishments. When the idea was first proposed Franklin D. Roosevelt was in office; he had reappointed Bates and his team and had confirmed the progressive direction they were heading. With characteristic political skill (plus some encouragement from the first lady), Roosevelt obtained support for the idea from the leadership of the American Federation of Labor and other union groups, and legislation was passed creating the Federal Prison Industries, Inc.[23] The act was signed into law by Roosevelt on June 23, 1934. Top ranking industry and labor representatives were appointed to the board, and Bates was appointed to represent the attorney general and provide important linkage with the Bureau. Bennett assumed administrative responsibility as commissioner of industries, while A. H. Conner became associate commissioner.

The new corporate format did not guarantee that opposition to prison products would end, but it protected the industries by granting them a degree of independence with their own working capital and an influential board. Both Bates and Roosevelt stressed the policy that prison industries must be broadly diversified, with no one product so extensively produced that it offered serious competition for private industry.

About the time that Bates yielded the directorship of the Bureau to Bennett new resources were opening for a special type of problem prisoner—the drug addict. Congress initiated the new program in 1929, at the same time so much other criminal justice legislation was enacted, but in this case, Congress conceived an institutional approach that would serve the Bureau of Prisons without being a part of it. The plan was to build two large hospitals that would offer the best-known treatment for drug dependence and, at the same time, carry out research on any aspects of addiction and its treatment. The institutions would accept both voluntary civil admissions and federal prisoners.

The hospitals were administered by the United States Public Health Service, and the Bureau of Prisons assigned addict prisoners as it wished. The first inmates to be transferred to the new facilities were the addict prisoners in the Leavenworth Annex, as this building had to be emptied by the end of that decade and returned to the army.

The first of the two hospitals, located near Lexington, Kentucky, to serve the eastern half of the country, opened in May 1935. The second, serving the western region, opened in Fort Worth, Texas, in October 1938. The large, very well-staffed facilities began with optimism and hope, but suffered disappointing experiences in the long term. The mixture of cases was one acknowledged problem. Often three different categories of patients were on hand at the same time. In addition to the regular sentenced inmates placed by the Bureau of Prisons, other patients, sometimes known as the shock probation cases, were sent directly by courts to undergo up to six months of study and treatment before final sentencing. The third group, and the most frustrating one, was composed of persons who committed themselves voluntarily. Anyone who had an addiction problem could be admitted, on request, for care and treatment. The problem was that these patients could also check out at any time, and a high percentage did leave soon after withdrawal, before the treatment program could have any effect. With no follow-up help in the community, the long-term effects were discouraging.

The problems inherent in operating these mixed programs inevitably led to administrative redesign; although the institutions lasted as USPHS hospitals for more than three decades, in the 1970s both became Bureau of Prisons facilities.

In Bennett's second year as Bureau director juvenile offenders were given new attention with passage of the Federal Juvenile Delinquency Act of 1938. This legislation was not intended to bring more juvenile offenders into federal facilities, but to confirm the direction Bates previously had taken in trying to divert them to state or local jurisdiction. The new act defined a juvenile as seventeen or younger (later amendments raised this to eighteen), and adopted a concept, then in use among the states, that permitted the young defendants to be charged with juvenile delinquency instead of a named criminal offense. Unlike most state laws, however, this procedure was optional; a youth could choose to be prosecuted for the specific criminal offense, particularly if he or she preferred a jury trial, an option not authorized under the general charge of delinquency. If a juvenile were convicted under the act, the court could use probation or other alternative measures, or commit the offender to the custody of the attorney general. Confining juveniles with adult prisoners was prohibited.[24]

In general, the act encouraged the courts to make more use of local agencies, foster homes, and private or state facilities. Juveniles who actually came into federal custody still went principally to the National Training School in Washington, and the numbers of these grew—not so much because of the act, but because of the country's population growth and the broader coverage of federal laws. When the Delinquency Act was passed, Congress also authorized a new prison in the western area, and construction began (with Public Works Administration funding) in 1938 at Englewood, Colorado. The institution was to serve as a jail, such as the one at Milan, but before it opened in July 1940, population pressures required its use for older teens and young adults. Accordingly, Englewood opened as a reformatory for inmates ages eighteen to twenty-one, with strong emphasis on education and vocational training. By 1946, the pressure of juvenile commitments resulted in a policy change, and Englewood began to take only boys under eighteen.[25]

Meanwhile, changes were underway at the National Training School. On July 1, 1939, as one result of the Federal Reorganization Act, the school's board was abolished and its administration was transferred fully to the Bureau of Prisons. Some changes were made immediately; a new superintendent was hired, programming was oriented more toward treatment concepts, corporal punishment was abolished, a new food services building was built, and medical services were provided by the USPHS. Soon, the notion grew that a satellite camp could be useful to the school. The U.S. Forestry Service turned over an abandoned Civilian Conservation Corps camp (CCC) in the George Washington National Forest, near Natural Bridge, Virginia. The empty barracks buildings were renovated, and the camp opened in the fall of 1944. The facility provided space for about sixty boys, in a beautiful, noncustodial setting that offered forestry work, remedial education, and some trade training.[26]

In 1950, Congress made one more comprehensive effort to improve the handling of youthful offenders when it passed the Federal Youth Corrections Act. Unlike the earlier Juvenile Delinquency Act, this legislation called for regular criminal procedure in prosecuting eligible youth, ages eighteen to twenty-two. An important feature was the decision to commit youth to the custody of the attorney general for an indeterminate period, thus allowing the parole board to grant release, within four years, whenever rehabilitation was deemed accomplished. Congress expected the Bureau of Prisons to keep these youthful offenders separate from adult prisoners and to provide them with intensified treatment programs. In addition, in recognition of the individual's improvement, the parole board could order a juvenile's conviction expunged from the record.

Although its intent was humane, the law was difficult to implement, and its results were disappointing. The Bureau did allocate certain institutions for the youthful offenders and did enhance the programming, but the rehabilitative results were not as impressive as were the persistent problems. One serious issue was the disparity in sentences; too often, because of their differing ages, codefendants were sentenced under different laws, and the youthful defendants usually served more time. Gradually, the purpose and effect of the act were defeated by the problems inherent in it, and the law was repealed in 1984.

During Bennett's first decade as director, the number of adult prisoners continued to grow alarmingly, due to more commitments and longer sentences. In his annual report for 1940, the attorney general noted that the average length of sentence for prisoners committed in 1937 was 14.7 months, while the average in 1938 was 16.5 months. He found that this increase in sentence length was responsible for raising the average daily federal prisoner population by almost two thousand. In view of this pressure and the loss of the Leavenworth Annex in 1940, the Bureau had reason to appreciate the addition of two new major institutions—prisons at Terminal Island and Terre Haute.

Terminal Island was on an unlikely site near Long Beach, California—a flat, compact, oblong parcel of land that was part of a navy base, surrounded by an intensely developed industrial area. The site had been built up incidentally as the army dredged a ship channel. The institution opened in 1938, but had to be given up less than three years later because of wartime necessities. When it was surrendered to the navy in 1941, Terminal Island was under its third warden, Henry L. Merry, champion of the ox teams at his previous post, El Reno. The site was returned to the Bureau in 1955, as a regular prison for men, but, unique for that time, it included a separate small unit for women.

The correctional institution that opened at Terre Haute, Indiana, in 1938 was a close adaptation of the Lewisburg penitentiary design. The facility was intended to serve prisoners from the Midwest who were not considered habitual or dangerous and were able to respond to rehabilitative services.

At this point, the Bureau was on the brink of institutional expansion that, forty years later, would bring the system to a total of nearly fifty institutions. Over that period, practice was to identify each institution by the city or town of its location. Eventually, the institutions were also put into certain defined categories, with most of them classified as federal correctional institutions. The new urban jails were metropolitan correctional centers; several maximum security prisons were penitentiaries; and the open, minimum-security facilities were federal prison camps. Later, a new category of institution, intended to detain deportable aliens for the Immigration and Naturalization Service, was designated as federal detention centers. Accordingly, the designation for each facility evolved into a simple use of the geographical name, preceded by the initials for its category; for example, FCI Danbury; MCC San Diego; USP Atlanta; FPC Allenwood; or FDC Oakdale (Louisiana).

By 1977, security level classifications had also been established, with the institutions defined as level 1 (open, minimum custody), level 5 (maximum custody), or graduated custody levels between those. The new, extra-secure penitentiary at Marion, Illinois (chapter 9), became an exception when, in July 1979, it was designated as level 6.

The Bureau's biggest surge of expansion started in 1938, when President Roosevelt released about $14 million in PWA funds to finance several institutions. In order to qualify for the money, the projects had to be under construction by the end of June, 1938. Bureau staff from that time recall that planners, draftsmen, and architects were assembled at headquarters, in large rooms with rows of temporary tables; jointly—informally and hurriedly—they helped each other design the physical plants and get the projects underway. As a result, the Terre Haute institution was finished, and the facilities at Ashland, Kentucky; Danbury, Connecticut; Englewood, Colorado; Seagoville, Texas; and Texarkana, Texas, were designed. These prisons all opened in 1940. In the rush to beat the deadline Bureau personnel adapted to the exigencies as necessary. At Danbury, for instance, they let the contract for the foundation and got it under construction without waiting for plans to be drawn for the buildings. Englewood was an even closer call. In order to claim that construction was underway by the deadline, a lieutenant was pulled out of another institution, sent to the untouched site near Denver, and told to buy some shovels, hire six laborers, and just begin digging.[27]

Altogether these experiences lent an exciting, heady quality to the end of the Bureau's first decade. By then, the agency had expanded its capacity enormously, so it could contend with the increased numbers of prisoners brought in under new federal crime laws, and it had also established a pattern of bureaucratic integrity and merit it would need most acutely in the decade ahead. Another world war was about to bring profound social changes that would rudely shake any complacency the custodians might still have about their customary ways of running prisons. And though the hasty, informal rush to design and begin new construction would not be repeated with such intensity, there would be other times when the demand for prison space would seem sadly endless.

9

PRISONS OF
LAST RESORT

On becoming U.S. President in 1933 Franklin D. Roosevelt appointed as his attorney general Homer S. Cummings, a scholarly gentleman who previously had been the state attorney general in Connecticut. Already there in the Department of Justice to work under him with effective mutual respect was the equally astute Director of the Bureau of Prisons, Sanford Bates, held over from the Hoover administration. One of their first collaborative efforts produced the most legendary of the federal prisons, an institution that seemed necessary and appropriate to a problem of the times.

It was an era when crime increasingly threatened the public peace. The Eighteenth Amendment was passed in 1919, and Prohibition spawned a ruthless hierarchy of gang leaders with immense resources. They were difficult to catch and more difficult to convict, even though many of them operated openly within easy public view. In Chicago, Al Capone dominated the bootlegging gangs during the 1920s, and he seemed arrogantly immune to any law enforcement efforts against him. But finally Capone was prosecuted by the Treasury Department and was convicted of income tax evasion; he entered the Atlanta Penitentiary in May 1932 with eleven years to serve.[1]

Stories of Capone's career and his conviction and sentencing were only part of a series of exciting crime stories that appeared in the early 1930s. Police agencies in the spring of 1933 were hunting for John Dillinger, the one-man crime wave in the Midwest. The prolonged hunt for the Lindberg kidnapper also aroused intense public concern. In June 1933, four federal agents and three local police officers were escorting an escapee to Leavenworth when they were ambushed at the railroad station in Kansas City, Missouri. Their prisoner, Frank Nash, a member of a gang of train robbers, had escaped from Leavenworth three years before. As the party moved from the train to a car, gunmen opened fire, killing the three local officers and one federal agent. Nash also was killed. "It was not clear whether the purpose of the murders was to rescue Nash or to kill him for underworld reasons."[2]

Five weeks later, a prominent Oklahoma oilman, Charles Urschel, was kidnapped and held for $200,000 ransom. Soon after the ransom was paid and Urschel was released, the FBI arrested George "Machine Gun" Kelly and several others for the crime.[3] Both Kelly and his wife were convicted and given life sentences.

Collectively, the crime news stories kept public excitement at a high pitch that year; it was an opportune time for the attorney general to capture attention for any crime-busting plans he might announce. For one thing, Cummings used the events to justify his requests for more support for the FBI, remarking that the underworld had more men under arms than the army and the navy.[4] For another thing, he found it an ideal time to propose a new type of tough prison for tough criminals.

It was only a few months after he took office that Cummings prepared an in-house memo that raised a provocative question. "In the agenda of things to be considered, when we get around to it, would it not be well to think of having a special prison for racketeers, kidnapers, and others guilty of predatory crimes, said prison to be in all respects a proper place of confinement. . . . It would be in a remote place—on an island, or in Alaska, so that the persons incarcerated would not be in constant communication with friends outside."[5]

A week later Bates responded with an estimate of the cost of taking over the military prison in San Francisco Bay; after another few weeks, the secretary of war signed a transfer for the property. On October 12, Cummings announced in a radio address that the Bureau of Prisons had acquired Alcatraz. His satisfaction led him to be a little more optimistic than was justified. "The current is swift and escapes are practically impossible. . . . It is in excellent condition. . . . Here may be isolated the criminals of the vicious and irredeemable type so that their evil influence may not be extended to other prisoners who are disposed to rehabilitate themselves."[6]

Despite the attorney general's enthusiasm, persistent but unrecorded memory is that Bates and other Bureau officials did not want

Alcatraz and had misgivings about it. However, any murmurs of opposition apparently were quickly repressed because of strong political expediency. Publicly, Bates always supported the attorney general's decision.

The government's need for a super-prison conveniently coincided with the availability of Alcatraz Island. Only a few months earlier, the War Department had announced it intended to close its disciplinary barracks at Alcatraz; the army had not originally intended to have a prison there, but circumstances, not planning, had diverted the site from its intended role as a fort. The strategic location of the rocky, barren little island, just inside the entrance to the San Francisco Bay, made it an ideal site for a fort, a plan authorized by President Millard Fillmore in 1850. Nine years later, the island had its impressive fortress in a state of readiness, with troops and powerful artillery.

No enemy ever challenged the Alcatraz guns, but though the threat of military action failed to develop, the need for space to hold military prisoners did increase. Military forces on the West Coast had no prison to hold their occasional offenders, and it was inevitable that the underused and secure island fort would be called into such service. During the Civil War, in the absence of any other facility, soldiers convicted of various offenses were held there. In fact, even some civilians, charged with disloyal activities during the war, were housed there.[7]

Years later, the Spanish American War brought still more prisoners, and by 1900, more than four hundred inmates were confined there. The transition of Alcatraz from fort to prison was completed with construction of a permanent new cellblock, started in 1909 and completed in 1912. For the next two decades, the island served as a useful military disciplinary barracks, but it was in an awkward location, it suffered steady deterioration from the salt air, and it was excessively expensive to operate. Increasingly, too, the army was embarrassed to have a penal facility with its forbidding character dominating the view from San Francisco. By 1933, the army was ready to give up the site.

When Cummings announced the new plans for Alcatraz, local reaction to the proposal was surprisingly like the objections often raised in regard to new prisons at other sites. The San Francisco public, led by various vocal county officials, expressed fear and annoyance at the prospect of having a collection of especially vicious criminals in the vicinity. Nor was the touted barrier of the island's surrounding water entirely convincing. Throughout the island's history, the impossibility of swimming through the cold water and dangerous currents of the Bay was a well-cultivated myth, and Cummings was quick to refer to it to reassure the Bay residents. But the opponents of the prison soon proved that the waters were not quite so forbidding. On October 17, Anastasia Scott, the seventeen-year-old daughter of an army staff sergeant stationed on Alcatraz, easily swam from the mainland to the island. Followed by three companions in a boat, she made the swim in forty-three minutes.[8]

The *San Francisco Examiner* saw the story possibilities in this sort of stunt and a few days later sponsored a swim by two other young women. As reporters and photographers followed in two boats, eighteen-year-old Doris McLeod and twenty-year-old Gloria Scigliano swam across to the island. Scigliano waded ashore by an Alcatraz dock, but McLeod swam nonstop, around the island and back to the mainland, with no apparent difficulty.[9] Realists could see that a young, well-trained athlete, swimming with an escort of boats was different from a hunted prisoner, unprepared and unconditioned, swimming alone. But in the end, the public preferred the myth. The feat of the young women who swam to the island was soon forgotten, while the idea of impassable waters firmly endured.

Having acquired the island, the Bureau of Prisons needed a warden who could take charge of the extensive process of renovating and preparing the buildings for their new use. The man selected was James A. Johnston, a shrewd, dry-of-personality, well-organized, nononsense businessman and prison administrator. Trained as a lawyer, he had been chairman of the California Board of Control when the state asked him, in 1912, to take over as warden of the prison at Folsom, then in a severe crisis condition. After one year at Folsom, Johnston was tapped to be warden at San Quentin. According to his own account, it was there that he first met Sanford Bates, then Massachusetts commissioner of corrections, who came to inspect the prison. After eleven years at San Quentin, Johnston retired to become a banker in San Francisco and was there when Bates asked him to take over Alcatraz.

Appointed in January 1934, Johnston found that Alcatraz was already obsolete in some respects. The main cellblock building, by then more than twenty years old, had not been built to the exacting security standards that were now necessary. Though Cummings had cheerfully asserted that the prison was in excellent condition, Johnston and a consulting engineer prepared extensive lists of costly changes that would be required before the facility could receive the new type of prisoners. New locking mechanisms were ordered for the cellblocks; most cell fronts, window sash and other metal barriers had to be replaced with tool-proof steel. Gun towers and new fences were built outside; gun galleries were built inside; a system of gas guns was installed in ceilings for instant use at strategic points; walk-through metal detectors, then a very new idea, were brought in; and an emergency electrical source was developed. Various noncustodial improvements were also made, including improved hospital, library, and kitchen facilities.[10]

The island had no water supply of its own, so the Bureau continued to bring fresh water by barge from Fort Mason and pump it into storage tanks ashore. To conserve the fresh water, salt water circulated through a separate system to toilets and fire-fighting hoses.

During the time that Warden Johnston was planning and supervising the extensive reconstruction, the army was still in charge and still had a few prisoners on hand. Thirty-two of the army's more serious offenders remained and became the first inmates in Johnston's custody when he took over the administration on July 1, 1934.

The Bureau decided that no newly committed federal prisoners would be received directly at Alcatraz, and none would be released from there. Prisoners for Alcatraz would be selected from those already in other federal prisons, and later, before release, they would be transferred again to other prisons. The first batch of transferees came from the McNeil Island penitentiary on August 11. This small group of fourteen arrived in Oakland by train, and the men were transferred to the island by the prison's launch. In accordance with another policy decision, the press was not notified and learned of the move four days later.

The next transfer, in the same month, was logistically more demanding; because of the size of the group, the distance traveled, and the extent and expense of security precautions, the move was the most involved and elaborate in the Bureau's experience, until then.

Fifty-three high-risk prisoners were loaded on a special train in the grounds of the Atlanta penitentiary. The Bureau's contract with the railroad had specified steel cars with modifications that included bars on windows and a cage for guards at each end of each car. The Bureau was concerned that outside confederates might attempt to hijack the train, so officials sent it by an unannounced, indirect route, across country to a railyard at Tiburon, in the northern portion of San Francisco Bay. The cars were rolled onto a barge, and the barge was towed across to Alcatraz. The shackled prisoners did not leave the train until then.

This time the press learned of the transfer. Excited by the fact that Al Capone, the country's most famous prisoner, was aboard, reporters and photographers by the boatload attempted to cover the action. However, government boats kept them at a considerable distance, and they made do with telephoto shots.

About two weeks later the procedure was repeated when 103 prisoners were transferred in from Leavenworth. Between these two large prisoner moves, a small group of eight had been sent from the District of Columbia reformatory which at that time was having problems.

It was a time when the whole prison system was overloaded—and getting more that way—so it was tempting to take advantage of the six hundred or so beds the new island prison offered. However, the Bureau of Prisons had designated a specialized institution to meet a special problem, and it was resolute in not compromising the principles built into the plan. "We are not regarding this institution as one to which transfers can be made to relieve overcrowding in other prisons."[11]

Another policy decision stipulated that rules would be strict, privileges minimal, and treatment programming virtually nonexistent. No other federal prison was ever so determined to shield its operation from outside scrutiny. The press was not welcome and the administration offered information about internal events only rarely. This policy inevitably contributed materially to the mystique and the public fascination with the island prison. Though that side effect was unintended, it served a practical purpose. The highly notorious gangster prisoners tended to be quite visible, even when incarcerated, and they would manipulate outside contacts in any possible ways if allowed.

Determined to frustrate such efforts, the prison administration drastically curtailed outside contacts for these inmates and prevented news about them from getting out.

One unusual security feature was how the inmates' mail was handled. Not only did prison staff censor all incoming and outgoing letters, they took the process a considerable step further. Original incoming letters were never delivered to the prisoners. Instead, to thwart communication by any secret ink or code, staff members typed complete copies of the letters and the prisoners received only these copies. In addition, during the institution's first few years, if an inmate wished to confer with a lawyer he had to obtain written permission from the attorney general. Family members were allowed to visit monthly, but always they were separated from the prisoners by a heavy glass partition and talked by telephone.

In a few cases, prisoner family members were also incarcerated. As already mentioned, the Bureau found that wives or other female confederates of crime figures were sometimes imprisoned and were a greater challenge than the prison at Alderson could safely manage. At one time the tight security unit built for these women at Milan held as many as four women who were wives of Alcatraz inmates.

In the early years of Alcatraz a rule of silence was enforced, with talking prohibited except where essential or unavoidable. Over a period of time there was a very gradual relaxation of the stricter rules, but even after more than a decade the rules included such as these excerpts.

- You are entitled to food, clothing, shelter and medical attention. Anything else that you get is a privilege.
- Short haircuts (reasonable) and no beards or mustaches.
- No gambling is allowed. You may play chess, checkers or backgammon. Authorized card games are Hearts, Cribbage and dominoes. No card game will be allowed if it is a "draw" type of game or does not use the full deck on the deal. [12]

In the midst of the general austerity, one bright spot was the food. The managers knew that food is a potent morale factor, especially in such an unprivileged prison as this. As a matter of self-serving practicality, the administration maintained a generous food budget at

Alcatraz and prisoners rarely complained about the quality of the meals. Despite this concern, during one period the kitchen apparently was not well managed. Inmates staged a serious food strike in 1952, with the result that a new food manager was hired to reorganize the kitchen operation.

The Bureau also provided a generous supply of reading materials; Warden Johnston opened the institution with a well-stocked library in place, and over the years it was gradually enlarged. In later years, the number of titles on hand increased to fifteen thousand. While the selection of both books and magazines was somewhat more classical than those readers would customarily choose for themselves, the library was appreciated and used heavily. One chaplain who supervised the library reported that the average usage was seven books and magazines each month for each prisoner. Such a figure is impressive, considering that prisoners could not actually go to the library but had to order books from a catalogue and wait for them to be brought by an inmate runner.[13] One inmate wrote that since the library was operated mostly by inmates, books were often misfiled or lost, and ordering from the catalogue could be uncertain and frustrating.[14]

Like other federal prisons, Alcatraz always maintained various industrial shops, although, at first, the prisoners were paid no wages. A large laundry operation did the washing for the institution and for some local army posts. There was also a shoe shop, a wood shop, a tailor shop, and a dry cleaning plant. Later, a clothing shop to make uniforms for federal prisoners and a furniture reconditioning shop were added. When World War II began the navy needed cargo nets, so a shop that made floor mats from old automobile tires was converted to a new use, turning out thousands of cargo nets for use in amphibious landings. Another shop repaired and reconditioned the buoys that were used for the anti-submarine net that protected the entrance to San Francisco Bay. These new industrial activities brought one welcome improvement; for the first time prisoners were paid wages. By the late 1930s, the rule of silence had been relaxed, musical instruments were available for an active ten-man orchestra, motion pictures were shown occasionally, and correspondence courses were available from the University of California.

In his relationships with the press Johnston kept his cool reserve and was never intimidated by reporters' aggressiveness or by accusative stories. He always refused to confirm or deny the stories about his prisoners or his practices, and this pattern continued, with very little change, through the terms of his successors. That policy was an attempt to counter the intense public interest in some of the notorious individuals who spent time there, particularly Al Capone who was there during the prison's first five years. When he arrived, Capone was a young man of thirty-five, a Chicago gang chieftain of immense wealth and power, accustomed to the limelight and to exercising influence wherever he chose. During his previous brief stay in Atlanta, Capone had regular contacts with his family members who took up residence at a nearby hotel, and he worked at corrupting guards and enlisting fellow prisoners as lackeys—allegedly with some success.[15] But at Alcatraz, Capone lost all his influence and privilege. He was assigned to menial jobs and was unhesitatingly punished with time in solitary when he broke rules. Though this treatment was strictly in accordance with the way other prisoners were treated, it was a remarkable accomplishment, considering the times and the prisoner.

Capone never again enjoyed prestige or power. He was already suffering from syphilis when he entered prison, and he made his own case hopeless by refusing to acknowledge his condition and its seriousness. When he left Alcatraz, he was already slipping into the mental confusion of paresis; and when he finally was discharged from custody out of Lewisburg, his family took him to Florida where he died at the age of forty-eight.

Among other early notorious prisoners were George "Machine Gun" Kelly and Alvin Karpis, who was the subject of J. Edgar Hoover's special wrath, after a flamboyant career of robbery and kidnapping with the Ma Barker gang. Karpis spent twenty-four years at Alcatraz where he was no model prisoner, but was clever enough to avoid overt trouble. When he eventually was transferred out to McNeil Island, he settled into a mellow, cooperative demeanor. In 1969, when he was finally released, Karpis was much like any quietly behaved, elderly retiree.[16]

The list of notorious Alcatraz residents is too long to inventory here, and their various careers are well covered in other writings. However, one more may be noted—an interestingly different character—atomic spy, Morton Sobell. In all the mythology of Alcatraz, persistent assertions emerge about J. Edgar Hoover's interest in Alcatraz and the ways he managed to influence the prison's operation and the assignment of prisoners to it. Such stories cannot be corroborated, but neither are they entirely denied. The Sobell case could be an example of Hoover's influence; Sobell did not fit the type generally chosen for Alcatraz, but he did fit a type particularly targeted by the FBI director. Sobell was arrested in 1950 and, along with four others, charged with selling atomic secrets to Russia. It happened in a time of strong public feeling against the perceived Communist threat. Sobell's friends, Julius and Ethel Rosenberg, were convicted and executed; Harry Gold was convicted and sentenced to thirty years in prison; Mrs. Rosenberg's brother, David Greenglass, confessed and was sentenced to fifteen years. Sobell was sentenced to thirty years.

Sobell alleged that J. Edgar Hoover dictated his placement in Alcatraz and arranged for him always to have a special mail censor.[17] In fact, no special censor was assigned to Sobell, but the regular censors did give him especially close attention. Whether or not Hoover had anything to do with it, a particular Bureau policy did apply to this class of prisoner. On one occasion, Director Bennett sent a memo to the warden at Lewisburg, reminding him of Bureau policy with respect to any prisoners in espionage, sabotage, or overthrow-of-government cases. By this policy, the warden was "instructed to delegate some supervisory or higher administrative official to observe every activity, such as correspondence and visiting, and to take part in any administrative decision respecting members of this group. . . . Any significant happening in respect to these cases should be reported to the Bureau without waiting for the next regular progress report."[18]

Alcatraz riots and escapes were of great interest to the public and a source of frustration to news reporters who tried to cover them. According to one news item, "Reporters have almost as hard a time getting into Uncle Sam's special penitentiary as the inmates have getting out."[19] But occasionally some excitement could be directly observed, as when escape attempts brought out extra patrol boats and other visible security measures. The most dramatic event occurred in May 1946, when six prisoners attacked officers, obtaining their weapons and some keys. The six men took over one cellblock without other staff knowing; then they waited for officers to come into the area and took them hostage, one by one. With nine hostage officers locked in cells, the armed inmates were in control of their immediate area but lacked the keys and the firepower to go anywhere else. Though the surviving hostages were shortly released, the several armed prisoners settled down to a spectacular siege; the Alcatraz custodial staff was reinforced by nearly thirty corrections officers brought in from other federal institutions, a dozen sent from San Quentin, and assault forces from the U.S. marines. For two days, crowds on the mainland could watch as troops assaulted the island and fired at the cellblock building. In the end, three inmates held out and took refuge in the plumbing access corridor where they were attacked by gunfire and by grenades dropped on them from above. All three were killed.

Two of the hostage officers had been killed and several were wounded. Three surviving prisoners were charged with murder; one was given an additional life term, and the other two were sentenced to death. The federal government arranged for the two executions to be conducted at the San Quentin prison by the state of California.[20]

While this was by far the most spectacular escape attempt, there were several others, though none succeeded. Among the more ingenious was an effort in June 1962 by two brothers and another inmate who carried out a long-term strategy, chipping away at the concrete walls adjoining the ventilator openings in their cells. Over time, even concrete deteriorates in the salt laden air from the Bay—and this made their job easier. Finally, when the openings were large enough, the three men wriggled through into the plumbing access area one night, leaving artfully designed dummies in their beds.[21] They climbed to the top of the cellblock, removed a roof ventilator, crossed the roof, slid down a drain pipe to the ground, and went on to the water's edge. The three men were never seen again, and in that sense the action might be called an escape. However, there is no indication that the men survived; given their desperate situation and their criminalistic qualities, they would soon have been much in evidence if they actually made it to the mainland shore.

Other serious escape attempts occurred, but none succeeded unless the try made by J. Paul Scott in 1962 could be classed a success. After sawing through bars of a kitchen basement window, Scott got off the island and swam to the rocky shore at the base of the Golden

Gate Bridge. However, he was seen as he attempted to climb out of the water and, in his exhausted state, was recaptured without difficulty.

The statistics, as summarized by the National Park Service, show that thirty-six prisoners were involved in fourteen separate escape attempts. One man drowned and seven were shot and killed. Five others are still missing and confidently presumed dead. The remaining twenty-three were captured, either on the island or nearby.

Over its nearly twenty-nine years as a civilian prison, Alcatraz had four wardens, and those four served under two Bureau directors. When Johnston retired in 1948, he was replaced by Edwin W. Swope, who entered the federal prison system as warden of the McNeil Island Penitentiary in 1934. He also headed the Terre Haute and Englewood institutions before being appointed to Alcatraz. With his exacting, intense emphasis upon secure custody and ruggedly enforced discipline, he should have been a popular choice of the custodial staffs in the several prisons where he successively worked. But Swope was not popular with any constituency. Subordinate staff were uncomfortable with him and inmates actively disliked him (to put it politely). Still, he competently administered Alcatraz prison for seven years. The next warden was a former Alcatraz officer, Paul J. Madigan, who was brought back from Terre Haute where he had been the warden for two years.

When Johnston first organized the island prison in 1933, choosing the most promising officers from other federal prisons, Madigan, then at Leavenworth, was one of his first selections. Eventually Madigan rose to be captain at Alcatraz, and in 1941 he distinguished himself by his cool effectiveness in thwarting a desperate escape attempt.[22]

Now the change of leadership, from Swope to Madigan, brought a pointed contrast in managerial styles. Over his many years in the federal system Madigan enjoyed a remarkable degree of respect from both staffs and inmates. The reaction of the Alcatraz prisoners to Madigan's return to the Island is interestingly noted by one veteran prisoner, Alvin Karpis, who was listed as public enemy number one at the time of his arrest. Though Karpis' usual view of his custodians is hardly to be trusted, in this instance his opinion seems well-founded. "Swope suddenly resigns to accept the job of Director of

Prisons in the New Mexico State Prison System. . . . For us it is a pleasant surprise but the Federal Bureau of Prisons must decide, almost overnight, on a replacement. The final decision is even more exhilarating than the announcement of Swope's retirement. 'Madigan will be the new warden.' . . . No one has a negative thought about Madigan. . . . Madigan is a bonus I hadn't expected."[23]

Although Madigan could firmly control and punish without hesitation when the situation demanded, he was noted more for his simple, utterly honest and unpretentious humanity. He liked people, and he treated everyone—staff and inmates alike—in an unfailingly considerate manner.

When Madigan departed for McNeil Island in 1961, the Island's last warden, Olin G. Blackwell, was appointed. It was during Blackwell's time that the three men cut through their cell walls, emerged onto the roof, and fled to the water where they disappeared. This escape did not cause the Bureau to think of closing the institution, but it did point up the vulnerability of the aging physical structure and helped underline some of the reasons why it should be abandoned. Not only was the structure becoming less secure, it was unacceptably expensive to renovate it, or even to continue to operate it. The prison projected a highly visible, negative image that the government was becoming self-conscious about. Even a decade earlier, Bennett had spoken of the need to build a replacement somewhere in the middle of the country. And so Warden Blackwell served for just one and one-half years, presiding over the prison's closing. The last prisoners left Alcatraz in March 1963, and Blackwell went on to become warden at Lewisburg and Atlanta penitentiaries.

Throughout Alcatraz's twenty-nine years, the Bureau yielded only slightly in its initial resolve to provide tight control with virtually no amenities. It yielded not at all on its resolve to limit the population to the most recalcitrant and not to use the prison to relieve crowding elsewhere. There were always unused cells, while other penitentiaries were overloaded. In all, the total number of prisoners admitted to Alcatraz was only 1,557; the average daily population of 302, reached in 1937, was its highest.[24]

Was Alcatraz really the savage, brutal place that sometimes was popularly depicted? The answer depends on whose opinion is considered. Departing inmates and a few former staff found their audiences eager to believe the worst, so what they reported tended to reinforce the image of "America's Devil's Island." On the other hand, many former inmates remember the institution as no worse—and in some ways better—than more conventional prisons. There is reason to credit the view that prisoners often served their own need to be seen as "tough guys" by convincing their listeners of the rough experience they had been through. Staff members, too, carried the aura; when they transferred to other prisons, they usually were seen as being particularly competent in stressful situations because of their Alcatraz experience.

On his departure from Alcatraz, Karpis said that it had done nothing to reform him. Undoubtedly, directors Bates and Bennett would have agreed that this prison was not intended for reformatory purposes; according to Bates, it was intended only to exercise unique control over the dangerous few who would otherwise disrupt the system. Warden Johnston tells of going to Washington to confer with Bates and the attorney general while the institution was first being prepared. "They wanted everything tight, firm, strict, but they wanted to make sure that we could at the same time, be just, decent and humane in our treatment of inmates. . . . Alcatraz would be a prison of maximum custody with minimum privileges."[25]

Whatever else may be said about Alcatraz, it always had—and still has—the capability to incite great interest. People hold widely diverging views in regard to its justification, its decency, its success, or its failure. And, as will be seen, the prison's successor institution has been no less provocative in eliciting vigorously opposed viewpoints.

With the closing of Alcatraz need still existed for some similarly secure facility to house the high-risk inmates who had been well controlled in the island prison. The search for a suitable site started in about 1955, with much of the responsibility for the planning carried by Myrl Alexander, then the assistant director. Among the five sites finally considered in 1959, the one situated between the southern Illinois towns of Marion and Carbondale proved the strongest contender, for several reasons. One observer ascribed it mainly to simple politics. "Senator Everett Dirksen, in addition to being Senate minority leader, was ranking Republican on the Judiciary Committee which has jurisdiction over federal penitentiaries, and he wished a federal facility in the southern tip of Illinois, where his strength lay and which at that time was suffering from economic depression."[26]

Actually the issue was not so simple; the strong interest of Southern Illinois University, in Carbondale, was an important factor, as was the availability of suitable land already owned by the federal government. The university had an effective and respected president, Delyte W. Morris, who saw splendid potential for interaction with a nearby correctional institution. So, the University not only campaigned for the facility, it also developed a new academic unit, the Center for the Study of Crime, Delinquency, and Corrections. Close at hand was a large federal wildlife refuge, Crab Orchard Lake, where the Fish and Wildlife Service was willing to give the Bureau of Prisons twelve hundred acres that previously had been used for an army ordnance loading plant.

When the final decision was made by a Bureau of Prisons team, Alexander listed the reasons the Crab Orchard site was selected: (1) the existence of a community environment with good recreational and educational facilities that would help in staff recruitment; (2) the presence of a major university with an active interest in being supportive; (3) the availability of suitable federal land; (4) the economic need of the area.[27]

About three months after Alcatraz closed, in March 1963, the new prison at Marion was opened; by the following year it was fully operational. By some accounts, it was to replace Alcatraz; by other accounts, it was not intended to be a new Alcatraz, but only later shifted into that role. But in fact, as Alexander attests, Marion was indeed intended to succeed Alcatraz; the contrary opinion arose partially from the fact that no Alcatraz prisoners were actually transferred to Marion. The Bureau of Prisons wanted to give the untried institution time to test its building and staff, time to be fully completed and fully competent. So the Alcatraz inmates were scattered out to other penitentiaries while Marion opened with a less disruptive type of prisoner.

It is pertinent to digress here enough to note one feature not found at either Marion or Alcatraz—a death row. If the Bureau of Prisons had maintained such a facility Marion would seem to be the logical place for it. However, it has not been needed, even though federal law provides the death penalty for several crimes. This book will not attempt to trace the complex pattern of legislative acts and appellate court decisions that define national policy on executions; suffice it to say that since the Supreme Court's 1972 decision in *Furman v. Georgia,* the federal death penalty statutes have been assumed not to meet constitutional requirements.[28] One exception would be any conviction for aircraft piracy in which a death occurs, but the death penalty has not so far been imposed for this crime.

The law provides that federal defendants, if so sentenced, are to be executed in the state where the sentence is imposed, and by the means that state customarily uses. The last execution conducted for the Bureau was carried out in Iowa, where the state provided its gallows to hang kidnapper Victor Feguer on March 15, 1963.

Feguer was the thirty-third person to be executed by the Bureau of Prisons. The first one was Carl Panzram, who was hung at Leavenworth because Kansas had no facilities for executions (chapter 4). Anthony Chebatoris was another one executed in a federal prison, on July 8, 1938, on a gallows set up in the prison at Milan, Michigan. The warden, who had to find and hire a hangman, was dismayed when the man showed up for the occasion too drunk to perform the job. Though the hanging was finally accomplished, it was a harrowing experience for the officials involved, including the Bureau director, Bennett.[29]

Other executions included the two men put to death in San Quentin's gas chamber in 1948 for the murders committed during the Alcatraz rioting; a man and woman executed together, for kidnapping and murder, in Missouri's gas chamber in 1953; and Julius and Ethel Rosenberg, electrocuted for espionage, in Sing Sing prison in 1953.

The first two Bureau directors, Bates and Bennett, were firmly on record as opposing the death penalty. In later years, after inmates committed several murders, the Bureau's fourth director, Norman Carlson, announced that he supported the death penalty for murder of prison employees.[30] In the two centuries since the first federal execution (chapter 1), although many such penalties have been carried out, it is impossible to document the exact number. However, recent research on U.S. executions generally has confirmed that, as of 1987, at least 345 federal (other than military) executions have occurred.[31]

In its original design and operation, the Marion penitentiary included the usual large recreation areas outside and gymnasium inside, the usual industries shops, and the usual treatment or activity programs. Prominent among these was the Asklepieion Society, a self-help adaptation of the transactional analysis concept, conducted by psychiatrist Dr. Martin Groder. But events in the larger society during the late 1960s and early 1970s forced the Bureau to reappraise the institution's mission, and the rehabilitative elements were eventually dismantled. Corrections administrators were influenced by research that showed institutional treatment programs usually were ineffective.

During this time, one particular event incited challenges to the Marion operation and to the Bureau of Prisons generally—the disastrous riot at New York's Attica prison in September 1971. Because it caused so many deaths and involved so much property damage, because it revealed so nakedly the underlying causes of the rage that fueled it, and because for four days it was front-page news that gripped the country's attention, Attica profoundly changed the general atmosphere in which prisons were administered. Other prisoners reacted, sometimes overtly, like the women at Alderson who rioted only a few days after the Attica uprising. But more important, the public became aware of prison problems, and prisoners were stimulated to initiate more challenges to the corrections systems.

Until the 1950s, the country's prisoners essentially had no access to the courts, for there was a general attitude that the courts should keep a hands off stance in respect to prison operations. The last important expression of this so-called hands-off doctrine regarding federal prisons came in 1954, when a Leavenworth prisoner sued the Bureau to allow him to deal directly with the U.S. Patent Office. The Tenth Circuit Court of Appeals flatly asserted that "courts are without power to . . . interfere with ordinary prison rules or regulations."[32]

However, even as that case was decided, other prison cases began to receive more sympathetic attention; and by the time of Attica, the courts accepted that they did indeed have both the power and the responsibility to interfere where a prisoner could claim to be unfairly treated. Before Attica, a steady trickle of prisoner cases came to the courts; after Attica, the trickle became a flood. And no federal prison was more certain to spawn new legal challenges than Marion, which housed a distillate of the most hostile among the Bureau's prisoners.

Access to the courts is an important element in the differences between the Alcatraz and Marion institutions.

One major legal challenge derived from the special custodial measures taken in 1972 at Marion, following a prisoner work stoppage. The prison established the "control unit," a tight grouping of cells for seventy or fewer inmates who were to be kept entirely separate from the general prison population. Architecturally, the unit comprised four ranges of cells, each bordered by a grillwork partition; behind this guards had remote control of cell door locks without entering the area.

When striking prisoners were confined in this unit, the National Prison Project of the American Civil Liberties Union filed suit, alleging that segregation was not conducted with procedural safeguards and that prisoner access to attorneys had been unreasonably curtailed.[33] As a result of the litigation, more formal procedures were developed for selection of inmates for the unit; rather than using it for punishment, it was designated "to confine, in a highly structured and secure environment, assaultive, predatory, or violent escape-prone offenders who have demonstrated they cannot function successfully in general population without threatening the safety of staff or inmates."[34]

Initially the prison managers attempted to provide employment for control unit inmates. In the open space opposite the cells, they placed a few locked cages in which individual inmates could perform benchwork production tasks. Nevertheless, many of the prisoners spent most of their time in their cells, where the grillwork fronts allowed noise to flow freely, often with disruptive effects. To reduce this problem, nine of the approximately seventy cells were equipped with a partitioned vestibule in front of each, to contain the noise. These, nicknamed boxcar cells, prompted another lawsuit that attacked control unit conditions and resulted in more exacting management practices, including periodic reviews of each case, a minimum of seven hours a week out-of-cell exercise, better cell lighting, and a policy of not closing the vestibule doors unless a prisoner requested it or unless disruptive behavior made it necessary. The suit alleged that the vestibules resulted in sensory deprivation (lack of light and sound), and for this reason the cells were redesigned to add more window space.[35]

The complex and protracted litigation in this case demonstrated how difficult it is to apply stringent control measures to such a resourcefully resistive prisoner group and, at the same time, to make sure the procedures safeguard against arbitrary or retaliatory staff actions. The Marion population, a concentration of the high-risk prisoners culled from the whole prison system, produced an astonishing series of events in which assaults, escapes, or attempted escapes were plotted and conducted with consummate ingenuity and gross disregard for human life. Inmates made handcuff keys and, in one instance, even a zip gun, using only the unlikely items they were able to acquire in these extremely guarded cells. Marion prisoners took regular advantage of the long-time prison ruse of carrying contraband hidden in the rectum.[36] In one instance, a prisoner returning from a court appearance was found to be carrying a rectal bonanza of hack saw blades, two handcuff keys, and five cellophane-wrapped packets of marijuana.[37]

Several dangerous and sometimes fatal episodes are particularly interesting and serve to indicate the kind and degree of threat this inmate group presented. For instance, in 1973 when five Marion prisoners opened the main entrance grill doors and walked out to temporary freedom, the escape was said to be the most sophisticated in the bureau's history—and probably in the history of U.S. prisons generally. The penitentiary is designed with a wide center hall inside its front entrance; the sally port includes three sets of sliding grills, only one of which was ever to be open at one time. Unlike more typical prison entrances, where a control room is placed on the same floor and adjoins the sally port, at Marion the controls were placed in a room above the hallway, and closed circuit television was used to observe traffic through the entrance area.

The control mechanism for the sally port doors had previously malfunctioned and had been removed to the maintenance shop for repairs. One prisoner maintenance worker, Edward Roche, was allowed (improperly) to assist with the repair work. A former prisoner had told Roche that the electronic lock controls could be defeated. Roche followed up with his own extensive reading about the technology and was ready to take advantage of his opportunity when it came. During the time the mechanism was in the shop, Roche occasionally was left working there alone. Surreptitiously, he made and added to the mechanism a device to override the regular electrical control, when activited by an audio signal of a certain tone. When the staff reassembled and reinstalled the repaired control panel, they were unaware that it contained this added element.

With the help of other prisoners included in the plan, Roche next made an audio tone generator. He designed it in three components that could be carried separately to the sally port area. On the evening of October 10, 1975, an inmate discussion group was scheduled to meet in a room near the front entrance, with correctional officer Lorin Deeds as the security person assigned to monitor the meeting. Roche and four other plotters attended the meeting; two of these men were serving life sentences, while the other three were serving sentences that totaled 114 years.

During the meeting one of the inmates asked for a bandaid and in this way lured Deeds into a nearby storeroom; two others followed and quickly locked Deeds in. The three components of the audio tone generator were quickly assembled and plugged into an electrical outlet in the immediate area of the microphone/speaker that served for communication between the control room and persons approaching the sally port. When the device was turned on, it emitted a continuous tone that in turn activated the mechanism hidden in the repaired control panel. All three sally port doors slid open. The five inmates simply walked out the main entrance and hurried off the grounds, into the night. Baffled staff members, who had never seen all three grills open at the same time, did not know how it happened or how to get the doors closed. It took time and detailed study to discover the gadgetry that defeated the locking mechanism.

Ironically, the inmates who built such sophisticated, technical equipment gave no thought to the escape strategy they would follow once they passed the prison door. Although they took clothing, guns, and a car from one nearby home, the men did not commit any other serious crimes. Authorities captured four of the escapees within three days. The fifth fugitive got as far as Chicago and remained at large for three weeks.

One other escape attempt, quite different but equally dramatic, occurred in May 1978, when a woman named Barbara Oswald tried to take inmate Garrett Trapnell out of the prison by helicopter. Oswald engaged the helicopter and pilot one morning at St. Louis, and after they were airborne she ordered the pilot, at gun point, to fly to the penitentiary; he was to settle into the recreation yard just long enough for Trapnell and two others to hop aboard. As they neared the prison the pilot caught the woman off guard and wrestled her gun away from her. When she produced another gun and continued to threaten him, the pilot shot and killed her. He recovered control of the craft in time to land it on the lawn, near the prison's front entrance.

That was not the end of the story; Oswald's teen-age daughter, Robin, took up her deceased mother's fascination with Trapnell and made her own attempt to get him out. The following December, Robin Oswald boarded a regular TWA flight in St. Louis. She claimed to be carrying explosives and ordered the pilot to land at the Williamson County Airport, near Marion. For the next ten hours Oswald held the passengers and crew hostage, all the while demanding that Trapnell be released and guaranteed safe conduct from the vicinity. At the end authorities persuaded her to surrender.

Such escape attempts, though dramatic and potentially dangerous to the community, were not as serious a problem as the internal events that began to characterize institution life during the 1970s and 1980s. In 1983, about one-third of the inmates were transfers from state or District of Columbia prisons; about one-fourth were serving life sentences and another one-fourth were serving thirty years or more.[38] By 1986, "almost ninety percent of the Marion population had a history of prison assault, and nearly 40 percent were involved in murder or attempted murder while in prison."[39] With these types of prisoners concentrated in one place, it is neither surprising nor remarkable that a chronology of persistent violence was suffered over a period of two decades. In the years from 1965 to 1983, inmates murdered three corrections officers and twenty-one inmates; they also perpetrated numerous nonfatal, but serious, assaults and attempted a variety of escapes.

At times, when a brief period of quiet occurred, the Bureau restored normal operations and allowed inmates to move in small groups to various activities. But just as frequently new violence erupted and tight restrictions were reimposed. By the mid 1980s, under the pressure of successive violent episodes, the Bureau developed the tight controls that came to characterize this "prison of last resort."

The changes affected the general population inmates as well as the more violent prisoners, with all prisoner movements limited to only one small unit at a time, with enhanced staff escort. The industries and other work programs were eliminated in order to remove opportunities for group actions or weapons making. The maintenance and housekeeping jobs had to be done only by the staff or by inmates from the adjoining minimum security camp.[40]

Within the control unit the tight procedures required that any inmate being moved from his cell to the shower, or any other place, was first handcuffed and then escorted by at least two correctional officers. But even that proved to be insufficient. The most unsettling event occurred in October 1983, when two officers were killed. Three officers were conducting an inmate, Thomas Silverstein, from the shower to his cell with his wrists handcuffed in front. While walking ahead of his three-officer escort Silverstein stopped at the grill front of another inmate's cell. He thrust his hands through the bars, only momentarily, then turned suddenly to confront the officers, with one hand free of the cuffs and holding a knife. Before the officers could recover from their surprise, Silverstein had fatally stabbed officer Merle Clutts.

Later the same day inmate Clayton Fountain, being escorted in the same way, made an identical attack; he stabbed and killed officer Robert Hoffman and injured two other officers. More episodes of violence occurred in the following days and the warden made the procedural changes that led to extreme lockdown conditions. Thereafter prisoners in the control unit were handcuffed with their hands behind them whenever they were escorted anywhere; necessary services were kept as close as possible to the housing units so inmates would not need to leave those areas. Law libraries were installed in the four ranges, chaplains visited the inmates at their cells, and medical personnel came to the cells to respond to any physical complaints. Staff heated and served food within the units and after each meal the prisoners returned all paper plates and utensils, and even the papers from the sugar, salt, and pepper. To ease the boredom of the long hours of cell time the administration supplied a black and white television set to each cell. Although inmates were allowed daily recreation time, only one man at a time was allowed to use the locked exercise area. All weight lifting equipment was removed and exercise was limited to walking, calisthenics, and using a chinning bar.

One highly provocative security measure was the digital rectal search, a procedure that seemed necessary after the several experiences with contraband concealment. Prison policy called for this type of search to be done whenever inmates left the control unit and then returned.

Under those conditions—with most industries shut down, with recreation curtailed, with confinement in cells for twenty-three hours a day, and with inmates subjected to occasional rectal searches, it is not surprising that strong protests would be heard from both prisoners and outsiders. A militant organization of attorneys and citizens based in Chicago and known as the Marion Prisoners' Rights Project, promoted litigation, held publicized meetings, and prepared mailings of accusatory material intended to promote public concern.

The National Prison Project of the American Civil Liberties Union accomplished more effective impact. That agency challenged the Marion conditions by filing the suits already mentioned. But unlike the other opposition groups that maintained a hostile aloofness, the National Prison Project staff was willing to engage in dialogue and negotiation.

With a prisoner population as volatile as that in Marion, provocations tended to escalate. In response to the murders and disorders in October 1983, the Bureau of Prisons temporarily sent in at least sixty more officers from other prisons, including the riot control group from Leavenworth. Inmates reacted intensely to the shakedowns that followed. In 1984, they filed a suit (*Bruscino et al. v. Carlson et al.*, CV84-4320) that demanded relief from alleged brutality and other violations of their constitutional rights. They asserted that "defendants have engaged in a systematic pattern and practice of assault, abuse, denial of access to the courts, racial and religious discrimination, property deprivation, and harassment of prisoners."

A centerpiece of the allegations related to the auxiliary officers and their shakedown activities. "During the initial stage of the lockdown, 60 guards equipped with riot gear, shipped in from other prisons, systematically beat approximately 100 handcuffed and defenceless prisoners."[41] The federal court gave special attention to this issue and found that one officer (who by then had resigned—in lieu of being fired) had used excessive force on one occasion, but it discovered no other evidence of beatings. In summary, the court found that the complaining inmates themselves were committed to using indiscriminate violence, were not credible witnesses, and were "bent on the disruption of the prison system in general and of USP-Marion in particular." The court repudiated the inmates' complaints and recognized the professionalism of the staff. Subsequently this finding was fully affirmed by the Seventh Circuit Court of Appeals.

This does not mean that the controversy went away. Marion continued to be a lightning rod for heated criticism. There was no shortage of critical observers, including experienced corrections experts who argued that the repressive regime at Marion was unnecessarily harsh and contributed to its own problems by exacerbating the anger and resistance of prisoners held there. Bureau officials were equally sure that the men held at Marion were there because they already were committed to violence and not concerned about the consequences of their actions.

All these opinions were aired thoroughly in congressional hearings held in 1984 and in 1985. Both the Bureau officials and a variety of earnest and articulate critics had every opportunity to record their views, but no official findings were issued and no congressional action was taken.[42] The institution settled down to operate as a place with permanent tight control; procedures were modified and refined in accordance with the strictures imposed by the courts in *Adams v. Carlson* and *Bono v. Saxbe.*

By 1987, Marion's population consistently ran at less than 1 percent of the total federal prisoner population, and this was usually the only federal institution that was not overcrowded. As with Alcatraz, the Bureau did not assign prisoners to Marion for the purpose of relieving crowding at other institutions and did not resort to double occupancy in these cells. Because of the extreme volatility of the population selected for Marion, the Bureau believed that this institution was not only a humane response to the problem behavior of its inmates, it also contributed to the safety of inmates throughout the system by removing the disruptive few who would otherwise jeopardize living conditions in other institutions. Marion's control unit attracted the most critical attention, but as the institution program finally developed, most inmates were housed in units that imposed less stringent conditions. Though the administration had closed the prison industry shops, it opened a smaller and different industry for those inmates who were in the final months of their Marion time. This was a cable workshop that operated as a satellite to the large electronic cable factory at the Lexington Correctional Institution.

After he had served twelve months with clear conduct, any prisoner in one of the three general population cellblocks could transfer to C unit; there his privileges would be increased modestly and he would begin training for work in the cable workshops. After six months of clear conduct in C unit, a prisoner would be transferred to B unit, the most privileged of the Marion units. After six months of good conduct in B unit, where he would work in the shops, the inmate would be transferred to another penitentiary.

Marion also maintained a separate and unique housing area called K unit. A strictly segregated set of seven cells, K unit was always occupied by men who were in need of the most exacting security— sometimes because of their dangerousness, sometimes because they needed protection. These men included unusually vulnerable, high-profile individuals who might be targeted for death (or sometimes for violent rescue attempts) by determined and resourceful criminal elements. Because these men had to spend substantial parts of their sentences in this very restricted area, the managers attempted to make it more livable than ordinary prison cells. About the size of an average living room, each of these cells had space enough for a bed, a washbowl, a toilet, a shower stall, and a workbench where this inmate too could participate in the cable work. As an exception to the usual Marion practice, the prison provided a room within the unit where these inmates could receive contact visits with family members.

As conditions at Marion stabilized through the mid-1980s, the Bureau no longer talked of having a "lockdown," a term implying a temporary condition pending resumption of normal operations. Instead, the institution had adjusted its regimen to permanently manage disruptive prisoners in a safe manner. The 1979 task force report had made recommendations that seemed too draconian at the time and so were not fully implemented then. But subsequent events caused the Bureau to accept the task force view that "an apparent increase in violence in our prison system has created a category of inmates that are recognized as unmanageable when they are placed in an open population in large groups. Level 6 inmates are generally violent and assaultive."[43] The task force had urged that Marion's primary and overriding purpose be to reduce violence in federal prisons and recommended that work and other programs be secondary, if they existed at all.

By 1983 it had come to that. The industrial production program was abolished, except for work done by the pre-transfer inmates in B unit and the prisoners in K unit. The usual maintenance or housekeeping jobs were eliminated, and that work was done by staff. Kitchen and grounds work was performed by the outside camp inmates. Activity programs were eliminated and recreation for control unit inmates was reduced to a bare minimum. Although conventional classroom educational programs were canceled, motivated inmates could pursue correspondence courses or instructional programs the institution provided on closed-circuit television.

Procedures to move control unit prisoners outside their cells were permanently shaped to the demands of complete control. The administration reduced the need for out-of-cell movement of prisoners as far as possible, and then moved only one inmate at a time, using a three-officer escort. Even then, before a prisoner was taken from his cell he was put in step-chains (leg irons) and his wrists were cuffed behind him. When family members visited, they were separated from the prisoner by a glass partition and used a telephone to talk.

Less restrictive measures were used for the general inmate population. Their privileges were gradually increased in an effort to encourage these men to move out to other institutions. Groups of up to eighteen inmates in C and B units were allowed weekly to use the gymnasium and the outside recreation area, with tennis courts and jogging track. Finally, B unit inmates could leave their housing area in groups, without personal restraints, to go to the shops or to eat in the dining hall.

Altogether, substantial control was accomplished. Assaults were drastically reduced, though not stopped entirely. Because prisoners had no contact with visitors, urine tests for drugs were negative in all cases—a unique record for any prison. With importation of drugs absolutely prevented, gang leaders were deprived of this source of power, permitting much more certain institutional order and control. Though it is a truism that all prisons must tolerate some sharing of the management with its prisoners, Marion became an undisputed exception. The staff was in control, and, considering the nature of the population, they achieved a high degree of safety.

Although the rate of assaultive incidents increased immediately after the administration imposed imposition of the high security measures in the fall of 1983—a predictable result of inmates' resentment over the new restrictions—this rate decreased after about six months. In three and one-half years after October 1983, inmates attacked and killed three other prisoners; they did not kill any staff. These figures compare favorably to the three and one-half years immediately previous to October 1983, when six inmates and two staff were killed.

Legal challenges and written criticisms continued. A Quaker group expressed a typical viewpoint (without visiting the prison). "Despite repeated evidence that lockdowns don't assure safety, the authorities at Marion continue to respond to every new proof of the failure of their policy with an escalation of brutality."[44]

Attorneys for the prisoners continued to assert that inmates had been beaten in retaliation after the 1983 murders, and since. The court examined this allegation extensively and thoroughly in the Bruscino case, and the charge was not sustained. Counsel for the plaintiffs complained that the court was biased and that it unfairly failed to accept the testimony of the prisoners.[45]

The most objective review of all the data tends to support the Bureau's integrity in this issue. Admittedly—and entirely consistent with general corrections experience—when officers must bring turmoil under control, in the stressful heat of the moment, some inmate or inmates may take some bruises. The most well-intentioned managers cannot be everywhere at once in the aftermath of a disturbance, and they cannot guarantee that angry staff members will not sometimes let inmates feel their resentment when no supervisor is looking. However, it is consistent with the whole history of Bureau leadership and policy to believe that management always attempted—by policy, by staff training, and by direct supervision—to enforce the use of the least provocative and least severe controls consistent with maintenance of order and safety. From the Bureau's beginning, its top management had known that humane procedures were clearly a matter of self interest.

After the 1983 murders, when extra teams were brought in from Leavenworth and other institutions, several top managers from Bureau headquarters were dispatched to Marion to participate in supervision of the shakedown and control activities in order to keep the measures objective and proper. In the years afterward, as both K unit and the control unit settled into their long-term, highly restrictive regimens, the warden, his regional manager, and an assistant director of the Bureau conducted bi-monthly, on-site reviews of individual cases. At these review sessions, each inmate was privileged to be present and to speak for himself if he wished.

In the summer of 1984, the Judiciary Committee of U.S. House of Representatives commissioned two outside corrections experts, David A. Ward and Allen A. Breed, to study the Marion situation. Their report recommended a number of measures to alleviate some of the conditions or practices of which the two authors were critical.[46] The report was professional and constructive in tone, but, not surprisingly, it did not entirely satisfy any of the interested parties. The Bureau management rejected some of the recommendations and accepted and complied with others. The opposition groups, especially the Marion Prisoners' Rights attorneys, were irritated and substantially disagreed with the report.

Inevitably, among the continuing general criticisms of Marion, some observers claimed that Marion seemed to be more violent and dangerous than Alcatraz had been—a complaint that implied that the Marion management was flawed or was somehow less competent. A comparison of the two prisons is useful, though a superficial review can easily be misleading. Complex differences existed between the two facilities—differences in prisoner types but, particularly, important differences in the times. Alcatraz functioned in a period when prisoners everywhere had far fewer privileges and, accordingly, lower expectations. Compared with the 1980s, prisoners fifty or more years earlier were confined under spartan conditions and had few amenities and no "prisoners' rights." Prisoners endured the harsh regimes and the absence of any legitimate avenues of protest because there was simply no real expectation that things could be otherwise.

If no other factors affected the comparison between Alcatraz and Marion, these still would go far toward accounting for the difference in the character of the prisoner populations.

The example of rectal searches helps to make the point about different expectations. These digital probings that proved to be so provocative for the Marion inmates (anal rape, they charged) and became the heated subject of litigation were hardly different from the procedures that provoked no noticeable protest from inmates at Alcatraz.

The authors of the Ward/Breed report were well aware of the contrast in the conditions of daily life between Marion and Alcatraz, particularly since Ward had been conducting exhaustive research on the history of Alcatraz. However, they addressed this point only briefly.

> The answer to the question of why the Marion prisoners are more assaultive toward staff than the Alcatraz inmates and why they are more likely to kill other inmates lies in a complex set of factors that relate to changes over the past two decades in the character of crime, the emergence of powerful white, black and Hispanic gangs organized within prisons or in outside communities, the dramatic growth of the drug trade and other changes in American society that go beyond the scope of this report.[47]

As of 1987, the situation at Marion was still controversial. The Bureau insisted that the tight controls were a necessary and successful response to the disruptive efforts of a few extremely dangerous prisoners from all parts of the country; critics insisted that repressive, brutal conditions persisted at Marion and that these conditions promoted the violent behavior. The Bureau asserted that the Marion regimen enabled other federal penitentiaries to operate more safely, and, thus, it had a salutary effect on the whole system. Critics maintained that the Marion inmates were not as intrinsically dangerous as painted; it would be more humane and effective to permit them a living situation nearer to normal and to deal with their hostilities through therapeutic programming.

On the other hand, some argued that the intense control was not at all inhumane. Prior to the Bruscino case, Dr. William Logan of the Menninger Clinic conducted an extensive study of the Marion inmates. On the basis of psychiatric interviews with about sixty-five inmates, Logan concluded that those in the control unit showed the least evidence of mental health problems, mainly because of the highly structured situation with its clear expectations.[48]

It may be enough to know that these restrictions do not make prisoners worse. But it might also be hoped that even a prison of last resort could go further and offer effective programs to encourage positive changes in its prisoners. There have been some experiences with intensive therapeutic programming that do encourage this hope. But even if such programs cannot guarantee permanent reform (as indeed they do not), they can at least make a positive contribution by normalizing and stabilizing life in the prison.[49]

However, the programmatic approach does have one problem that is seldom fully appreciated or mentioned by its advocates. A therapeutic program depends entirely for its effectiveness upon the skill and charisma of the therapist. It depends further upon the sustained understanding, enthusiasm, and managerial support of the warden and other supervising officials. Therapeutic programming is a fragile procedure; if the therapist falters in handling a crisis or is hired away by another agency, the program is lost, to be rebuilt only slowly, if at all.

No correctional system has found a way to guarantee that it will recruit, deploy, and retain the right combination of managerial and therapeutic leadership. Therapeutic programming may be the most humane approach to a disturbing problem, but it remains forever a gamble—even with the most promising prisoner. In addition, there seems to be consensus that most of the hard-core inmates may be unreachable by any techniques we know.

The more certain alternative, then, is to rely on masonry, hardware, restraints, and control procedures to manage the persistently disruptive prisoners. These measures do not rehabilitate, but they endure, they survive staff changes, and, as rigorous as they are, they can be applied with considerable decency and fairness, untainted by brutality. This approach is not ideal, but given the volatile nature of the prisoner population at Marion in the 1980s it may be argued that the Bureau of Prisons was appropriately realistic in opting to use control measures as the most dependable, safe approach.

PRISONS IN
WARTIME

Within weeks after the Japanese attack on Pearl Harbor, in December 1941, the shops at the McNeil Island penitentiary began to receive tangled masses of electrical cable salvaged from destroyed ships and shore installations. Prisoners tackled about eighty-five tons of the scrap every month, stripping it of damaged insulation and reconditioning it for return to the navy, ready to be reused. Other McNeil Island shops were converted quickly to manufacture rope cargo nets for the navy, while the cannery produced great quantities of foodstuffs for military use, including six thousand pounds of dehydrated potatoes each day.

Even before the United States entered the war, the prison system built up its production capacity in anticipation. The attorney general's annual report for 1941 declared, "Defense needs and activities have seized the imagination of both staff and inmates to so marked a degree that our production of cotton textiles, metal products, shoes and other industrial materials has more than doubled." The Atlanta penitentiary increased its already large output of mattresses and canvas goods; the Leavenworth shoe factory, producing shoes for the army, had turned out 125,000 pairs in the three months before war was declared, but in the next three months it produced more than 181,000 pairs. The Lewisburg metal products plant turned to the production of bomb fins and bomb racks, and all other prisons similarly increased their production.[1]

While director Bennett was proud of the Bureau's response, it was not in the production shops that the more significant and enduring effects were seen. Just as the war created profound social changes generally, it also disrupted prisoner management, largely due to the influx of nontraditional inmates who challenged many prison practices.

The prisons got a foretaste of the dilemma during World War I, when a few war objectors were sent to the new civilian prisons of that time. Ammon Hennacy was a good example of the type of prisoner that appeared in far greater numbers in World War II. Hennacy, a militant socialist, arrived at the Atlanta penitentiary in 1917, to serve a two-year sentence. In prison, he maintained the same stubborn adherence to principle that caused his offense. The custodians were frustrated in dealing with this prisoner who was never deceitful or dangerous, never an escape risk, but who was scornful of any procedure or rule he considered illogical. "Hennacy's prison experience portrays many of the difficulties which the correctional system faces when dealing with political offenders and the manner in which traditional penal techniques of appealing to an inmates's self-interest (either to avoid punishment or to obtain reward) have little impact upon the 'politicals.' "[2] Later, World War II, the Korean War, and the Vietnam War brought their pressures for prison administration to change.

The Selective Service Act of 1940 created an influx of World War II objectors by requiring male citizens to register for possible military service. Such sweeping legislation inevitably snared persons with all kinds of disordered lives, including some criminals, who, perhaps, avoided registration in hopes that their "wanted" status would not be revealed. Many were clearly mentally disturbed. "No statute ever brought to the Federal correctional system so many definitely insane persons as did the Selective Service Act." During World War II, at least 175 such persons were transferred to the Springfield institution for psychiatric care, while another twenty were released by the courts because of their mental condition.[3]

Among the wartime prisoners were those simply too inept to respond properly to the registration notice, "the careless, the ignorant, the socially irresponsible who knew little about the war, the world situation and the Selective Service Act." However, the Bureau of Prisons found that the leftover stereotype of the World War I "draft dodger"—the weak, the cowardly, the selfish—was not a valid concept. No truly typical type existed, but many more people than expected avoided service as a deliberate expression of principle—however strained and unpatriotic that principle might seem to more conventional people.

Since the government had established an alternative service program for those who conscientiously opposed military service, it seemed unnecessary for any ordinary objector to go to prison. The fact that so many did enter prison was a sign of the infinite variety and complexity of the human conscience. Jehovah's Witness adherents comprised the largest homogenous group. By 1944, when the federal prison system held over four and one-half thousand Selective Service violators, more than half of these were Jehovah's Witnesses. Their violation of the law did not stem from an unwillingness to register, but from their insistence that all members of their church were ministers and should be classified as exempt from military duty. Although this principle denied them recourse to alternative service, in effect these people did choose another option for service—as prisoners.

After they were convicted of violating the Selective Service Act and were imprisoned, the Jehovah's Witnesses saw no further need to rebel; they made no effort to escape and were tractable, cooperative, and willing to work. The Bureau assigned them to its open camps or other minimum security placements, and the various wardens often asked for more of them when they needed prisoners who could be trusted on outside work details. Altogether, from 1941 to 1946, the federal prisons admitted 4,050 Jehovah's Witnesses.

Among other types of objectors were those whose principles were not so much religious as political or philosophical. Some were well educated and professionally accomplished, and many were ahead of their time and impatient to accomplish social reform. Writing afterward about their prison experience, two men commented accurately that prison "magnifies and exaggerates race-related political and social forces which are at work throughout the society." They also noted, "Political prisoners tend to be far less racist than the average white inmate. Therefore, when confronted with evidences of white racism, they have a gnawing desire to attempt to mitigate these expressions of hate."[4]

Alfred Hassler was one of the most perceptive and articulate of the objectors. He remembered his time at West Street and spoke of that "jimcrow institution," where black inmates "must go into one of two specified dormitories no matter how crowded it may be, or how empty one of the others." The races mixed as they walked in line toward the dining room serving tables, but then whites and blacks were routed to separate sections to eat. "When I spoke to the lieutenant about changing things, he said policy was set in Washington and the local authorities could not do a thing."[5]

In fact, however, the practice was not actually policy in the formal, written-down sense. It was a classic case of a custom having been followed so long that it was generally thought to be policy. Before the Bureau of Prisons was created racial segregation had been so solidly in place in society generally that its rightness was not questioned in the several federal prisons. But later, the Bureau leadership became concerned; in 1943 Bennett wrote an advisory memo to his wardens about "the efforts of some of the extremist conscientious objectors to force us to permit indiscriminate intermingling of the white and colored groups." Obviously, he was not anticipating desegregation, but he took a position ahead of most prison practice of that day. He insisted that all living conditions be equal. "The colored men have the same opportunities for work, for vocational training and for recreation as do the whites. . . . They ought to work on the same details. Particularly 'dirty' jobs or poor paying jobs should be equally divided."[6]

The Bureau's conscience on racial issues developed steadily, but slowly; a few years later, staffing decisions reflected an awareness of racism. "Myrl E. Alexander, leading a panel discussion on personnel management at the wardens' conference of 1948, pointed out that Black personnel were employed in only ten institutions and constituted about one percent of the total institutional personnel complement. He called for more active recruitment of minority employees."[7]

Though pressure for change continued to build, even those wardens sympathetic to desegregation remained cautious. Some of the prisons were in the south and surrounded by a social environment hostile to any desegregation efforts. Wardens also were aware of the attitudes of some of their custodial officers who, with sons or other family members in the armed services, resented the war objector prisoners and their viewpoints. Time and the momentum of change on the outside would be required to nudge the prisons toward desegregation. The Supreme Court did not rule against school segregation until nine years after the end of World War II (1954), and it was after that when Rosa Parks sat in the white section of a public bus in Montgomery, Alabama (1955), and Martin Luther King, Jr., picked up that issue and began his crusade. It was still later (1957) when

President Eisenhower sent federal troops to the schools in Little Rock, Arkansas; when Congress passed the Civil Rights Act of 1960; when federal marshals were sent to protect the right of James Meredith to enter the University of Mississippi (1962); and when Governor George Wallace blocked enrollments of blacks at the University of Alabama (1963).

The slow march of these events had its effect as the Bureau of Prisons began a process of desegregation that started with the Supreme Court's school desegregation decision. The move received extra impetus from actions of the Truman administration (from 1948 through 1951) to integrate the military services. Director Bennett prepared a questionnaire in 1954, asking all wardens a series of questions about their racial integration, in terms of dormitory housing, cellblock housing, honor block assignments, hospital beds, recreational activities, work details, educational classrooms, church choirs and services, seating in dining rooms, visiting rooms, and television rooms or auditoriums. He asked the wardens about their efforts to train staff and their plans to complete the integration process. But he made it clear that while the change must be accomplished expeditiously, it must be consistent with safe operation. "I realize on the other hand that there are some deep-seated prejudices which are going to be difficult to overcome, but if the Army and Navy can break down these time-honored distinctions so can we."[8]

In 1956, Frank Loveland, an assistant director, presided at a Bureau conference on the subject. His report afterward showed much progress had been made, though it was uneven and incomplete. Loveland was explicit about giving the Bureau's position. "We need no argument as to whether we are going to proceed with integration. . . . Integration is the policy of the executive branch of our government. We are part of the executive branch and we are proceeding and will proceed to further the integration."[9]

In 1954, just three prisons—Englewood, La Tuna, and Tucson—were fully integrated; by 1956, six more had complied. All others were progressing, but reported that pockets of segregation remained. Some wardens were frustrated in getting their dining rooms integrated because inmates tended to cluster in groups of their own race. This situation changed gradually as dining rooms were remodeled to use smaller tables, and as housing units were desegregated.

The Atlanta penitentiary reported a problem in integrating their baseball team. They had integrated their intramural teams, but had to maintain single-race teams for outside games; other teams would not play against an integrated team. For the most part, integration brought little trouble, often surprising the fearful staffs. A few hostile prisoners were put in punitive segregation or transferred to different institutions, but these were minor problems that soon subsided. No overt disturbances occurred. Resistant staff members presented some problems but with only brief and minor consequences. As one of the men reported in the 1956 meeting, "One of the greatest problems we faced in integration at Texarkana was obtaining cooperation of personnel. However, the warden announced a policy of 'integrate or migrate,' so the matter proceeded without difficulty."

The Bureau also had one memorable chance to be involved in the integration struggle outside of its institutions. During the violent rioting at the University of Mississippi, when James Meredith enrolled there in 1962, the Department of Justice relied mainly on U.S. marshals to keep order. But the furor on the campus got out of hand, and the besieged marshals needed reinforcements. Volunteer correctional officers from Leavenworth and El Reno saw some desperate action as they carried fresh supplies of tear gas and weapons to the scene of the disturbance, through mobs bent on stopping them by any means possible.[10]

Racial discrimination was not the only issue pursued by the war objectors. As Bennett commented in his treatise on the wartime experience, "A few members of this group continued to fight everything except the war." Rebellion seemed to manifest itself in a bewildering variety of ways. "What leads one pacifist to draw the line here and another there, depends entirely on the individual. Many of such prisoners are bewildered and frustrated in their efforts to find a constructive answer to the complex problems of a world in conflict, and finding none, satisfy some inner need through protest and escape from reality." The protests took endlessly varied forms, and staffs were required to be flexible and adaptive. Hunger strikes were common; mostly these were temporary, but sometimes they were so prolonged that tube feeding was necessary. Two prisoners "adopted a non-violent form of protest whenever their requests were denied by lying down on the floor until carried away by prison officers. A few refuse to be vaccinated voluntarily but will submit after protest. One young man declined to drive a farm tractor because it was equipped with rubber tires, but had no objection to using a tractor with steel wheels. Another group refuses to submit to photography because pictures are a form of 'graven image' forbidden by the Bible."

Since the draft did not require females to register, the Selective Service Act violators included virtually no women. However, another act brought females into the system—the May Act prohibiting prostitution in the area of any military base. Most women convicted of this violation were sent to Alderson, and most were the unsophisticated, opportunistic prostitutes who gravitated to bases near their rural homes. Alderson personnel found them to be unsocialized, often even illiterate, "dejected looking creatures, bedraggled, full of vermin, undernourished and frightened." These prisoners brought no militant challenge of policies, but only a pathetic need for social and physical health care.

World War II was the first war during which the United States had its own federal prisons for civilians; thus, for the first time, war objector civilians could be incarcerated separately from military personnel convicted of other offenses. Fortunately, the stressful experience of the previous war—having to mix the two types in military prisons—did not need to be repeated. However, whether in war or peace, military and civilian prison managers always opted for practical cooperation. During World War II, this was seen mainly when the Bureau of Prisons accepted army (and a few navy) personnel who were convicted of serious felonies. Generally, these were men whose crimes disqualified them for further military service, and most of them received fairly long sentences, along with dishonorable discharges. The Bureau had received an average of about forty army prisoners every year until the outbreak of the war, when these commitments began to rise. In the peak year of 1946, the Bureau's institutions received 2,216 army prisoners. Bennett noted that most of these young men had no previous criminal records, yet their sentences averaged fourteen and one-half years. They were persons who, for various reasons, did not adapt to military life; he believed that through their resultant crimes they, themselves, became casualties of war.

Later wars stirred other problems. By 1967, the American public began an anguished appraisal of its involvement in Vietnam, and from then until the nation withdrew from that conflict six years later, persistent social turmoil jeopardized public respect for many of its basic institutions—including prisons. As militance in the streets became endemic, it brought a new militance to the prisons. McNeil Island penitentiary, for instance, had been one of the more orderly federal prisons, but in 1971 the inmates staged a work strike, supported by a noisy crowd on the nearby mainland and by student demonstrators at the University of Washington. Prisoners demanded an end to the censorship of mail, liberalized visiting rules, and elimination of hair and beard restrictions.[11]

The issue of beards and hair length serves to delineate the mood of the times and the complex factors that opposed each other as pressure for policy changes built up. Because beards could substantially change a prisoner's appearance, the Bureau's policy had long been that no beards were allowed. A successful attack on the policy came with the wartime presence of men who were war objectors because of religious beliefs—beliefs that, in some cases, called for beards to be uncut.

Despite the Bureau's refusal to bend on the matter, beards became an issue that would not go away. Finally, in 1972, the Bureau made a small concession and permitted beards for men whose religion clearly required them. At first the rule stipulated that this would apply only to those whose religions and beards were evident when they were admitted to prison. Inevitably, someone already in prison claimed to be converted to a beard-wearing religion, and he wanted to let his beard grow. That soon led to a court decision that the prisons could not properly discriminate between a religion acquired before incarceration and one acquired after incarceration.

The Bureau's response to this, in 1976, was to return to its original position that prohibited beards for anyone, religion notwithstanding. By then, however, the momentum for change was too strong; once again, a prisoner brought a suit; and once again, a court ruled that while the need for security was important, it could not outweigh the First Amendment right of freedom of religion. That concluded the contention; Bureau policy was changed and hair styles and beards were no longer restricted.[12]

At the same time that these aspects of religion were being tested, conflict arose about the basic question of when a religion is a religion.

Prisoners could no longer simply be divided into the categories of Catholic, protestant, and Jewish. As the country's blacks began to win their civil rights battles, they acquired new pride in their cultural identity, and one unexpected result was the sudden popularity of the Black Muslim religion. This development deeply worried wardens, both state and federal, for it came in the context of disturbing events outside the prisons—and these could all too easily come inside. Angry black inmates throughout the prisons demanded the right to hold religious meetings and ceremonies, to eat certain foods, and to receive certain printed religious materials—and all in the name of a strange religion that seemed to the custodians less like a religion than a potential rallying point for disruptive group action.

As the Black Muslims gained definition and strength they took their case to court in the District of Columbia, in 1962. The court agreed that the group's beliefs constituted a religion, but that was only the beginning. More Muslim cases were filed in various jurisdictions, on various points of law, and the Muslims usually succeeded in obtaining the recognition they sought. Many side issues had to be settled. For instance, in one suit, the court ruled that chaplains' reports were not to be submitted for consideration in parole decisions. Other cases had to decide fine points about such issues as reasonable meal times and food preparation. Jewish prisoners brought a case in which the court decided that the Bureau must provide sufficient food to sustain a person in good health without violating dietary law.[13]

In due time, the Black Muslims developed an accepted, settled existence in the prisons; Muslim ministers came in from outside to conduct weekly services, and asterisks on dining room menu boards showed items that met the Muslim dietary requirements.

One maverick "religious" group was not as successful in gaining recognition. In 1970, the Atlanta penitentiary was host to Harry W. Theriault, an ingenious (and sometimes violent) prisoner. Theriault bent a clever mind to the task of formulating his own unique religion, complete with scriptural writings, dietary requirements, ordained church officials, and himself as its head with the title, Bishop of Tellus. While the name he selected—Church of the New Song—had a certain elegance, its commonly used initials—CONS—rather baldly suggested something less than devout seriousness. Theriault gained considerable publicity, especially for his stipulation that the periodic ceremonial meals were to include porterhouse steaks and Harvey's Bristol Cream sherry.[14] The Bureau was not receptive to Theriault's request that it order an initial supply of one hundred bottles of the sherry.

Not surprisingly, virtually all the church's adherents were prisoners, though gradually a few ex-prisoners accumulated to support it from outside. By 1972, the popularity of Theriault's church led him to claim membership of several thousand, with sixteen chapters in various federal prisons, twenty-seven chapters in state prisons, and several in the free world. Former prisoners in Iowa published a periodical, *The Penal Digest International,* to serve the church's interests. Unexpectedly, when Theriault brought suit for recognition of his contrived religion, he actually won the first round. The U.S. District Court, Northern District of Georgia, ruled that CONS should be given the same privileges and proportionate support as other religious groups in the prisons. The Bureau of Prisons deemed it essential to challenge that decision; in 1975, the appellate court reversed the previous decision, stating, "The Church of the New Song appears not to be a religion, but rather as a masquerade designed to obtain First Amendment protection for acts which otherwise would be unlawful." After commenting that the purpose seemed to be to disrupt prison discipline just for the sake of disruption, the court added that "the unmistakable stench of the skunk is found emanating from that which petitioner has declared a rose."[15] Once it was established that CONS enjoyed no official recognition, its membership rapidly dissolved.

One practice, common in the prisons during World War I but later repudiated, was to utilize prisoners for medical research. Atlanta penitentiary inmates were used for many years to study the effects of malaria. More than nine hundred inmate volunteers participated, and the work reputedly resulted in development of a drug to suppress malaria. At both Chillicothe and Atlanta researchers carried out studies of polio; elsewhere they tested prisoners for tolerance of DDT; and at McNeil Island, experiments with hepatitis treatments were conducted. Inmate volunteers received small amounts of money or extra days of "good time." Medical research carried some patriotic cast during the war, and the extent of its general acceptance is suggested by the lack of any noticeable public concern when two

McNeil Island inmates died from the hepatitis with which they were infected.[16]

But times and attitudes change. When the Bureau of Prisons issued a report on its medical research programs in 1960, its tone was one of pride in its contribution to medical science.[17] Ten years later, however, a newly militant generation found much to dislike and oppose in the criminal justice systems, and protesters decried the exploitation of prisoners for medical research.

During the early 1970s, the country's custodians gradually stopped allowing employment of prisoners as research subjects. The change could not be made abruptly, as the various experiments were contracted and had to be phased out, one by one. Accordingly, in 1974, when Congress inquired about the Bureau's research practices, Bureau personnel could report that while a few prisoners were still being monitored in the last stages of certain research projects, policy was in place to prohibit any more such studies.[18] The last research subjects were several prisoner volunteers in a drug addiction research program at Lexington, and this was finally phased out in 1976.[19]

From one war to another, and on into the 1970s, many people remained angry about many issues. The Vietnam War was especially provocative, civil rights issues led to civic disturbances, and prison systems caught their share of fallout from the younger generation's alienation from the "establishment." Some protesters insisted that all prisoners were political prisoners and all prisons should be emptied. Generalized anger and frustration typically seek a target—either tangible or symbolic—and, at times, the prisons served handily; they were highly visible and one was always near at hand. Occasionally, the focus might be narrowed to a one-person target, and at times the Bureau of Prisons director served this purpose. Attacks were usually rhetorical and appeared in the opposition literature, but once, the assault was more ominous. In August 1980, fortunately while the Carlson family was away, three shots were fired into the Carlson home. The assailants also shot at the nearby home of Carlson's executive assistant. Police soon arrested two men, both former federal prisoners; they were convicted of the shooting and returned to federal prison.[20]

EXPERIENCES WITH PROGRAMMING

James Bennett's seventieth birthday, August 11, 1964, was also his last day as director of the Bureau of Prisons. Attorney General Robert Kennedy paid a surprise visit that morning, and several others also came to help Bennett end his career with a complimentary flourish. To give the retirement party the proper festive spirit, the attorney general had brought along a large cake which Bennett was encouraged to cut and serve. The director took knife in hand and proceeded to slice pieces for everyone. And the hilarious high point of the action came when he found baked inside the cake—a hack saw blade!

The *New York Times* editorialized that Bennett was "one of the most far-sighted men in the enforcement of criminal law."[1] Generally, his peers expressed similar sentiments. The informal, private assessment of the few who knew the Bureau intimately was that, in his later years, Bennett was becoming less effective, less innovative, and more concerned with defending his record. That belief was reflected in Kennedy's refusal to grant Bennett's request to extend his time in the job. But to be fair, Bennett's career must be viewed as a whole. Appraisal must include his nearly thirty-five years with the Bureau, when he proved to be a strong leader in a conventional mode, a person of impeccable integrity and sound management ability. He also was notably adept at keeping the respect of key political and bureaucratic figures in Washington.

The day after Bennett's retirement party, a new director took office; Kennedy had persuaded Myrl E. Alexander to return to the Bureau from his new academic career, started three years earlier as head of the Center for Study of Crime, Delinquency, and Corrections at Southern Illinois University at Carbondale. Alexander owed no

214

thanks to Bennett for the appointment, for Bennett was frank about his preference for another long-time Bureau manager and ex-warden. "I did all in my power to have one of my deputies, a fellow named Fred Wilkinson appointed. I told that to the attorney general."

When the attorney general made his own decision to appoint Alexander, the disappointed Bennett saw it as unfortunate evidence of a new interest in education over experience.

> [Wilkinson] didn't have the education, he didn't have a college degree, but he was an excellent administrator. . . . He had come up through the service, he had come up from a guard, up through the ranks, to being a warden, to being my deputy. . . . Mr. Alexander, on the contrary—in contrast, shall I say—had a college degree and he represented, shall I say, the theoretical group. He was all right, and so on, but he had become at that time a professor of criminology, he had retired from the Bureau. I didn't like that because he had walked out on us when he got what he thought was a better job, and then wanted to come back when the climate changed. Fred Wilkinson had stuck with me.[2]

Bennett's comment downplayed too much the solid experience that Alexander had in rising through the ranks. When he was twenty-one years old, Alexander started work as one of Sanford Bates's junior wardens' assistants, serving initially at the Atlanta penitentiary. From then until he retired in 1961, he progressed through a succession of responsible assignments in institutions, in parole and jail services, and as assistant director before he left to teach at the university.

The six years of Alexander's administration are not easily separated from the administration that followed; a continuity of accomplishments spanned the next two decades, without significant interruption. Corrections experts might expect that Alexander's administrative record would reflect the traditional, custody-oriented approach of the conventional prison managers he worked with several decades earlier, but, in fact, he appreciated progressive ideas and worked to liberalize the Bureau's practices and policy. Commenting on his decision to retire at age sixty, Alexander said, "It wouldn't be fair for me to make commitments of the Bureau for years from now and not be around that long. Our whole program of corrections is ready for radical change."[3] It was an honest expression and it reflected the progressive inclinations of three important executives of the time, Attorney General Kennedy, Alexander, and Norman Carlson, Alexander's successor.

During the 1960s, many of the country's correctional systems instituted special treatment programs, in an optimistic hope that the behavioral sciences could diagnose individual criminal cases and devise corrective strategies. It was a time of widespread creative experimenting in rehabilitation.[4] The Bureau of Prisons was not the first to move in innovative directions, and when it finally did, a significant impetus for new strategies came from outside, from the busy mind of the attorney general. Soon after he was appointed in 1961, Kennedy urged the Bureau to plan new approaches to its work, and he offered to find funding to help. Acting on that incentive, Bennett and his staff conceived and implemented three programs that were developed and extended under the Alexander and Carlson administrations. One was a special education project operated at the facility for youthful offenders in Englewood, Colorado. Another, at the National Training School in Washington, was known as the Demonstration Counseling Project, a program for developing correctional officers as counselors. The third was a project to inaugurate prerelease guidance centers, the Bureau's first move into the use of community-based halfway houses.

The latter program started in 1961 with three prerelease guidance centers located in New York City, Chicago, and Los Angeles. Young men, committed as youthful offenders, could be released to these halfway houses during the last three to six months of their prison terms. The number of centers gradually increased when the Prisoner Rehabilitation Act was passed, and in 1965, the plan was extended to adults. After that, the residences were called community treatment centers (CTCs), and Norman Carlson was appointed to head this program. Carlson came to the Bureau in 1957, taking an entry-level job as a counselor at Leavenworth, and later holding a similar position at Ashland.

To Alexander's considerable credit, he was concerned with providing an effective succession, and to this end, he gave Carlson every opportunity to develop professionally. When Alexander retired, the attorney general, John Mitchell, was considering several prospective appointees from outside the Bureau whose names had been supplied by various politicians, but Mitchell, with only a hint from Alexander, made his decision in favor of Carlson.

In 1964, some of the Bureau managers had been disappointed about the administrative transition from Bennett to Alexander. Bennett had tended to promote people on a seniority basis, and when he retired there were some hopeful careerists at hand, some distinguished more by longevity than by brilliance. Alexander's appointment prompted several disappointed people to retire, thinking it was unprofitable to stay and try to adjust to a rather different sort of director. As a result, Alexander was able to fill key posts with younger men and start a process of new professional growth for the Bureau. Six years later, during the transition from Alexander to Carlson the process was distinctly smoother. Carlson, at age thirty-six, was identified particularly with the new community-based program, and brought the likelihood of more new program strategies.

One new penitentiary, a prison at Lompoc, California, was added during Alexander's last year as director. The former army disciplinary barracks at Vandenberg Air Force Base was transferred to the Bureau and was ready to open just a few days after Alexander's retirement. By then, prisoner populations once again were excessive, and the new Carlson administration had to move swiftly to expand prison capacity. In Carlson's first five years as director, he opened six major prisons and several camps.

One significant institutional change was the closing of the National Training School for Boys, in May 1968. The obsolete plant, in a residential area of Washington, soon was sold and condominiums were built on the site. The following January, a sleek, modern new institution for youthful offenders was opened at Morgantown, West Virginia. The Robert F. Kennedy Federal Correctional Institution was the only one of the federal institutions to be named for a person. This facility was, in many respects, the most favored of the federal institutions, with the ultimate in teaching equipment, a handsome chapel, an impressive gymnasium, and a swimming pool—but also a sophisticated concept of classification and treatment programming.

Under its last superintendent, Roy Gerard (who became the first warden at Morgantown), the National Training School implemented dynamic designs for treatment. In addition to the demonstration counseling project, there had been a program called CASE (contingencies applicable to special education), using a token economy in an elaborate system to motivate students toward education. The apparent success of the technique was indicated by tests showing that students advanced an average of nearly one and one-half school years in less than half a year.[5]

As the old institution closed and the new one opened, another innovation developed under the guidance of Dr. Herbert C. Quay, a psychologist from the University of Illinois. Quay designed a system to classify both staff members and inmates, so counselors could be assigned to students in matchings that assured maximum effectiveness. This classification procedure, plus the quality of the academic and vocational education program, made Morgantown the Bureau's showpiece. Furthermore, the need for the facility was urgent, because, in addition to the NTSB, the Bureau also closed Chillicothe, the reformatory that Mabel Walker Willebrandt had promoted so earnestly. In 1966, the Chillicothe facility was vacated and transferred under a lease to the state of Ohio. It had been a richly programmed, vibrant part of the Bureau's resources for young offenders, but its physical plant was not designed for the style of operation and the demands made on it in later years. Its young and volatile inmates were hard to control under crowded conditions, with about half of the population housed in packed, open dormitories. After the reformatory closed, the youthful offenders went mainly to the newer institutions at Englewood and Ashland.

Easily the most significant institution to be planned during the Alexander administration was the facility that struggled into existence on the site of a former prisoner of war camp, near the small town of Butner, North Carolina. Its development became a case study in the politics of correctional planning during a time of social stress. In fact, the intensity of the controversy nearly aborted the institution.

The idea to establish Butner started with Bennett, who decided the system needed a prison with psychiatric services to diagnose and treat disturbed, unpredictably violent prisoners. During Bennett's last three years, congressional authorization was received, and the site was acquired. Years of delay followed before sufficient funds were appropriated to equal the increasing construction cost estimates. Meanwhile, the original concept of the institution was reconsidered, and it evolved into a plan for a research center to study methods of treating offenders with personality disorders. The Bureau had fostered several smaller research projects, including one at Chillicothe to study psychopaths.[6] The Butner scheme seemed a natural extension of these efforts—an entire institution devoted to this sort of laudable purpose. But the events that occurred over the next few years seemed to confirm the so-called principle that says, "If anything can go wrong it will."

By the time Carlson took office in 1970, a new appropriation was on hand; plans for the institution were completed, and in late 1972, a construction contract was let. Building did start, but suffered endless delays. Finally, in May 1976, the institution was ready to be dedicated. The programmatic plans proved to be especially provocative. With the best of intentions, the Bureau had planned to conduct research to diagnose disruptive behavior types and to devise corrective therapy. But the name originally chosen for the institution—The Center for Behavioral Research—generated intense opposition to the facility. While Bureau officials knew that the research would be on *program methods*—not on *people*—many disaffected outsiders did not believe this and took an extremely negative view. At that time the public was extremely sensitive to anything that might suggest racism. The opposition started with the fact that blacks were represented disproportionately in prison populations, and critics argued loudly that the Bureau of Prisons must be planning to use surgery, drugs, brainwashing, and hypnosis on helpless black offenders.

The illusion was strengthened by the selection of the first warden, Dr. Martin Groder, a psychiatrist who had been well regarded on the staff at Marion, where he created the Asklepieion treatment program. Groder, already in North Carolina to hire staff and plan the programming, underestimated the intensity of the opposition and proved to be more scrappy than reassuring. When the church-based Commission on Racial Justice (from New York) sounded a national alarm about the ominous plans for Butner, it was soon apparent that the new prison was in trouble—even before it opened. Groder invited members of the Commission on Racial Justice and other interested groups to meet with him at Butner. They accepted, but the results were far different than Groder expected. When they came, in February 1974, the critics were in no mood to listen to rational explanations; they wanted only to provoke more publicity for their angry opposition.

The politics of the situation demanded change—a change of name and a change in the basic program plans. An inevitable side effect was a change also of warden. The Bureau was unable to persuade Groder to accept the modified planning and directed him to transfer to Springfield. At that point, in March 1975, Groder publicly criticised the Bureau—and then resigned.[7]

The institution suffered one more setback. Following Groder's resignation, the Bureau appointed an educator from headquarters to be the next warden. He proved to be the reassuring, diplomatic sort who could calm the hostile outside groups, but he was inept in the main task of administering the institution. With staff and program in a disorganized condition, the warden resigned. He was replaced in 1977 by a third appointee, and under him the institution grew to be effective in its specialized function.

Altogether, it was a deeply frustrating gestation for the institution, but it may have been the better for it. Much of its programmatic design was derived from ideas of Norval Morris, a University of Chicago law school professor whose humane concepts were in sharp contrast to the popular fears of forced behavior control. In a soundly reasoned book, Morris asserted that prisoners cannot be forcibly rehabilitated; they can be helped only when they volunteer to be involved. Repetitively violent prisoners being sent to Butner, Morris argued, should go only voluntarily in the first place, and once there should have the option of leaving the treatment program after ninety days.[8]

A relaxing, normalizing factor at Butner, as prescribed by Morris, was that prisoners could move easily and freely among the buildings and in the open landscaped areas between. The principal custodial restraint was in the perimeter, where double fencing, electronic detectors, and roving patrols were a sufficient bar to escape. Following Morris' suggestions, a high proportion of women were included on the staff, and staff training emphasized that the prisoners should be allowed to express their hostile feelings freely, to anyone, as long as they did not take any assaultive action. Finally and importantly, the name of the institution was changed to avoid any suggestion of behavior research; it became simply another correctional institution. Nevertheless, Butner was recognized worldwide as an innovative prison concept, and it attracted a continuous stream of impressed visitors from other correctional systems.

The institution plan proved to be a valid concept for therapeutic management of disturbed prisoners. Considering the disruptive potential of this type of prisoner, the facility operated with surprisingly few problems. In addition to its usual population of committed prisoners, Butner also served federal courts in the east by accepting defendants referred for temporary holding and clinical study, to enable the courts to make sound sentencing decisions.[9]

Butner was not the only institution under attack by outsiders who saw sinister "thought control" intentions in the Bureau's treatment programming. It was a time when behavior modification techniques offered intriguing hopes to corrections programmers, but when others were strenuously opposed on principle. As the foundations were laid for the Butner institution, the hospital prison at Springfield saw the inception of an experimental program intended to rehabilitate particularly unmanageable prisoners. The program, initiated in October 1972, was called START (special treatment and rehabilitative training); it was conducted in a separate, self-contained housing unit and was limited to twenty or fewer inmates, selected on the basis of their persistently disruptive behaviors. The plan was to house these men separately from the general prison population, in a unit where improved behavior was encouraged by increasing privileges and providing daily group counseling.[10] But the program drew intense criticism because its strategy was to start each prisoner with virtually no privileges, a condition critics asserted was punishment, not therapy. They also complained that the selected prisoners were coerced into participation.

In a report on the general subject, Senator Sam J. Ervin, Jr., reflected both congressional and popular concern when he observed, "To my mind the most serious threat posed by the technology of behavior modification is the power this technology gives one man to impose his views and values on another." Other testimony on the same occasion criticized the Bureau's projects because they were conducted "under guidelines and procedures which are ineffective at best. . . . The Department of Justice has made virtually no effort either to provide the necessary monitoring of research projects or to resolve important questions relating to individual liberties."[11]

Due both to the relentless criticisms from without and various operational problems within, the Bureau discontinued the START program after sixteen months—but not before the National Prison Project of the ACLU took court action to oppose it. The suit alleged that while the Bureau called the program therapy, the effect of placement in the program was, in fact, punishment; inmates should be entitled to a hearing before they were assigned and should have the right to refuse the treatment. When the program was closed, many of the points in the suit became moot, but the court agreed with the plaintiffs that "the selection and transfer of a prisoner into a future behavior modification type of program patterned on START . . . should be and is hereby declared a violation of the law as guaranteed by the Fifth Amendment to the Constitution."[12]

The Bureau's experiences with Butner and START coincided with new research into correctional treatment programs that seemed to prove such therapeutic techniques yielded no provable benefits.[13] But the attacks on research designs and behavior modification programs were just part of the Bureau's many-sided problems with the intense social issues of the 1970s. Carlson came into the director's job just in time for the general social ferment to make him the Bureau's most controversial leader. Ironically, this did not reflect any radical quality in his administration; rather, it was the result of his very orthodoxy in a time when radical rethinking of correctional philosophy put orthodoxy on the defensive. Carlson's job was to run the government's prisons, and this meant building additional facilities as they were needed to meet the demand—and that was the heart of the problem.

The movement against prison construction actually started within conventional circles, advocated by experienced corrections leaders who urged a first use of all feasible alternatives. In 1973, the National Advisory Commission on Criminal Justice Standards and Goals, funded by the Law Enforcement Assistance Administration (LEAA), issued a report that recommended, "Each correctional agency should adopt immediately a policy of not building new major institutions . . . unless an analysis of the total criminal justice and correctional systems produced a clear finding that no alternative is possible."[14]

This concept was soon picked up by other groups. These groups were consultative or advisory organizations, not operational agencies, and as such they could afford to be militant in advocating alternatives.

The result was the development of a general movement recognized as the National Moratorium on Prison Construction (NMPC). The respected National Council on Crime and Delinquency (NCCD)—founded more than half a century earlier as the National Probation Association—was the most prominent of the several agencies that promoted the moratorium. After 1972, through its director, Milton G. Rector, the NCCD opposed the Bureau of Prisons on two points; it argued that construction of new institutions should be halted, and it urged the Bureau to encourage and use improved state corrections services, rather than pursue its own construction plans. The term moratorium did not mean that prisons should be eliminated; it meant that alternative measures should be pursued first, and new construction should be a last resort.[15]

The most prominent, and most energetic, of the groups allied with the NCCD was the Unitarian Universalist Services Committee, a group that was aggressive in opposing the Bureau's expansion and in discrediting Carlson personally; the group attacked him "because he is 'always ready to do the will of Congress'; . . . because he is a consummate bureaucrat who will always blow with the prevailing wind."[16]

The most visible event in the moratorium campaign was its opposition to constructing what became the federal correctional institution at Ray Brook, New York. The 1980 Winter Olympics were scheduled to be held at nearby Lake Placid, and the United States needed to contrive housing for the visiting athletes. In the interests of economy the government proposed to build a prison that could be used first for Olympic housing and afterward revert to its permanent purpose. Government planners saw the idea as admirable economy, while the moratorium agencies saw it as an opportunity to exploit a rallying point. Moratorium advocates mounted a tremendous campaign around the slogan "STOP the Olympic Prison!" The issues involved became mixed as moratorium advocates, whose true rationale was that no more prisons should be built, advanced the idea that the United States was insulting the athletes by offering to house them in a prison. The issue seethed through 1978 and 1979, while the NMPC urged United Nations member countries to boycott the games if the prison plan was not canceled.[17]

The campaign generated heated rhetoric for months, but neither

Congress nor the Bureau management was influenced; the campaign did not impede the prison plans. On schedule, as soon as the games were over, the Bureau completed construction details on the new facility at Ray Brook, and it opened as a prison in January 1981.

The 1970s witnessed the unfortunate drama of highly principled and genuinely humane men and women—motivated to serve the public good—working to defeat each other's efforts because they held differing views on how best to solve the social problem that engaged their hopes and energies. Carlson stayed steadily on his course, maintaining a well-managed prison system with the most constructive impact possible on its inmates; the several leaders of the moratorium movement thoughtfully but uncompromisingly opposed the Bureau's building program while they called for what they believed to be workable and more civilized alternatives. In the end, the moratorium was defeated—not by Carlson and the Bureau, but by the overwhelming statistics of crime. As one of the most astute moratorium leaders observed, crimes and convictions climbed so excessively during the 1970s that "a national hysteria about crime and criminals was born and many legislatures, prosecutors and judges responded to democratic pressures with more certain and more punitive prison sentences. . . . In this hysterical stampede, the moratorium movement was trampled to death."[18]

In all fairness, Bureau of Prisons managers took no pleasure in seeing the prisoner population grow and the list of prisons expand. New prison construction was driven by relentless social trends that neither Carlson nor the moratorium leaders could thwart. And just as the increasingly punitive public attitudes forced the building of more prisons, the negative appraisals of treatment programs forced a permanent change in the Bureau's approach to rehabilitation.

The result was not to discontinue treatment efforts, but to stop coercive imposition of treatment on anyone. The healthy new philosophy was framed by Carlson in a directive to the wardens. "We are not abandoning our efforts to assist inmates. What we are doing is abandoning the 'medical model' which implied that we had the ability to diagnose and treat criminal behavior. In a real sense the 'new philosophy' will require that we develop more and better programs if we hope to interest inmates in helping themselves."[19]

While Congress generally supported the Bureau's goals and management, the relationship was sometimes strained during the antigovernment militance of the Vietnam era. Early in Carlson's tenure, the Berrigan brothers made themselves highly visible at Danbury, stridently criticizing the way they were treated there and attracting the anxious attention of Congressman Ronald V. Dellums, who demanded the right to go to Danbury and investigate. The Bureau managers believed they had the right to administer the system without interference and felt that allowing a hostile congressman to visit and investigate was too much like surrendering control. However, Carlson decreed that the Bureau, as a servant of the public, must be open to critical inspection by Congress. But that did not imply the agency was giving up its right—in fact, its responsibility—to administer as it saw fit. Accordingly, Dellums was free to visit the prison and to talk to whomever he chose. No repercussions resulted; instead, the controversy was effectively defused.

Carlson's tenure also was noted for certain other attitudes that, in some respects, seem picayune, but they were significant. For instance, he laid an unrelenting emphasis upon sanitation as a basic aspect of good property maintenance and decent treatment of prisoners. Federal prisons became models of clean, well-managed physical plants, and the attitude extended itself to promote pride of good management in all other operational areas. Carlson was sharply critical of the old tendency of institution staffs to take advantage of the "perks," a practice that had drifted into outright corruption in some state systems. Wardens were told they could not use government automobiles, except for official business; wardens and other staff no longer could use inmate servants, and this edict of "no house-boys" became a sort of signature rule with the Carlson directorship. The rule was part of an overall emphasis on professional, efficient management and high personal integrity as standards for wardens and other managers.

A similar issue concerned the use of staff dining rooms. Carlson favored the idea that prison personnel must be constantly involved with inmates; good and safe prison management called for staff to be available to inmates and to avoid a "we-they" attitude. The prison at Butner was the first to be designed without a staff dining room, and after that, all new federal prisons were built with dining areas where staff and inmates could come together to eat without distinction.

Many persons observed that visitors coming to a modern federal prison found it difficult to distinguish inmates from staff. The staff members, however, always knew, and the overall effect was to promote a relaxed, comfortable quality of life—one that resulted in safer prisons.

Finally, one Carlson policy of some broad significance was the attitude of easy cooperation with state correctional systems. Frequently, states have emergencies when sometimes quite large groups of inmates must be moved out quickly. Sometimes, too, a single inmate becomes too difficult for a small state system to handle. And, other times, a state needs impartial outside help with planning or troubleshooting. Carlson was invariably helpful. He believed that the federal system was a servant of the public, and it should not hesitate to help states with their stickier problems.

Carlson constantly imparted this attitude to the federal wardens; it was, in fact, well accepted by them and was possibly the outstanding evidence of the Bureau's maturity as a model system.

12

DIVERSIFICATION
AND EXPANSION

In September 1971, the state prison at Attica, New York, erupted with its famous and tragic riot. Smaller disturbances were triggered by it at other institutions, including a noisy one a few days later at the women's prison at Alderson. That incident led to an exciting new experience for the Bureau of Prisons—the inauguration, under conditions of severe stress, of a new institution mixing both male and female prisoners in its population.

Although the states had housed men and women in the same penal institutions since their beginnings, the practice had never been a matter of integration; the two sexes were kept apart, in separate sections. J. Ellen Foster was adamant about the importance of this separation (chapter 5), and her view reflected the general orthodox attitude. Other than the high-security female unit that operated at Milan, the only other example of co-correctional operation within the federal system was the prison at Terminal Island, California, where, from 1000 to 1977, the Bureau operated a small unit for women within the grounds, but quite segregated from the main institution.

By 1970, the Bureau was aware of some experience with mixed-sex institutions in other countries and was making careful plans to try the idea. Two prisons were picked as the first sites for the co-correctional experiment. One was the new youth facility at Morgantown, and the other was a soon-to-be-opened institution at Fort Worth, Texas. The plan started in the spring of 1971, when several carefully selected younger women from Alderson were quietly and uneventfully placed at Morgantown. As planned and hoped, the women settled into the arrangement uneventfully. By contrast, the Forth Worth opening a few months later was a baptism of fire.

The bitter outburst at Alderson in late September necessitated the immediate move of some of the most rebellious women. A bus was loaded with forty-five of the most disruptive inmates, and, after a one month stop-over in Seagoville, the women, still angry and noisy, were delivered to Fort Worth. There the Bureau was just finishing the conversion of a large hospital complex it had acquired from the U.S. Public Health Service.

Fortunately the warden had the needed understanding and skill; he welcomed the challenge.

> It provided a dramatic illustration of how much people are inclined to respond according to the way they are treated, as well as a compelling demonstration of the powerful influence of expectations. We had no reasonable choice but to tell these women we needed their help, that a large share of responsibility for the co-correctional experiment would be resting on their shoulders. Apprehensive though we were, we behaved toward them as if we couldn't have been more delighted to have them. Forty-five rowdy, foulmouthed women responded to this treatment magnificently. We had some tense and difficult times then and during the months thereafter, but to observe the growth of these women in dignity and self-respect was a tremendously gratifying experience.[1]

Over the next few years the Bureau refined its experience with co-corrections, extending the plan to other institutions and operating them with an emphasis upon casual, normal living. Inmates who tried any intimacy beyond hand holding could expect that both would be transferred to one-sex institutions. Not surprisingly, women sometimes became pregnant, but the Bureau's calm response was that, while these cases were unfortunate, many more pregnancies would have occurred if the inmates were outside.

In addition to the Morgantown and Fort Worth institutions, those at Lexington, Kentucky, and Pleasanton, California, also were mixed for several years. Morgantown reverted to a single-sex mode in 1975, but again began to accept females in 1981. The other three facilities also reverted in later years, in response to changing population pressures within the system.

Female prisoners were also affected by a policy change during the 1950s that related to those who deliver babies while incarcerated. In the first thirty or so years of its existence, Alderson regularly permitted inmate mothers to keep babies born there. After that practice was discontinued, newborn babies were sent to family members or put into the temporary custody of welfare agencies; new programming was developed to allow generous visiting opportunities for families that brought children. In the 1960s, the "Sesame Street" program started, with long visiting hours for the adults and supervised playroom space for the children. A privately operated hospitality house in the community accommodated visiting families, providing overnight lodging and transportation to the institution.

One aspect of the Alderson experience points up the Bureau's cooperative relationship with nonfederal jurisdictions. In its earlier history, in regard to its criminal defendants, the District of Columbia was treated as a federal jurisdiction. The attorney general was responsible for its jails and its inmates, as much as he was for any other federal prisoners. A series of developments early in the current century gradually gave the District its own correctional system, but did not remove it entirely from some degree of dependence on the federal prison system.

The District's first separate facility for women came when it acquired property near the towns of Occoquan and Lorton, in nearby Virginia. The District opened a workhouse for men in 1910, and two years later, on adjoining property, opened a workhouse for women. In 1966, a court decision that public intoxication should be treated as a public health problem resulted in such a decrease in workhouse populations that these facilities were reorganized and combined as an alcoholic rehabilitation center.[2] Most of the women felons were accepted by the Bureau of Prisons and transferred to Alderson.[3] The remaining women were removed first to a cellblock at the D.C. jail and later to the Women's Detention Center on North Capital Street, in Washington. At a later date, in response to a civil suit, an agreement with the District of Columbia Board of Corrections specified the terms on which the D.C. women could be placed in other federal facilities for women, even though this would sometimes mean placing them at a distance from their homes in Washington.[4]

Many of the District's male prisoners were also regularly placed in federal prisons. When the District opened its new reformatory at Lorton, in 1916, the first prisoners admitted were sixty D.C. men who were transferred from Leavenworth, and fifteen men moved from Atlanta. After that, in most cases the District housed its own male prisoners. After the Federal Youth Corrections Act was enacted in 1950, however, youthful offenders were sent to the federal system. Eventually, age, overcrowding, and poor management of the District's institutions prompted some critics to insist that the Bureau of Prisons take over the District's penal system. Carlson was firmly opposed. However, to relieve the situation, he agreed to take into the federal system those men convicted of U.S. Code violations (as opposed to D.C. Code violations). "This means an annual increase of approximately 500 adult males coming into the Bureau of Prisons in addition to females and YCA cases we have been taking over the past several years."[5]

The Bureau's position had long been that it should take prisoners from nonfederal jurisdictions only in cases of special need. Sometimes prisoners were accepted because they were in danger, or because they themselves were dangerous, or because they were escape-prone. Some of the more violent prisoners at Marion were these state "boarders." Similarly, the Bureau sometimes found reason to board out certain federal prisoners to selected state facilities.

At times, the Bureau accepted sizable groups of prisoners in response to crises; for example, 348 state prisoners were transferred to Bureau facilities following the disastrous riot at the New Mexico penitentiary, in February 1980. The most fateful and demanding influx of prisoners, however, resulted from the impulsive hegira of something more than 125,000 Cubans who fled their country through the fishing port of Mariel, in 1980. As the "Marielitos" arrived in Florida, the Immigration and Naturalization Service (INS) screened them hurriedly and separated out those who should be incarcerated as apparent criminal offenders. The procedure was uncertain and difficult because the INS had no records and the screening had to be accomplished entirely through interviews. In the original processing more than two thousand probable offenders were identified and routed to federal prisons. The dilemma was deeply disturbing for a country that sets high standards for civil rights; the imprisonment of people who had committed no crimes here, and whose crimes elsewhere were not proven here by any due process procedure, was tolerated only because no alternative seemed possible. The penitentiary at Atlanta soon had nearly fifteen hundred Cubans, while at least seventeen hundred more were in various other federal prisons.

In 1984, Fidel Castro relented in his determination to be rid of the troublemakers and agreed to allow nearly twenty-eight hundred of them to return to Cuba. An airlift was organized, but after five planeloads (a total of 201 prisoners) had gone to Cuba, propaganda broadcasts from Radio Marti in Florida so angered Castro that he cut off the return flow.

The Marielitos dilemma was gradually resolved. The INS continued to screen the Cubans, and most were released; eventually about one hundred people were retained with no prospect of release. Two different categories of Marielitos were defined in the federal prisons. One was made up of "prisoners"—those who committed new crimes after they were released and who were back inside serving sentences imposed by courts here. The other group comprised "detainees"—persons held because the INS considered them too dangerous to be released. Often inmates who completed their sentences as prisoners were kept in custody as detainees because it was deemed too risky to release them. In these cases, detention or release was decided upon by a panel appointed by the attorney general for that purpose. Altogether, the numbers remained high; in the late 1980s, about thirty-five hundred were in the prisoner category, and about twenty-five hundred were in the detainee category. The situation was constantly fluid; most of the Marielitos were distributed among federal facilities, but many were housed in state or local institutions.

Though the United States made the difficult decision in 1891 to build its own prisons for federal offenders, federal jails were a different matter. The Bureau of Prisons did not construct a true modern jail until 1974. One important aspect was the utilization of appropriate urban sites. Instead of being located on out-of-town sites, like Milan, the new generation of jails appeared in midtown locations, adjacent to, or conveniently near, the busiest federal courts. The extremely limited ground space available at these locations dictated high-rise buildings of twelve to fourteen storeys. Radical new designs included unobtrusive custodial features that avoided the usual steel grills and clanging doors. Most prisoners were housed in individual rooms, grouped in units of manageable size; each unit had its own spaces for visiting, eating, and staff counseling. The architects made a point of giving the living spaces attractive colors and design.

The first of these unique jails (called metropolitan correctional centers) was opened in San Diego, in late 1974, and others opened the following year in New York and Chicago. At the same time, the obsolete West Street jail in New York was closed. Typically, the new facilities were built to house about five hundred inmates, both men and women. They served a true jail function, taking primarily pre-trial or unsentenced federal prisoners. Usually the only exception was a small maintenance cadre of sentenced prisoners, assigned there on a longer term basis, to tend to maintenance. At the same time, the system always needed additional quasi-jail type space for a variety of detention requirements. Prisoners in transit or others who needed to be held temporarily, were kept in several of the regular correctional institutions, designated as federal detention centers. In such institutions management operated a separate wing or cellblock as the detention facility, and among its prisoners were the typical pre-trial cases, held there in the absence of a federal jail in that area.

The Bureau adopted the new jail designs as part of a general new approach to prison planning, in the 1970s. Designers wished to break from the traditional prison architecture, with its massive, impersonal cellblocks, and instead to develop designs that would enhance privacy and bring more warmth and human feeling into the hard prison atmosphere. But the architecture was only part of the radical departure from traditional jail operations. Small industrial shops were also installed in the metropolitan correctional centers. Inmates were allowed to stay out of their cells during the day to work in the shops or participate in other activities, as is typical in regular prisons. Such efforts to soften and normalize the environment proved highly desirable and were soon copied by other corrections planners. After that, all of the Bureau's new facilities were designed with less obtrusive security features, smaller living units to facilitate the use of the unit management plan, and more use of wood and attractive colors.

From time to time, the Bureau of Prisons has taken some ribbing for its "country-club" prisons, the prison camps where, presumably, the prominent white-collar offenders serve their time in relaxed, open settings. But, in fact, most of these prisoners are the usual unknown, ordinary offenders, though not assaultive or escape-prone types.[6] Indeed the minimum custody camps easily incite the scorn of those who presume that all prisoners need and deserve a taste of "durance vile," and that minimum security camps are the ultimate in coddling of prisoners. However, the Bureau of Prisons, while receiving many of the most criminalistic and dangerous of the country's offenders, also receives many who are in no degree escape risks, but are stable, reliable workers. Such inmates do not need expensive high-security prisons. Throughout this century, federal prisons have been hosts to former governors (at least nine), mayors, ex-congressmen, judges, and other government officials. The Watergate scandal resulted in one of the most ironic of these cases, that of John Mitchell, the attorney general who appointed Norman Carlson as director of the Bureau of Prisons. In 1975, following his conviction for conspiracy to obstruct justice, Mitchell became one of Carlson's prisoners and was placed in the federal prison camp at Montgomery, Alabama. Mitchell was assigned as a clerk in the law library and always was a helpful and cooperative inmate.

A review of their operating costs reveals the substantial economic advantage of having these open camps. In 1987, the annual cost per inmate in four of the typical minimum custody camps averaged less than eight thousand dollars, while that cost for four of the maximum security institutions averaged nearly twelve thousand dollars. The contrast is further enhanced by the greatly reduced initial construction costs of the camps. When the first camps were acquired early in the Bates administration, they were particularly cheap, with minimal construction and few amenities. The facilities were oriented to very basic work opportunities, such as "constructing or repairing roads; clearing, maintaining, and reforesting public lands; building levees." In some cases the camps could be moved to new locations, according to work requirements. "Most of the living quarters were surplus army tents and temporary buildings constructed from whatever materials could be found."[7]

By 1938, the Bureau reorganized the camps into a system, with physical improvements, coordinated management, more exacting qualifications for staff, and such advantages as social services, classification, and educational programs.[8] In more recent years, the living conditions were upgraded by the addition of permanent and comfortable buildings, while cost savings were still gained by locating many of the camps adjacent to the major correctional institutions so they could share utilities and maintenance.

During the 1960s and 1970s, rapid growth of the federal prison system and an ever-widening variety of institutional and community programs necessitated improved management methods, including regionalization, unit management, and greatly improved staff training.

For overall government purposes, the federal Office of Management and Budget (OMB) divided the country into ten regions, and in 1973, some of the Bureau's central office staff proposed that the Bureau should also regionalize, in order to bring management closer to the widely scattered institutions. Carlson agreed to try the idea and so a pilot region was set up in the south-central area, based in Dallas. With positive reactions from the wardens after one year of experience with this, Carlson went ahead with the full plan. However, the ten OMB regions were considered too many for the Bureau's purpose, so they were combined to make five regions, based in Dallas, Kansas City, Atlanta, Philadelphia, and San Francisco. Thereafter, each regional office employed a manager and other specialists to supervise their institutions and community programs.

Another development of special importance was unit management, an idea instituted in the 1960s to facilitate internal institutional operations. The earliest form of unit management was in the demonstration counseling project at NTSB, where each housing unit developed an interdisciplinary staff team to manage its cottage and inmate group. Soon afterward, the plan was tried at Englewood; then, the new institution at Morgantown was designed especially to utilize the unit management concept. One by one, other institutions adopted the plan until eventually it was in effect and well accepted throughout the system.

In implementing unit management, "the essential components of a unit are a small number of inmates (50 to 120) who are permanently assigned together and a multidisciplinary staff (unit manager, case manager(s), correctional counselor(s), full- or part-time psychologist, and clerk-typist) whose offices are located adjacent to the inmate housing unit, and who are permanently assigned to work with the inmates of that unit."[9] The staff generally accepted this plan and agreed that it usefully divided inmate populations into manageable groups, with a sense of group identity; it increased the frequency of staff/inmate contacts, allowing earlier detection of incipient problems; it enhanced understanding of case dynamics and fostered responsive prisoner management in general by utilizing a combination of staff disciplines and shared professional attitudes. Its value became evident when state prison systems borrowed extensively from the idea.

Record keeping in the 1980s became a sophisticated process that would have amazed the pre-Bureau wardens who had to use inmate clerks even to process inmate records. With over forty institutions and more than fifty thousand inmates, the Bureau of Prisons would have been virtually unmanageable without a computer-operated system to store and retrieve information. Installed in 1977 and named "Sentry," the system was developed to track all inmates and to contain the data necessary to make case decisions. The capability to make initial institution assignments, for instance, was a primary requirement. Personal and demographic data was entered for each new inmate, and the system was programmed to indicate to which security level and to which institution that person should be assigned. In addition to the initial placement decision (which, of course, management staff could override in special cases), Sentry served to expedite the continuing classification process. The system was even used to maintain the voluminous information needed to plan expenditures, prepare budgets, and facilitate communication between all units of the system.

Classification and placements within the system included one unique category of inmates, those under the "witness protection" program. Witness protection was similar to, but not the same as, "protective custody" sections commonly found in state prisons. Usually, the ordinary protective custody inmates were handled in the federal system by being shifted, as necessary, among the various institutions. But the Bureau received a number of prisoners who had informed against members of gangs or organized criminal groups and were in danger of reprisals. In 1966, a crime commission appointed by President Johnson recommended that the Department of Justice develop "safe houses," to shelter and protect persons who were in serious jeopardy as witnesses. The idea was further spurred by the passage of the Organized Crime Control Act of 1970.[10] At the same time, the Bureau set aside part of one floor at the metropolitan correctional center in New York City, as the first protective unit for witnesses who were prisoners. Other units were established at the prisons in Otisville, New York, and Sandstone, Minnesota. Finally, the first new building designed especially for that purpose was included as part of the facility opened in Phoenix in 1985. The witness protection units were self-contained, so that these prisoners never mingled with general population prisoners. Entrance vestibules were equipped with one-way windows so that that prisoners could inspect and identify visitors before they were admitted. Prisoners who asked for this type of protection were screened carefully before they were assigned and the process included a polygraph test. Such measures were essential to be sure of the applicant's motives, in order to keep out anyone who wanted only to get access to someone he intended to harm. Inside the units, the general practice was for the inmates to use only their initials, rather than their names. The program was successful in preventing assaults; by 1987, about four hundred prisoners had been through the witness protection units, and no prisoner so protected had been attacked.

A heightened concern for victims was an issue closely related to the witness protection program. In 1984, when Congress passed the Victims of Crime Act, the Bureau responded with its "inmate financial responsibility program," a computerized method to track all inmate obligations for fines, restitution, or family support. Fully implemented in early 1987, the system collected an impressive amount of money from inmates' earnings in order to enforce their obligations. The Bureau also developed procedures to notify any relevant witness or victim about the release or furlough of a prisoner.

The extension and upgrading of staff training was as important as any other instrument for improving the system. When Jesse Stutsman started the staff training school in New York in 1930 (chapter 6), it was a hopeful and significant step in professionalizing the service, but, unfortunately the program was aborted by Stutsman's death and by limited funds. Subsequently, the Bureau tried to inaugurate staff training in several of its institutions, starting at Lewisburg. By the late 1930s, six of the prisons were designated as regional training centers.[11] At first, these served only correctional officers, but the training was soon expanded and by 1940 included courses for cooks, bakers, shop foremen, and clerical personnel. In 1949, a new course,

"Advanced Training for Experienced Employees," began at the El Reno Reformatory. These efforts contributed to the quality of staff, but progress often was frustrating and difficult. Training was conducted in the prisons, where exigencies of work with high prisoner populations competed heavily for the time of the trainees, and it was impossible to guarantee they would complete the prescribed courses. It became essential to plan a separate central training center. [12]

In 1970, the Bureau attempted to establish a training center with residential facilities. El Reno was picked as the site because it was centrally located and because it had a building that could be adapted for classroom purposes. There the Bureau began to shape the curriculum to provide systematic training for all job classes, rather than for corrections officers only.

The El Reno program proved to be a good beginning for a comprehensive residential training center, but the experience showed the need for a better location and better facilities. At El Reno, trainees were housed in motels, and they had to provide for their own meals. There were no recreational opportunities, and community attitudes sometimes presented problems for minority trainees. The Bureau tried to provide parts of the training at other sites, but finally, the search for a satisfactory training center ended at the small Atlantic coast site of Glynco, Georgia, where the Treasury Department had taken over a former naval air station. The facility had been developed into a training center for federal agencies that had law enforcement functions; in 1982, the Bureau became one of the participating groups and it used the center to provide basic training for all its personnel. The plan was to have all new employees, even office personnel, come to the center within forty-five days of their being hired and take the three-week basic instruction course. The program included physical self-defense and firearms use, as well as more academic subjects in human relations and philosophy of corrections. The approach pointedly avoided the custody versus treatment dichotomy that has long made a problem in prison management, and instead was designed to develop corrections generalists who could work closely in team relationships.

The Glynco Training Academy brought most staff training into one place. Though the center conducted specialized training courses (prison industries operations, locksmithing, personnel management, and others), the Bureau also conducted a few specialty courses elsewhere. Oxford, Wisconsin, hosted the food service training; management and supervision training was located at Aurora, Colorado; Fort Worth, Texas, supplied training in commissary operations and inmate accounts.

The availability of work for all employable prisoners was always a crucial element of improving prisons. After the earlier prison industries controversies, the Bureau's industrial shops of the 1980s were efficient, highly productive, and well accepted. By the time Alexander came to the administrative post, the issue of competition was mostly resolved, and he could concentrate on modernizing the shops and seeking improved marketing techniques. To this end, Alexander instituted product research and equipment replacement planning. But where the Bureau had faced resentment from private industry in the 1930s, it faced a different sort of resentment in the 1970s; the general "anti-establishment" unrest of those times brought the country's prisons their full share of critical opposition. When several work strikes occurred in federal prison shops, one articulate critic asserted that "the injustice of paying pitifully low wages while [federal prison industries] earns large profits is apparent to all prisoners, and is an issue in virtually every strike."[13] As the militant unrest in the streets subsided so did the prison work strikes, with almost none occurring in the 1980s.

At times the Bureau was criticized because the industries were not designed to train inmates for employment outside, and that could be a valid point if the industries were intended, in fact, to provide such training. One critic, previously quoted, complained, "Whatever may have been its original intentions, work and training as supplied by FPI has little to do with providing benefits for prisoners. As presently constituted, its function is to serve the interests of the federal prison bureaucracy."[14] The key point to note in considering this charge is that, while the *bureaucracy* does make some profit (using profits to capitalize new industrial shops as new prisons are built), *bureaucrats* as individuals do not profit. The Bureau never attempted to justify prison industries as trade training, beyond the hoped-for intangible benefit of practice in good work habits. When Carlson reported extensively on the industries in a congressional hearing, he made no mention of the idea of trade training. He believed that the industries were justified for their contribution to the stability and good order of prison operation. "Without viable work programs, the Federal Bureau of Prisons would quickly become unmanageable."[15]

At that time, the Bureau took steps to modernize industry marketing strategies, by adopting a new name and a new logo to simplify the program's identity and sharpen its image. In 1978, the corporation renamed itself *Unicor*. It was widely diversified, well managed, and—in accord with its critics' accusations—profitable. The industries not only paid wages to prisoner employees, but, as Carlson added, "Those inmates who work in other assignments are also eligible for a wage which is generated from the profits of Federal Prison Industries. Last year, for example, $5 million of the Federal Industries profit was used to pay inmates who work in the food services, the hospital and other service aspects of the institution." And while the Bureau did not claim that the training prepared inmates for outside jobs, its profits were used to finance other vocational training programs for prisoners. "In 1986, $3 million was allocated to funding pre-industrial and experimental training programs."[16] For many years, industries profits were used also to purchase gift packages that were distributed to inmates at Christmas. An interesting refinement, instituted in 1950, was the policy of allowing "vacations" for the industry workers. Any inmate who worked for a year in an industry job was eligible to take one half-day vacation for each month worked. After the first year, vacation time was accrued at the rate of one day per month. Inmates could use their vacations to stay off the job, take more recreation, or just plain loaf, and they still received full pay.

Prison industry work supervisors were more important than might be realized. Evidence of their constructive influence was gained incidental to a massive research project, financed by the Ford Foundation at Bennett's behest. Bennett saw the project as an opportunity to bring useful attention to the Bureau's work. The research, designed to evaluate the effectiveness of the system generally, was directed by sociologist Daniel Glaser of the University of Illinois. Beginning in the late 1950s, Glaser and his team undertook to gain in-depth knowledge of the prison experience by conducting interviews with inmates in five federal prisons. The data about staff-inmate relationships, consistent throughout the system, showed "at all prisons, the work supervisors were the most liked of all officers." Glaser also interviewed former inmates and found that their good feelings for work supervisors had little to do with learning a trade. "It is striking that about 90 percent of the remarks by the successful releasees on the rehabilitative influence of their work supervisors do not mention vocational teaching by these men; instead they stress only their personal relationship to the work supervisor."[17]

One inevitable change in the work programs was the virtual disappearance of prison farms. These had been a staple from the beginning; starting with the three penitentiaries at the turn of the century, the adjacent prison farms had been a feature taken for granted at most of the prisons. But farming was not cost effective when staffs worked forty-hour weeks, nor was it useful to urban-oriented inmates. One by one, the farms were discontinued, and by the late 1980s only two were left in the federal prison system—Lompoc and El Reno (no longer, however, with Warden Merry's oxen).

The federal prison system, responding to rapidly increasing population pressures in the 1980s, built new facilities at a prodigious rate; by late in the decade, the Bureau had added fourteen camps and over fifty prisons of various types and security levels. One of the institutions being planned was to be a sophisticated, state-of-the-art maximum security facility designed to take the high-risk cases from Marion. In addition to a growing population of the usual repetitively violent prisoners that were typical at Marion, the Bureau increasingly had to accept affluent drug kingpins, terrorists, or others with the resources and outside support to threaten even the best prison security. The new institution, planned for a site in Colorado, would presumably have the capability to meet the most severe security challenges, allowing Marion to revert to the status of a regular penitentiary.

The proliferation of programs and management devices needed to operate an agency such as the Bureau of Prisons is too complex and fluid to be captured here in detail; only a few specific developments can be noted—those that might be termed "signs of the times."

Many of the new trends were common to all correctional services, state and local as well as federal, and one of the most significant and encouraging was an accreditation system. In 1974, the Commission on Accreditation for Corrections was organized under the parentage of the American Correctional Association, a little more than a century after that organization began as the National Prison Association. The penitentiary at Terre Haute was the first federal prison to be accredited, in 1979. By 1989, thirty-seven of the institutions within the Bureau of Prisons were accredited.

Changes in the chaplaincy services reflected new concepts of denominationalism and the professional function of chaplains. In the early years of the century, a chaplain was, typically, a nearby minister who might be paid a few—very few—dollars to come to the prison on Sunday and preach. Later, when full-time chaplains were employed, their role still was not well defined; they were called on for many duties that were not assigned to others, such as recreational and educational services. However, the chaplains of the later years were true, full-time professionals (about eighty-five of them were in the system in 1987) and no longer were recruited on a strict denominational basis.

Work release was another concept early prison wardens could not have imagined. The Prisoner Rehabilitation Act of 1965 authorized both furloughs and work release programs.[18] Alexander promptly implemented both program concepts, and only a year later, seven hundred prisoners earned work release status, while another two hundred or so were allowed emergency furloughs.[19]

One very different sign of the times was the invention of the helicopter and the new element of risk it brought to the practice of prison security. As early as 1975, the director urged the wardens to begin planning measures to defeat such escape attempts, but at the same time he instituted the policy that helicopters would not be fired upon.[20] Perimeter walls or fences were no longer sufficient when helicopters could easily drop into the large open recreation yards of prisons. Fortunately, most of the escape attempts were defeated, but hopeful prisoners and their outside friends kept trying. In January 1981, a helicopter unsuccessfully attempted to pick up an inmate from the roof of the high-rise federal jail in New York City. In July 1986, the FBI infiltrated the plot and defeated the elaborate plan to pick up two inmates from the yards of the Lewisburg penitentiary.

The first successful helicopter escape from a federal prison occurred in November 1986 at the co-correctional institution at Pleasanton, California. A male prisoner who had been a military helicopter pilot escaped while on transfer to another institution; some days later, he hijacked a helicopter and dropped into the Pleasanton grounds to pick up one of the women. The operation was completed smoothly in a matter of seconds. The two completely disappeared, but they were both caught a few weeks later, when they went shopping for a wedding ring. Within another year, most federal prison yards were defended by tightly strung overhead wires, placed to obstruct helicopter landings.[21]

Personnel policies presented other significant signs of the times. The nationwide trend toward broader opportunities for women brought them into the nontraditional jobs of correctional officers, along with such worries as staff competence, security, and fairness in personnel practices. The Bureau decided not to hire female correctional officers for the traditional cellblocks of penitentiary-type prisons, but to hire them at any other correctional institutions, where they would be expected to carry out any assignments except strip searches.[22] In January 1976, the institution at Lompoc (which had not yet been classified as a penitentiary) hired Elonye Wilkins who was pleased to note that she was the first female correctional officer to be hired in any federal prison for men.[23]

The Bennett administration had urged the hiring of non-white personnel years before, but the trend was slow to take hold. In 1970, two management staff persons wrote a proposal to institute an affirmative action program, and Carlson promptly approved the plan. He hired an affirmative action program manager who was charged to stimulate the recruitment of females, Hispanics, Indians, and blacks. The manager's task was not easy, but efforts were gradually effective. In 1972, slightly less than 10 percent of employees, systemwide, were women or racial minorities, but by 1987 that number had increased to nearly 26 percent, with 519 women in correctional officer positions.

In 1971, Lee B. Jett, at the Englewood institution, became the first black warden, and after that the number of blacks, Hispanics, and women hired for upper-level management positions gradually increased. The first female warden of a prison for males was Margaret Hambrick, appointed at Butner in 1981.

Management and institutional personnel especially welcomed one new personnel policy—the co-called 20/50 rule; this provided that employees could retire after twenty years of service and on reaching age fifty. The plan applied to the Bureau and to other federal law enforcement agencies, but it was especially appropriate for people who worked in the stressful climate of prison operation. Although an employee could choose to work beyond age fifty, retirement was mandatory at age fifty-five.

In 1987, at age fifty-three, and with thirty years of service (seventeen years as director), Norman Carlson retired and moved west to take a teaching post at the University of Minnesota. He had presided during a period of social unrest that made him controversial at times; but the attacks ostensibly aimed at Carlson during the militant seventies were really aimed at the system as a whole—indeed at just the concept of imprisonment in general. Even the most aggressive opponents did not question the quality of Bureau management. Carlson, as did his three predecessors, retired with an impeccable reputation for integrity. Fortunately unhampered by any ego needs, he proved able to manage with decisive objectivity and skill. His acknowledged stature contributed to a smooth transition, for the attorney general accepted Carlson's recommendation and appointed a deputy director, J. Michael Quinlan, as the new director.

Quinlan had served for fifteen years with the Bureau, including positions as superintendent at Eglin, and warden at Otisville. He was the third attorney to fill the director's post.

During the 1980s, the Bureau was caught in the rapid growth of prisoner populations nationwide, a trend fueled by the runaway drug culture and punitive social attitudes. Much of the Bureau's energy was absorbed by the need to meet a projected growth rate equivalent to about four thousand new prison beds every year. The agency constantly searched for new prison sites, renovating closed-down military installations, schools, or other properties to serve as custodial facilities. The staff training program was geared to recruit and train new management personnel; Unicor scouted for new products to make and market. The Carlson administration unquestionably built an overall system of institutions, with high standards of cleanliness, good order, competent security, and humane prisoner care. Staff morale was high, and, in general, the system was held in uniform respect by Congress and by correctional peers.

Though rehabilitation programs seemed to have been subordinated to a concern for security and control, prison managers came to believe that the best contribution to an inmate's rehabilitation just might be the well-controlled, basic decency of his daily living. Treatment programs were by no means eliminated, however. The mature federal prison system was ready to offer a good mix of self-improvement programs—vocational and academic education and special problem counseling—without pretense that treatment programs could reform prisoners unless they were motivated to use that help. A cogent, interesting aspect of the philosophy was expressed well by one earlier manager in the system who wrote, "The correction of the individual offender will always be a difficult process, and perhaps we should not have it any other way. If by chance someone did discover a sure and quick method of changing human behavior, it would represent more of a threat to mankind than a boon."[24]

NOTES
INDEX

NOTES

1. THE FIRST CENTURY: AT THE MERCY OF THE STATES

1. Willard S. Randall, *A Little Revenge: Benjamin Franklin and His Son* (Boston: Little, Brown & Co., 1984), 438.

2. Jonathan Trumbull to John Hancock, 5 May 1777, *Papers of the Continental Congress 1774–1789*, M247, roll 80, 333, NA.

3. John C. Fitzpatrick, ed., *The Writings of George Washington* (Washington, D.C.: Government Printing Office, 1933), 8:474–76.

4. Fitzpatrick, *The Writings of George Washington* 4:155–56.

5. *Connecticut Courant,* 24 February 1777. Letters and data regarding New Gate prison are in the Simsbury archives at the Connecticut Historical Commission, Hartford.

6. John P. Frank, "Historical Bases of the Federal Judicial System," in *The Courts in American Life,* ed. Kermit L. Hall (New York: Garland Publishing, Inc., 1987), 357.

7. Henry J. Bourguignon, *The First Federal Court: The Federal Appellate Prize Court of the American Revolution 1775–1787* (Philadelphia: The American Philosophical Society, 1977), 22–25.

8. Julius Goebel, Jr., *History of the Supreme Court of the United States* (New York: MacMillan Co., 1971), 1:147.

9. *Journals of the Continental Congress, 1774–1789* (Library of Congress, 1906), 5(1776): 594. Although the language here refers to "the state prisoners," it is from a time when today's more explicit meanings of "state" and "federal" had not yet evolved.

10. Negley K. Teeters, *The Cradle of the Penitentiary: The Walnut Street Jail at Philadelphia 1773–1835* (Philadelphia: Temple University, 1955), 23.

11. Negley K. Teeters, *They Were in Prison* (Chicago: The John C. Winston Company, 1937), 17.

12. The several referenced letters and petitions are found in *Papers of the*

Continental Congress 1774–1789, M247, roll 54, vols. 4, 21, 33, 37, 50, 244, NA.

13. Bourgingnon, *The First Federal Court,* 328–30.

14. Goebel, *History of the Supreme Court,* 457.

15. Edwin C. Surrency, *History of the Federal Courts* (New York: Oceana Publications, Inc., 1987), 676.

16. 1 Stat 96, 23 September 1789; Homer Cummings and Carl McFarland, *Federal Justice* (New York: The MacMillan Company, 1937), 352–53.

17. Goebel, *History of the Supreme Court,* 456.

18. Luther A. Huston, *The Department of Justice* (New York: Frederick A. Praeger Publishers, 1976), 6–9.

19. Secretary of State, Miscellaneous letters received, 1789–1825, M179, roll 4, 53, NA.

20. Criminal case files of U.S. Circuit Court for Eastern District of Pennsylvania, 1791–1840, roll 2, NA Philadelphia; and Negley K. Teeters, *Scaffold and Chair: A Compilation of Their Use in Pennsylvania 1682–1962* (Philadelphia: Temple University, 1963), 45.

21. Criminal case files, roll 1, NA Philadelphia.

22. County Prison, Prisoners for Trial Docket, 1790–1797, Philadelphia City Archives.

23. Goebel, *History of the Supreme Court,* 622–23.

24. The information on federal admissions for the New York prisons is developed from registers of those institutions in the New York State Archives and Records Administration, Albany.

25. Minute Book of Board of Inspectors of Eastern State Penitentiary 1829–1840, minutes of February 21, 1830, RG 15, Pennsylvania State Archives.

26. Virginia Executive Papers, June 30, 1807, letters received, box 145, Virginia State Archives.

27. Paul W. Keve, *The History of Corrections in Virginia* (Charlottesville: University Press of Virginia, 1986), 63–64.

28. Milton Lomask, *Aaron Burr: The Conspiracy and Years of Exile 1805–1836* (New York: Farrar, Straus, Giroux, 1982), 226.

29. Letters received, 1846, by Secretary of Treasury 1829–1899, RG 56, NA. It seems evident that most marshals responded and that most of the reports survived. However, we cannot be sure the numbers are complete, only that the count of prisoners shown by the table is probably a good indication of the total volume.

30. Cummings and McFarland, *Federal Justice,* 143.

31. Cummings and McFarland, *Federal Justice,* 146.

32. Cummings and McFarland, *Federal Justice,* 225–27.

33. Cummings and McFarland, *Federal Justice,* 375.

34. Zebulon R. Brockway, *Fifty Years of Prison Service: An Autobiography* (1912; reprint, Montclair, N.J.: Patterson Smith, 1969), 43–50; and David Dyer, *History of the Albany Penitentiary* (Albany, N.Y.: J. Munsell, 1867), 21.

35. David W. Lewis, *From Newgate to Dannemora: The Rise of the Penitentiary in New York, 1796–1848* (Ithaca, N.Y.: Cornell University Press, 1965), 111–56.

36. Lewis, *From Newgate to Dannemora,* 218–19.

37. First Annual Report of the Inspectors of State Prisons of State of New York, 29 January 1849 (Albany: Weed, Parsons & Company, 1849).

38. Brewster Cameron to Isaac V. Baker, Jr., 13 June 1882, Criminal record letter book #2, Records of the General Agent, RG 60, NA.

39. Attorney General to U.S. marshal, Nashville, 12 January 1881, Criminal record letter book #1, Records of the General Agent, RG 60, NA.

40. U.S. attorney, Memphis, to attorney general, 18 April 1882, Records of the General Agent, correspondence, 1877–1901, RG 60, NA.

41. Chief clerk, Department of Justice to U.S. marshal, Providence, 10 January 1881, Criminal record letter book #1, Records of the General Agent, RG 60, NA.

42. Brewster Cameron to warden, Iowa penitentiary, 18 March 1882, Criminal record letter book #2, Records of the General Agent, RG 60, NA.

43. Brockway, *Fifty Years of Prison Service,* 81.

44. Brockway, *Fifty Years of Prison Service,* 86.

2. THE DEMAND FOR FEDERAL PRISONS

1. Department of Justice, *Annual Report of Attorney General,* 1875, 5.

2. Forty-ninth Cong., 2d sess., Act of 23 February 1887.

3. U.S. Commissioner of Labor, Convict Labor 2d Annual Report, 1886, (Washington, D.C.: Government Printing Office, 1887), 4.

4. Glen A. Gildemeister, *Prison Labor and Convict Competition with Free Workers in Industrializing America, 1840–1890* (New York: Garland Publishing, Inc., 1987), 30.

5. For details of the practice in two states see, Mark T. Carleton, *Politics and Punishment: The History of the Louisiana State Penal System* (Baton Rouge: Louisiana State University Press, 1971), 22–31; and Keve, *The History of Corrections in Virginia,* 72–85.

6. Carleton, *Politics and Punishment,* 7.

7. Arlin Turner, *George W. Cable: A Biography* (Durham, N.C.: Duke University Press, 1956), 125–26.

8. Roeliff Brinkerhoff, *Recollections of a Lifetime* (Cincinnati: Robert Clark Co., 1900), 258–59.

9. George W. Cable, *The Silent South* (1889; reprint, Montclair, N.J.: Patterson Smith, 1969), 153.

10. Cable, *The Silent South*, 175.

11. Louis D. Rubin, Jr., *George W. Cable: The Life and Times of a Southern Heretic* (New York: Pegasus, 1969), 111.

12. F. B. Sanborn, "E. C. Wines and Prison Reform," in *Prison Reform*, ed. Charles R. Henderson (New York: Russell Sage Foundation, 1910), 64–87.

13. E. C. Wines and Theodore W. Dwight, *Report on the Prisons and Reformatories of the United States and Canada* (1867; reprint, New York: AMS Press, Inc., 1976). For discussion of Wines' national organizing efforts see, Blake McKelvey, *American Prisons: A History of Good Intentions* (Montclair, N.J.: Patterson Smith, 1977), 88–92.

14. E. C. Wines, *The State of Prisons and of Child Saving Institutions in the Civilized World* (1880; reprint, Montclair, N.J.: Patterson Smith, 1986), 88.

15. McKelvey, *American Prisons*, 144.

16. Brinkerhoff's biography is a comprehensive source for the details of his varied career interests.

17. Brinkerhoff, *Recollections of a Lifetime*, 244.

18. Brinkerhoff, *Recollections of a Lifetime*, 262–63.

19. Brinkerhoff, *Recollections of a Lifetime*, 263.

20. Brinkerhoff, *Recollections of a Lifetime*, 264.

21. Brinkerhoff, *Recollections of a Lifetime*, 304.

22. Department of Justice, *Annual Report of Attorney General*, 1871, 6.

23. Blake McKelvey, "The Prison Labor Problem: 1875–1900," *Journal of Criminal Law and Criminology*, 25 (1934): 258.

24. Department of Justice, *Annual Report of Attorney General*, 1887.

25. Cummings and McFarland, *Federal Justice*, 353.

26. Register of State Prison at San Quentin, 31 August 1889, California State Archives.

27. James S. Easby-Smith, *The Department of Justice: Its History and Functions* (Washington, D.C.: W. H. Lowdermilk and Co., 1904), 33.

28. United States Statutes at Large, 26 Stat., 839, Public Law PL 51-529, 3 March 1891.

29. This and the succeeding excerpts from the debate in the House are found in the Congressional Record for 27 January 1890, 873–93.

30. Letter of 16 January 1890, George F. Hoar Papers, box 114, Massachusetts Historical Society.

31. *Congressional Record*, Senate, 28 February 1891, 3563.

3. THE FIRST THREE PRISONS

1. Detailed descriptions of this penitentiary may be found in William Crawford, *Report on the Penitentiaries of the United States* (London: House of Commons, 1834), 101–3; and Stephen Dalsheim, *The United States Penitentiary for the District of Columbia, 1826–1862* (Washington, D.C.: Records of Columbia Historical Society, 1959, vols. 1953–56), 135–44; and Laurence F. Schmeckebier, *The District of Columbia: Its Government and Administration* (Baltimore, The Johns Hopkins Press, 1928), 88–90.

2. John W. Partin, ed., *A Brief History of Fort Leavenworth 1827–1983* (Ft. Leavenworth, Kans.: U.S. Army Command and General Staff College, 1983), 39–40.

3. Secretary of war to attorney general, 19 December 1894, Department of Justice central year files (folded), #2256-1891, RG 60, NA.

4. Elvid Hunt, *History of Fort Leavenworth: 1827–1927* (Ft. Leavenworth, Kans.: General Service Schools, 1926), 208.

5. James W. Pope to attorney general, 15 June 1895, Department of Justice central year files (folded), #2256-1891, RG 60, NA.

6. Frank Strong to attorney general, 17 May 1895, Department of Justice central year files (folded), #2256-1891, RG 60, NA.

7. House Committee on the Judiciary, 54th Cong., 1st sess., 1895, Report #1443.

8. Department of Justice, *Annual Report of the Attorney General*, 1896.

9. Department of Justice, *Annual Report of the Attorney General*, 1898, 152.

10. Rules issued by Attorney General John W. Griggs, Department of Justice central year files, (folded), #2556, 17 September 1898, RG 60, NA.

11. Rules issued by Griggs.

12. James W. French to Frank Strong, 11 October 1895, Department of Justice central year files (folded), #2256-1891, RG 60, NA.

13. William S. Eames to R. V. LaDow, 29 August 1908, Papers of R. V. LaDow, RG 129, NA.

14. William S. Eames to attorney general, 23 February 1897, Department of Justice central year files (folded), #2256-1891, RG 60, NA.

15. *Topeka Daily Capital*, 20 November 1905.

16. *Kansas City Journal*, 17 May 1897.

17. James W. French to attorney general 19, May 1897, Department of Justice central year files (folded), #2256-1891, RG 60, NA.

18. *The Leavenworth Times,* 19 May 1897.

19. McKelvey, *American Prisons,* 194.

20. *Annual Report of the City of Atlanta, Year Ending 31 December 1898.*

21. William S. Eames to attorney general, 7 September 1899, file 33-11-62, folder 1, RG 60, NA.

22. Department of Justice central files, file 33-11-62, folders 4 and 5, RG 60, NA.

23. Department of Justice central files, file 33-11-62, folder 9, RG 60, NA.

24. *Annual Report, City of Atlanta,* 1903.

25. R. V. LaDow to attorney general, 31 March 1903, Department of Justice year files (folded), #5136-1903, RG 60, NA.

26. R. W. McClaughry to attorney general, 12 October 1903, Department of Justice central files, 33-11-62, folder 3, RG 60, NA.

27. For a full history of this prison see Paul W. Keve, *The McNeil Century: The Life and Times of an Island Prison* (Chicago: Nelson-Hall, Inc., 1984).

28. Keve, *The McNeil Century,* 59.

4. THE EXPERIENCE WITH PENITENTIARIES

1. R. W. McClaughry to general agent, 21 August 1907, Papers of R. V. LaDow, RG 129, NA.

2. Douglas G. Browne and Alan Brock, *Fingerprints: Fifty Years of Scientific Crime Detection* (New York: E. P. Dutton & Co., 1954), 126.

3. Richard Gid Powers, *Secrecy and Power: The Life of J. Edgar Hoover* (New York: The Free Press, 1987), 149, 155.

4. See for instance, R. V. LaDow to J. Ellen Foster, 22 October 1909, letter book, Papers of R. V. LaDow, RG 129, NA.

5. House Committee on Expenditures in the Department of Justice, 62nd Cong., 1st sess., 13 June to 24 June; 1 July 1912, 867.

6. *Leavenworth Times,* 17 and 26 June 1910.

7. House Committee on Expenditures in the Department of Justice, 62nd Cong., 1st sess., 13 June to 24 June; 1 July 1912.

8. T. W. Morgan to Francis H. Duehay, 28 October 1914 and 27 March 1915, Warden's letter book, Leavenworth Penitentiary.

9. T. W. Morgan to Francis H. Duehay, 18 May 1915, Warden's letter book, Leavenworth Penitentiary.

10. *Indianapolis News,* 2, 28, 30, 31 December 1912.

11. Letter of 10 October 1918, Warden's letter book, Leavenworth Penitentiary.

12. FBI report; *U.S. Penitentiary, Leavenworth, Kansas: Inspection and Investigation, May 14, 1925*, 2–9.

13. T. W. Morgan to Francis H. Duehay, 11 October 1918, Warden's letter book, Leavenworth Penitentiary.

14. William D. Haywood, *Bill Haywood's Book* (New York: International Publishers, 1929), 332.

15. FBI report, 6.

16. *National Geographic* 174 (1988): 387–413; and 177 (1990): 44–61.

17. Roland Huntford, *The Last Place on Earth* (New York: Atheneum, 1986), 537.

18. Haywood, *Bill Haywood's Book,* 330–32.

19. Thomas E. Gaddis, *Birdman of Alcatraz* (New York: Random House, 1955).

20. Robert Stroud, *Diseases of Canaries* (Kansas City, Mo.: Canary Publishers Co., 1933), and Robert Stroud, *Stroud's Digest on the Diseases of Birds* (Minneapolis: L. G. Marcus, 1943).

21. Paul W. Keve, *The McNeil Century,* 222–24.

22. Karl A. Menninger, *Man Against Himself* (New York: Harcourt, Brace & World, Inc., 1938), 205.

23. Menninger, *Man Against Himself,* 207.

24. *Proceedings, Annual Congress of American Prison Association,* 1908, 81.

25. R. V. LaDow to R. W. McClaughry, 1 July 1908 (untitled file on working hours, box 14), Papers of R. V. LaDow, RG 129, NA.

26. R. W. McClaughry to Cecil Clay, 30 January 1907 (untitled file on working hours, box 14), Papers of R. V. LaDow, RG 129, NA.

27. William H. Moyer to Cecil Clay, 17 January 1907 (untitled file on working hours, box 14), Papers of R. V. LaDow, RG 129, NA.

28. William H. Moyer to R. V. LaDow, 21 March 1910 (untitled file on working hours, box 14), Papers of R. V. LaDow, RG 129, NA.

29. *New York Times,* 3 January 1912, and House Committee on Expenditures in the Department of Justice, 13 June to 24 June, 1 July 1912, 1042.

30. R. V. LaDow to William H. Moyer, 30 April 1910, letter book, Papers of R. V. LaDow, April 1910–July 1910, RG 129, NA.

31. *New York Times,* 8 February 1912.

32. *New York Times,* 22 May 1912.

33. *New York Times,* 6 September 1912.

34. *Atlanta Constitution,* 3 April 1915.

35. *Good Words* (Atlanta prisoner publication), 1 February and 1 May 1913.

36. *Proceedings, Annual Congress of American Prison Association,* 1927, 159.

37. Julian Hawthorne, *The Subterranean Brotherhood* (New York: McBride, Nast & Company, 1914), 79, 178, 191.

38. *New York Times,* 29, March 1915.

39. Isabel C. Barrows, *A Sunny Life: The Biography of Samuel June Barrows* (Boston: Little, Brown & Co., 1913), 154, 182.

40. Extensive records of Barrows' work on behalf of prisons and probation and parole may be found in the Barrows papers, Houghton Library, Harvard University.

41. Details of the law and its initial applications are discussed in a speech by Attorney General George W. Wickersham, *Proceedings of Annual Congress of American Prison Association,* 1911, 221–38. See also *Rules and Regulations Governing the Paroling of Prisoners from U.S. Penitentiaries* (Washington, D.C.: Government Printing Office, 1910); and Second Annual Report, Boards of Parole, in *Annual Report of Attorney General,* 1912, 369.

42. R. W. McClaughry to J. Ellen Foster, 12 February 1910, Papers of R. V. LaDow 1907–10, RG 129, NA; and *Proceedings of Annual Congress of American Prison Association,* 1910, 119.

43. House Committee on Expenditures in the Department of Justice, *United States Penitentiaries,* 14 May 1912, 731–32.

44. Alpheus T. Mason, *Harlan Fiske Stone: Pillar of the Law* (New York: Archon Books, 1956), 154.

45. Sartain inmate file, Federal Record Center, Suitland, Maryland.

46. *Atlanta Constitution,* 1 March 1927.

47. Dorothy M. Brown, *Mabel Walker Willebrandt: A Study of Power, Loyalty and Law* (Knoxville: University of Tennessee Press, 1984), 65.

48. *New York Times,* 25 June 1925.

49. Brown, *Mabel Walker Willebrandt,* 94.

50. *Atlanta Constitution,* 2 November 1928. Extensive further details are given in the issue of 18 March 1929. The correspondence between Snook and Borah is found in the Borah papers, box 281, Library of Congress.

51. Brown, *Mabel Walker Willebrandt,* 96; and *New York Times,* 25 April 1926.

52. Brown, *Mabel Walker Willebrandt,* 177.

53. *Tacoma Times,* 3 August 1934.

54. For details on this and other points in the history of this prison see Keve, *The McNeil Century.*

5. PLACES FOR WOMEN, PLACES FOR YOUTH

1. J. Ellen Foster to attorney general, 2 April 1910, folder of correspondence and reports of J. Ellen Foster, box 1, Papers of R. V. LaDow; and R. V. LaDow to J. E. Matthews, 3 May 1910, letter book, Papers of R. V. LaDow, RG 129, NA.

2. Biographical details regarding Foster are found in *Notable American Women 1607–1950* (Cambridge: Harvard University Press, 1971), 651–52; and in Ruth Bordin, *Woman and Temperance: The Quest for Power and Liberty 1873–1900* (Philadelphia: Temple University Press, 1981).

3. J. W. French to attorney general, 15 May, 25 May, and 6 June 1896 and 12 December 1897, Department of Justice central year files (folded), file #2256-1891, RG 60, NA.

4. Keve, *The McNeil Century,* 61, 145.

5. House Committee on Expenditures in the Department of Justice, 62nd Cong., 2d sess., June and July 1912, Hearing, 18.

6. R. V. LaDow to R. W. McClaughry, 5 January 1909, letter book, Papers of R. V. LaDow, RG 129, NA.

7. R. V. LaDow to R. W. McClaughry, 3 May 1910, letter book, Papers of R. V. LaDow, RG 129, NA.

8. Joseph F. Fishman, *Crucibles of Crime* (1923; reprint, Montclair, N.J.: Patterson Smith, 1969), 102–3.

9. Mary Belle Harris in her book, *I Knew Them in Prison* (New York: Viking Press, 1936), 260–62, says that Willebrandt had been alerted to the needs of female prisoners by hearing Foster speak. It is a convincing assertion even though the occasion would have to have been at least twelve years before Willebrandt was appointed assistant attorney general

10. Heber H. Votaw to Mabel Walker Willebrandt, n.d., file 4-9-01, box 659, RG 129, NA.

11. Undated paper, folder of correspondence and reports of J. Ellen Foster, Box 1, Papers of R. V. LaDow, RG 129, NA.

12. Archival records, Federal Correctional Institution, Alderson.

13. *Notable American Women: The Modern Period* (Cambridge: Belknap Press of Harvard University Press, 1980), 315–17. See also Harris, *I Knew Them in Prison,* 267; and Joseph W. Rogers, "Mary Belle Harris: Warden and Rehabilitation Pioneer," *Criminal Justice Research Bulletin,* Sam Houston University, Vol. 3, #9, 1988.

14. Heber H. Votaw to attorney general, memo of 9 January 1923, file 4-9-01, Bureau of Prisons, RG 129, NA.

15. Claudine SchWeber, "The Government's Unique Experiment in Sal-

vaging Women Criminals," in *Judge, Lawyer, Victim, Thief,* ed. Nicole Hahn Rafter and Elizabeth Stanko (Boston: Northeastern University Press, 1982), 285.

16. A useful description of the refuges is found in Robert M. Mennel, *Thorns and Thistles: Juvenile Delinquents in the United States 1825–1940* (Hanover, N. H.: University Press of New England, 1973), chapter 1.

17. Department of Justice, *Annual report of Attorney General,* 1908. See also *Joint Select Committee to Investigate the Charitable and Reformatory Institutions in the District of Columbia,* 69th Cong., 2d sess., 14 February 1927, Senate Document 207, 95–101.

18. Wines, *The State of Prisons and Child Saving Institutions,* 215.

19. *Joint Select Committee to Investigate the Charities and Reformatories in the District of Columbia,* 55th Cong., 1st sess., 21 July 1987, 160.

20. Department of Justice, *Annual Report of Attorney General,* 1881, 18–119, and 1899, 241.

21. James V. Bennett, *The Federal Penal and Corrections Problem* (a monograph published by the Bureau of Efficiency, March 1928).

22. Department of Justice, *Annual Report of Attorney General,* 1922, 377.

23. Department of Justice, *Annual Report of Attorney General,* 1881, 121.

24. Schmeckebier, *The District of Columbia,* 231–33.

25. Albert Deutsch, *Our Rejected Children* (Boston: Little, Brown & Co., 1950), 102.

26. Brown, *Mabel Walker Willebrandt,* 91.

6. BUREAUCRACY ACHIEVED

1. House Committee on Expenditures in the Department of Justice, *United States Penitentiaries,* 14 May 1912, 727.

2. The full report may be found as an appendix to Senate Subcommittee on National Penitentiaries, Committee on the Judiciary, *The Federal Prison System—1964,* 88th Cong., 2d sess., 22 January 1964 (Washington, D.C.: Government Printing Office, 1964).

3. *New York Times,* 23 January and 1 February 1929.

4. House of Representatives, *Report on Federal Penal and Reformatory Institutions,* 70th Cong., 2d sess., 31 January 1929, 4.

5. Records of Hart's career are found in the Delinquency and Penology file, Russell Sage Foundation Archives, Rockefeller Archive Center, Tarrytown, New York.

6. House of Representatives, *Hearing of Special Committee on Federal*

Penal and Reformatory Institutions, 70th Cong., 2d sess., 7 to 15 January 1929, 150.

7. The analysis of Bates' career development is derived from several sources including chapter 1 of Sanford Bates, *Prisons and Beyond* (Freeport, N.Y.: Books for Libraries Press, 1936); Thomas Carens, "Uncle Sam's Chief Jailor," *New York Herald Tribune Magazine,* 1 July 1929; and interview with Betty Nichols (Bates' daughter), 1 April 1987.

8. Mabel Walker Willebrandt, letter to Herbert C. Parsons, 11 October 1926, and memo to attorney general, 20 September 1926, Bureau of Prisons, Speeches, Publications and other papers of the Director, RG 129, NA.

9. Sanford Bates to William D. Mitchell, 22 March 1929, Bureau of Prisons, Speeches, Publications, and other papers of the Director, RG 129, NA.

10. James V. Bennett, *I Chose Prison* (New York: Alfred A. Knopf, 1970), 86. Further details on the key individuals are supplied by tape recordings of interviews conducted in 1980 by Myrl Alexander with many of the retired management personnel from the 1930s, available in BOP archives. See also *Fiftieth Anniversary 1930–1980,* a BOP monograph, 1980.

11. Myrl Alexander, letter to author, 15 December 1989.

12. A useful single source of information on the camps is an article by the person who was the superintendent over the camp system for some time, Robert H. Armstrong, "Prison Camps for Rehabilitation," *Federal Probation,* 6 (April–June 1942): 38–41.

13. *Handbook of Correctional Institution Design and Construction* (Washington, D.C.: Bureau of Prisons, 1949), 73.

14. *Federal Offenders 1935–36,* BOP publication, 59.

15. *Federal Offenders 1935–36,* 4.

16. *The Kansas City Star,* 2 August 1929; and *New York Times,* ? August 1929. On 4 August the *New York Times* ran a lengthy feature article on causes of prison riots, authored by Hastings H. Hart.

17. The Panzram career is the subject of a book by Thomas E. Gaddis and James O. Long, *Killer: A Journal of Murder* (New York: The MacMillan Company, 1970).

18. *Fiftieth Anniversary 1930–1980,* 5–7.

19. Russell Sage Foundation Archives; and Thomas Schade, "Prison Officer Training in the United States; The Legacy of Jesse O. Stutsman," Federal Probation, 50 (December 1986): 40–46.

20. Department of Justice, *Annual Report of the Attorney General,* 1933, 116.

21. *Fiftieth Anniversary 1930–1980,* 7.

22. Sanford Bates to Mary B. Harris, 16 March 1932, Bureau of Prisons class 4 correspondence, box 658, RG 129, NA.

23. Sanford Bates to Mary B. Harris, 10 January 1936, Bureau of Prisons files 4-9-03, RG 129, NA.

24. Department of Justice, *Annual Report of Attorney General*, 1934, 151.

25. Bennett, *I Chose Prison*, 132.

26. Operating agencies rarely, if ever, kept written records of their discriminatory practices. These comments on the subject are based mainly on the author's interviews with former staff members.

27. Claudine SchWeber, "The Government's Unique Experiment in Salvaging Women Criminals," 288, 289.

28. There are many sources regarding the escape, two of the most useful are Verdon R. Adams, *Tom White: The Life of a Lawman* (El Paso: Texas Western Press, University of Texas, 1972), 108–16; and Mary Ann Jones, "The Leavenworth Prison Break," *Harpers* 191 (July 1945): 54–63. The record of the reimbursement requests may be found in *Relief of Certain Claimants at Leavenworth, Kansas for Damage to Property Inflicted by Escaping Prisoners*, 10 May 1934, Senate Report 951, 73rd Cong., 2d sess.

29. Katherine Lenroot to Harrison Dobbs, 19 February 1930, Records of Children's Bureau, Correspondence and Reports Relating to Surveys and Programs, 1917–54, RG 102, NA.

30. Department of Justice, *Annual Report of Attorney General*, 1933, 165; and 1935, 122.

31. Hamlet, act 2, sc. 2, lines 552–58. From "Shakespeare as a Penologist," an unpublished article among the Bates papers, Sam Houston University.

7. DISSENTER PRISONERS

1. R. G. Brown, et al., *To The American People: Report Upon the Illegal Practices of the United States Department of Justice* (Washington, D.C.: National Popular Government League, May 1920).

2. Richard Suskind, *By Bullet, Bomb and Dagger* (New York: The MacMillan Company, 1971), 134.

3. Powers, *Secrecy and Power*, 63. A detailed airing of the charges and counter charges resulting from the raids, including Palmer's extensive defense of his actions, comprises the full report; Senate Committee on the Judiciary, *Charges of Illegal Practices of the Department of Justice*, 66th Cong., 3rd sess., 19 January to 3 March 1921.

4. Barbara Tuchman, *The Proud Tower* (New York: The MacMillan Company, 1962), 63.

5. *Congressional Record*, 53rd Cong., 2d sess., 9 May 1894, 4513–14.

6. Donald McMurray, *Coxey's Army* (Boston: Little, Brown and Co., 1929), chapter 10.

7. Department of Justice year files (folded), #4017-1894, box 763, folder 7, RG 60, NA.

8. Berkman recounts the event and the subsequent prison experience in Alexander Berkman, *Prison Memoirs of an Anarchist* (New York: Mother Earth Publishing Co., 1912).

9. Dorothy M. Brown, *Setting a Course: American Women in the 1920s* (Boston: Twayne Publishers, 1987), 112.

10. *The Nation,* 104 (28 June 1917): 766–67.

11. Alis Kates Shulman, *Red Emma Speaks: An Emma Goldman Reader* (New York: Schocken Books, 1983), 3.

12. Powers, *Secrecy and Power,* 86–87.

13. Haywood, *Bill Haywood's Book,* 335.

14. A, V. Anderson to superintendent of prisons, 27 February 1920, Warden's letter book, Leavenworth Penitentiary.

15. Ralph Chaplin, *Wobbly: The Rough and Tumble Story of an American Radical* (New York: Da Capo Press, 1972), 271.

16. Winthrop D. Lane, "The Strike at Fort Leavenworth," *The Survey,* 15 February 1919, 41–42. Also Lane, "Military Prisons and the C.O.," *The Survey,* 17 May 1919, 42–47.

17. Ray Ginger, *The Bending Cross: A Biography of Eugene Victor Debs* (New York: Russell and Russell, 1949), 168.

18. Ginger, *The Bending Cross,* 390–91.

19. Eugene V. Debs, *Walls and Bars* (New York: Socialist Party, 1927), 106.

20. Robert K. Murray, *The Harding Era* (Minneapolis: The University of Minnesota Press, 1969), 168–69.

21. Ginger, *The Bending Cross,* 407–8.

22. Murray, *The Harding Era,* 169.

23. *Atlanta Constitution,* 26 December 1921.

24. Page Smith, *The Rise of Industrial America* (New York: McGraw-Hill Book Co., 1964), 6:522.

25. Kate Richards O'Hare, *In Prison* (New York: Alfred A. Knopf, 1923), appendix.

26. Philip S. Foner and Sally M. Miller, eds., *Kate Richards O'Hare: Selected Writings and Speeches* (Baton Rouge: Louisiana State University Press, 1982), 218.

27. Foner and Miller, *Kate Richards O'Hare,* 237.

28. Emma Goldman, *Living My Life* (New York: Da Capo Press, reprint, 1970), 677.

29. O'Hare, *In Prison,* 221.

30. B. N. Ganguli, *Emma Goldman: Portrait of a Rebel Woman* (Bombay: Allied Publishers Private Limited, 1970), 5–6.

31. Robert E. Burke, *Olson's New Deal for California* (Berkeley: University of California Press, 1953), 181–82.

32. Norman Thomas, *Is Conscience a Crime?* (New York: Garland Publishing Inc., 1972), appendix.

33. Nicholas N. Kittrie and Eldon D. Wedlock, *The Tree of Liberty: A Documentary History of Rebellion and Political Crime in America* (Baltimore: Johns Hopkins University Press, 1986), 299.

34. Alfred Hassler, *Diary of a Self-Made Convict* (Chicago: Henry Regnery Company, 1954).

35. Kittrie and Wedlock, *The Tree of Liberty,* 297.

36. *Time,* 7 June 1968, 62.

37. *Danbury News-Times,* 9 and 12 August 1971.

38. Sherna Gluch, ed., *From Parlor to Prison: Five American Suffragists Talk About Their Lives* (New York: Vintage Books, 1976), 242–43.

39. *New York Times,* 19 July 1917.

40. Doris Stevens, *Jailed for Freedom* (Freeport, N.Y.: Books for Libraries Press, 1920), 141.

41. Ross Netherton and Nan Netherton, *Fairfax County in Virginia: A Pictorial History* (Norfolk, Va.: The Downing Company, 1986), 141.

42. Heywood Broun and Margaret Leech, *Anthony Comstock: Roundsman of the Lord* (New York: Albert and Charles Boni, 1927), 128–44.

43. Smith, *The Rise of Industrial America,* 277.

44. D. M. Bennett, *Champions of the Church: Their Crimes and Persecutions* (New York: Liberal and Scientific Publishing House, 1878).

45. Broun and Leech, *Anthony Comstock,* 171–72.

46. Kenneth E. Davison, *The Presidency of Rutherford B. Hayes* (Westport, Conn.: Greenwood Press, 1972), 161.

47. Davison, *The Presidency of Rutherford B. Hayes,* 162.

48. D. M. Bennett, *From Behind the Bars* (New York: Liberal and Scientific Publishing House, undated).

49. Smith, *The Rise of Industrial America,* 285.

8. A PERIOD OF GROWTH

1. Department of Justice, *Annual Report of Attorney General,* 1933, 108.

2. *Ye News Letter,* Bureau of Prisons Probation System, June 1936.

3. As told by Victor H. Evjen, "The Federal Probation System: The

Struggle to Achieve It and Its First 25 Years," *Federal Probation*, 39 (June 1975): 3–7.

4. Among useful sources for details on the story of Isaac Parker and the unique Fort Smith jail are, Glenn Shirley, *Law West of Fort Smith* (Lincoln: University of Nebraska Press, 1968); and S. W. Harman, *Hell on the Border: He Hanged Eighty-eight Men* (Fort Smith, Ark.: The Phoenix Publishing Co., 1898): and H. Wayne Morgan and Anne Hodges Morgan, *Oklahoma: A Bicentennial History* (New York: W. W. Norton and Co., 1977).

5. The experience with the Alaska jail system is detailed in "Correspondence and Monthly Reports," found in *Alaska, Reports—Monthly Narrative,* BOP Central Administrative Files, RG 129, NA.

6. Extensive papers covering the life of John Joy Edson are available at the Historical Society of Washington, D.C.

7. The commission's full report is found in *Message of the President of the United States,* Senate doc. 648, 60th Cong., 2d sess., 11 January 1909. It is also extensively reported in the *Washington Evening Star* for the same date.

8. Department of Justice, *Annual Report of Attorney General,* 1933, 120.

9. *Federal Offenders, 1935–36,* BOP publication, 13.

10. *Proceedings, Annual Congress of the American Prison Association,* 1933, 90. For a graphic account of one federal prisoner's jail experience see W. E. Laite, Jr., *The United States vs. William Laite* (Washington, D.C.: Acropolis Books LTD, 1972), chapters 4, 5.

11. Louis N. Robinson, *Jails: Care and Treatment of Misdemeanant Prisoners in the United States* (Philadelphia: The John C. Winston Company, 1944), 241.

12. Robinson, *Jails,* 163.

13. Robert V. LaDow, "United States Prisons and Prisoners," in *Penal and Reformatory Institutions,* ed. Charles R. Henderson (New York: Russell Sage Foundation, 1910), 174.

14. *Federal Offenders,* 135–36, 6.

15. Frank Loveland, "The Classification Program in the Federal Prison System: 1934–1960," *Federal Probation,* 24 (June 1960): 7–12.

16. Bennett, *I Chose Prison,* 53–59.

17. *Thirty Years of Prison Progress* (a monograph of the Bureau of Prisons, n.d.), 10.

18. Robinson, *Jails,* 245.

19. Myrl E. Alexander, in letter to author, 15 December 1989.

20. Ronald J. Stupak, "Taking Charge of the Future," *Federal Prisons Journal,* 1 (Fall 1989): 13.

21. House of Representatives, *Report on Employment for Federal Prisoners,* 68th Cong., 1st sess., 1 January 1924, Report #21, 1.

22. Bennett, *I Chose Prison,* 88.

23. Bennett, *I Chose Prison,* 86–89.

24. Federal Juvenile Delinquency Act, 1938, 18 USC 5031-5037; Youth Corrections Act, 1950, 18 USC 5005-26; Federal Juvenile Justice and Delinquency Prevention Act, 1974, 18 USC 3401-2.

25. *Federal Prisons, 1946: A Report of the Work of the Federal Bureau of Prisons* (a monograph of the Bureau of Prisons, 1946), 21.

26. H. G. Moeller, "The Natural Bridge Camp," *The Bulletin Board* (a publication for BOP employees), Washington, D.C., 10 (July 1948).

27. Description of the construction planning activities comes from an interview many years later between Myrl Alexander, former director of the Bureau, and R. D. Barnes who had been an architect responsible for design work at the time. Tape and transcription, BOP archives.

9. PRISONS OF LAST RESORT

1. John Kobler, *Capone: The Life and World of Al Capone* (New York: G. P. Putnam's Sons, 1971), 344.

2. *St. Louis Post-Dispatch,* 18 June 1933.

3. Powers, *Secrecy and Power,* 188.

4. *New York Times,* 20 March 1934.

5. Office memo to Special Assistant Joseph B. Keenan, 1 August 1933; Carl Brent Swisher, *Selected Papers of Homer Cummings* (New York: Charles Scribner's Sons, 1939), 29.

6. Swisher, *Selected Papers of Homer Cummings,* 36.

7. James P. Delgado, *Alcatraz Island: The Story Behind the Scenery* (Las Vegas: K. C. Publications, Inc., 1985), 14.

8. *San Francisco Examiner,* 18 October 1933.

9. *San Francisco Examiner,* 20 October 1933.

10. A thorough account of these technical details is provided by an unpublished document, Erwin N. Thompson, "The Rock: A History of Alcatraz Island, 1847–72" (Denver, Colorado, Historic Preservation Division, U.S. National Park Service, 1979).

11. Department of Justice, *Annual Report of the Attorney General,* 1935, 151.

12. USP Alcatraz, *Institution Rules and Regulations, 1956,* 1–2, Bureau of Prisons archives.

13. Thompson, *The Rock,* 423.

14. Martin Sobell, *On Doing Time* (New York: Charles Scribner's Sons, 1974), 383.

15. Kobler, *Capone,* 350.

16. Keve, *The McNeil Century,* 231–35.

17. Sobell, *On Doing Time,* 317.

18. Memo of 21 December 1954, individual case file, David Greenglass, Federal Records Center, Suitland, Maryland.

19. *Newsweek,* 1 February 1936, 16.

20. The "Battle of Alcatraz" is reported in detail in many sources, including the daily newspapers of the time. See James A. Johnston, *Alcatraz Island Prison and the Men Who Live There* (New York: Charles Scribner's Sons 1949), chapter 19; and Thompson, *The Rock,* 446–52. For one entire book on this event alone, see Clark Howard, *Six Against the Rock* (New York: Dial Press, 1977).

21. The dummy heads are in the possession of the U.S. National Park Service; a good picture of them accompanies the brief story of the escape in Delgado, *Alcatraz Island,* 35.

22. Johnston, *Alcatraz Island Prison,* 216.

23. Alvin Karpis, *On The Rock: Twenty-five Years in Alcatraz* (New York: Beaufort Books, 1980), 263.

24. Thompson, *The Rock,* 415.

25. Johnston, *Alcatraz Island Prison,* 15.

26. Ben H. Bagdikian, *The Shame of the Prisons* (New York: Pocket Books, 1972, 72.

27. Myrl E. Alexander, in a speech at Southern Illinois University, 25 April 1961, University Archives, Carbondale, Illinois.

28. 408 U.S. 238 (1972).

29. Bennett, *I Chose Prison,* 161.

30. "Interview With Norman A. Carlson," *Corrections Today,* December 1986.

31. Information furnished by Watt M. Espy, Capital Punishment Research Project, Headland, Alabama.

32. Banning v. Looney, 213 F2d 771 (1954).

33. Adams v. Carlson, 488 F2d 619 (1973).

34. Loren Karacki, "An Assessment of the High Security Operation at USP Marion, Illinois" (Bureau of Prisons monograph, May 1987), 2.

35. This suit, *Bono v. Saxbe,* became protracted through successive hearings, with the key decisions reported at 450 F. Supp. 934, 462 F. Supp. 146 (ED Ill., 1978), and 620 F 2d (7th Cir., 1980).

36. The practice is well described in accounts of the penal colony in French Guiana. See Henri Charriere, *Papillon* (New York: William Morrow and Company, 1970), 27; and Rene Belbenoit, *Dry Guillotine* (New York: Blue Ribbon Books, 1940), 23, 122–25.

37. Norman A. Carlson to Rep. Robert W. Kastenmeier, 25 April 1985, BOP records.

38. Karacki, *An Assessment,* 3.

39. Karacki, *An Assessment,* ix.

40. "A Report on the Mission of the U.S. Penitentiary, Marion, Illinois, and the Findings of the Program and Procedure Review Team" (Bureau of Prisons document, November 2–5, 1981).

41. From a distributed leaflet giving the agenda for "A Conference For Education and Action on the Second Anniversary of the Marion Prison Lockdown" (Chicago, The Committee to End the Marion Lockdown, October 26, 1985).

42. House Subcommittee on Courts, Civil Liberties, and the Administration of Justice, Committee on the Judiciary, *Marion Penitentiary—1985,* 99th Cong., 1st sess., Oversight Hearing, June 26, 1985.

43. "Proposal—To Convert Marion from an Open Population to a Closed, Tightly Controlled, Unitized Institution," BOP Task Force Report, 1979.

44. Mark Mauer, "The Lessons of Marion: The Failure of a Maximum Security Prison: A History and Analysis, with Voices of Prisoners" (a monograph from the American Friends Service Committee, Philadelphia, n.d. [circa 1985]).

45. Donna Kolbe, plaintiffs' attorney, interview with author, 13 September 1987.

46. House Subcommittee, *Marion Penitentiary,* Oversight hearing, 25–41.

47. House Subcommittee, Oversight hearing, 41.

48. Dr. William S. Logan, interview with author, 24 October 1988.

49. For a thorough description of one such program in a prison setting, see Bruno M. Cormier, *The Watcher and the Watched* (Montreal: Tundra Books, 1975).

10. PRISONS IN WARTIME

1. The wartime activities of the system are extensively described in *Gearing Federal Prisons to the War Effort,* BOP monograph, 1942.

2. Kittrie and Wedlock, *The Tree of Liberty,* 299.

3. Quoted material on this subject, unless otherwise referenced, comes from a typed manuscript by James V. Bennett, "History of the Activities of the Bureau of Prisons of the United States Department of Justice During World War II," Reports and Memorabilia Relating to Bureau-wide Operations and Programs, RG 129, NA. A published, summarized adaptation of this

material is found in *Federal Prisons* (Washington, D.C.: Bureau of Prisons 1946), 10–14.

4. Howard Levy and David Miller, *Going to Jail* (New York: Grove Press, Inc., n.d.), 131, 129.

5. Hassler, *Diary of a Self-made Convict,* 28, 34.

6. James V. Bennett to wardens, 9 September 1943, file, Wardens letters, 1 February 1937 to 26 August 1964, Carlson subject files, BOP archives.

7. H. G. Moeller, *Fiftieth Anniversary* (Bureau of Prisons monograph, 1980), 28.

8. Bennett, 10 June 1954, Carlson subject files.

9. Conference of associate wardens, 11 June, 13 June 1956, USP Terre Haute, mimeographed minutes, BOP archives.

10. The story of the action is detailed in a memo by Lt. John W. Edwards to Warden A. E. Pontesso, 6 October 1962, FCI El Reno files.

11. *Tacoma News Tribune,* 25 February 1971.

12. The relevant court decisions on beards are *Maguire v. Wilkinson,* 405 F. Supp 637 (D. Conn. 1975); and *Moskowitz v. Wilkinson,* 432 F. Supp 947 (D. Conn. 1977).

13. The first Muslim case mentioned is *Sewell v. Pegelow,* 304 F 2d 670. The case on Jewish dietary requirements is *Kahane v. Carlson,* 527 F 2d 492 (C. A. 2, 1975). For further discussion of these issues see Clair Cripe, "Religious Freedom in Prisons," *Federal Probation,* 41 (March 1977: 31–35.

14. *Chicago Tribune,* 3 June 1972: *Los Angeles Times,* 28 May 1972; *Newsweek,* 9 October 1972.

15. 391 F Supp 578 (W. D. Tex, 1975).

16. *Tacoma News Tribune,* 6 October 1952.

17. "Medical Research Projects in Federal Penal Institutions," *The Progress Report,* 8 (July–September 1960), BOP, Washington, D.C.

18. Norman A. Carlson to Sen. Sam J. Ervin, Jr., 19 February 1974, BOP archives.

19. "The Director's Letter," 17 March 1976, BOP archives.

20. *The Washington Star,* 11 September 1980.

11. EXPERIENCES WITH PROGRAMMING

1. *New York Times,* 17 August 1964.

2. Oral History Interview with James V. Bennett by Joan-Ellen Marci, November 11, 1974, 17; Robert F. Kennedy Oral History Program, John F. Kennedy Library, Boston.

3. *New York Times,* 6 January 1970.

4. For a review of the many programs and techniques of that era see Paul W. Keve, *Imaginative Programming in Probation and Parole* (Minneapolis: University of Minnesota Press, 1967).

5. H. L. Cohen, I. Goldiamond, J. Filipczak, and R. Pooley, *Training Professsionals in Procedures for the Establishment of Educational Environments* (Educational Facility Press; Institute for Behavior Research, 1968), 53.

6. One notable study of a criminal psychopath derived from the work of a BOP psychologist at the Lewisburg Penitentiary. See Robert M. Lindner, *Rebel Without a Cause* (New York: Grune & Stratton, 1944).

7. Steve Gettinger, "Dr. Martin Groder: An Angry Resignation," *Corrections Magazine,* 1 (July/August 1975): 27.

8. Norval Morris, *The Future of Imprisonment* (Chicago: University of Chicago Press, 1974).

9. For further descriptions of Butner and its programs see *Federal Correctional Institution, Butner* (BOP monograph, 1981); Gilbert L. Ingram, "Butner: A Reality," *Federal Probation,* 42 (March 1978): 34–39; and Robert B. Levinson and Donald A. Deppe, "Optional Programming: A Model Structure for the Federal Correctional Institution at Butner," *Federal Probation,* 40 (June 1976): 37–44.

10. Director Carlson gave a detailed description of START, as well as the rationale for the Butner program, in the principal testimony, Subcommittee on Courts, Civil Liberties, and the Administration of Justice, Committee on the Judiciary, *Behavior Modification Programs, Federal Bureau of Prisons* 27 February 1974, 5–6. In the same document is Dr. Groder's description of his program at Marion, 13.

11. Senate Committee on the Judiciary, *Individual Rights and the Federal Role in Behavior Modification,* 93rd Cong., 2d sess., November 1974, iii, 31.

12. *Clonce v. Richardson,* 379 F. Supp, 38 (W. D. Mo. 1974).

13. Two of the influential research reports were, Robert Martinson, "What Works: Questions and Answers About Prison Reform," *The Public Interest,* 35 (Spring 1974): 22–54; and Gene Kassebaum, David A. Ward, and Daniel M. Wilner, *Prison Treatment and Parole Survival* (New York: John Wiley and Sons, 1971).

14. William G. Nagel, "The Prison Moratorium Movement—Its Birth and Death," *Jericho,* no. 44, Fall 1987.

15. *New York Times,* 5 May 1972.

16. Michael A. Kroll, *Jericho* editor, in letter to author, 29 June 1981.

17. *Jericho,* no. 18, Fall 1979.

18. Nagel, *Jericho,* no. 44.

19. The Director's Letter, 17 March 1976, BOP files.

12. DIVERSIFICATION AND EXPANSION

1. Charles F. Campbell, in John Ortiz Smykla, *Coed Prison* (New York: Human Sciences Press, 1980), 88.

2. *Easter v. District of Columbia,* 361 F 2nd 50 (D.C. Cir., 1966).

3. As authorized by D.C. Code, Sec. 24-423, 24-424, 24-425.

4. The terms were stipulated in settlement of the suit, *Garnes v. Taylor et al.* Civil No. 72-0159, U.S. Dist. Ct., District of Columbia.

5. The Director's Letter, 7 November 1972, BOP archives.

6. For one example of the "ribbing" see a pretended Baedeker Guide to the country clubs, "Clubs Fed: A Guide," *Harpers,* 274 (April 1987): 25–28.

7. From an undated BOP brochure, Federal Youth Camp, Tuscon, Arizona.

8. Robert H. Armstrong, "Prison Camps for Rehabilitation," *Federal Probation,* 6 (April/June 1942): 38–41.

9. Douglas Lansing, Joseph B. Bogan, and Loren Karacki, "Unit Management: Implementing a Different Correctional Approach," *Federal Probation,* 41 (March 1977): 43–49.

10. 18 U.S.C. 3521.

11. *Federal Offenders,* 1938–39, 7.

12. See *The Bulletin Board,* January 1947, April 1947, July 1949, January 1951, BOP archives.

13. Robert Mintz, "Federal Prison Industry: The Green Monster," *Crime and Social Justice* (Fall/Winter 1976): 41–48.

14. Mintz, "Federal Prison Industry."

15. House Subcommittee on Courts, Civil Liberties, and the Administration of Justice, Committee on the Judiciary, *Prison Industries Improvement and Federal Correctional Education Assistance,* 98th Cong., 2d sess., Hearing, 2 August 1984, 24.

16. Unicor Annual Report, 1986, BOP, Washington, D.C.

17. Daniel Glaser, *The Effectiveness of a Prison and Parole System* (New York: The Bobbs-Merrill Company, Inc., 1964), 147, 142.

18. 18 USCA 4082 (1965).

19. Lawrence A. Carpenter, "The Federal Work Release Program," *Nebraska Law Review,* 45, no. 1966, 691.

20. The Director's Letter, 10 June 1975 and 22 July 1975, BOP archives.

21. News acounts of the helicopter attempts may be found in the *New*

York Times, 26 January 1981; the *Washington Post,* 16 July 1986; the *San Francisco Examiner,* 6 November 1986.

22. The Director's Letter, 26 November 1975, BOP archives.

23. The Lompoc Record, 20 January 1976.

24. Carpenter, "The Federal Work Release Program," 700.

INDEX

With a master's degree in social work, *Paul W. Keve* has been a career corrections administrator, serving in the states of Virginia, Delaware, and Minnesota. He has held appointments as director of the corrections departments of the latter two states. Since 1977 he has been on the faculty of Virginia Commonwealth University and now is Professor Emeritus. After writing several books on various aspects of corrections programming and management, he became interested in historical research, the present book being his third on corrections history topics.